ESCAPE FROM CORREGIDOR

EDGAR D. WHITCOMB

PAPERBACK LIBRARY, Inc.
New York

PAPERBACK LIBRARY EDITION

First Printing: *December, 1967*

Copyright © 1958 by Henry Regnery Company
Library of Congress Catalog Card Number 58-6754

This book is dedicated to the defenders of
Bataan and Corregidor.

*Paperback Library books are published by Paperback Library, Inc. Its
trademark, consisting of the words "Paperback Library" and associated
distinctive design, is registered in the United States Patent Office.
Paperback Library, Inc., 315 Park Avenue South, New York, N.Y. 10010.*

CONTENTS

I have read *Escape from Corregidor* with a great deal of interest. This straightforward narrative of the trials and vicissitudes of an American boy caught in the defense of the Philippines early in World War II is that of thousands of other American boys similarly enmeshed, including my son Bill Harris. It was he who made the all-night swim with the author through the shark-infested waters from Corregidor to Bataan and escape.

It paints the picture of the transition of a normal American boy from an average American home to war at its worst. The picture on the canvas shows:

The young navigator's early enthusiasm and pride in being a member of the longest mass flight in history of B-17's from the United States to the Philippines;

The frustration of my old friend Gene Eubank, the commander of this group of B-17's, as he stood in the unprotected open and saw his group disintegrate before his eyes from a Japanese attack;

The hope and belief that our great country would send succor to this little band of trapped warriors in the Philippines;

The realization that no help was coming and that only death or capture lay ahead;

Then, after the surrender on Corregidor, the determination to escape, followed by the successful swimming of the waters separating Corregidor from the mainland, and temporary freedom.

Such are the scenes which, when assembled, give

a vivid picture of how an American civilian adjusts himself to a totally foreign way of living—that of war—meets almost insurmountable obstacles, hurdles them with determination, and keeps going forward.

This ability of our American youth to adjust from the quiet American home to the hardships and grimness of the battlefield is a quality that I have often marveled at and long admired. He has been described in some quarters as soft and not able to take it. However it has been my observation that, given the proper tools and training, he is the equal, perhaps the superior, of any fighting man in the world. Maybe it is our competitive sports and competitive way of life that develop this quality, but whatever it is, the American serviceman is tops in my book.

An item of especial interest to me was noted. The author makes this statement: "Many of the men had never so much as fired an Army rifle and I was one of them." He was referring to some Air Force personnel ordered to take infantry training on Bantaan for defense purposes. This matter of whether or not to train Marine Corps aviation personnel in the use of the rifle has been debated in our Corps for years. However, it has always been decided that they should be so trained, pilots and everybody. In Korea we were awfully glad that we had this training. In North Korea, when things were rough we didn't have anybody except aviation personnel to protect our air installations. We were glad then that we knew how to use the rifle. I shall go further and add that I consider it the heritage of every American boy to be able to shoot a rifle and to do it well.

The latter part of the book deals with the trials and problems of the author after his recapture, and his ultimate return to the United States. Some of the happenings are fantastic and just couldn't happen, yet they did.

The culmination of this saga is the author's return to the Philippines as a member of a medium bomber group and his participation in bombing attacks on the enemy.

Some of the readers may wonder what happened to my son, Bill Harris, after he and the author separated. He and several companions were able to sail as far south as Morotai Island on their way to Australia. Only one more leg remained to complete their journey. Unfortunately, the natives betrayed them there, and they were turned over to the Japanese. This was in September 1943. From there Bill was flown to Japan and stayed in Japanese prison camps until the end of the war. He had the satisfaction of observing the Japanese surrender on the U.S.S. Missouri in August, 1945, and I had the pleasure of flying him from Guam to Washington and freedom. Later he was killed, leading his battalion in the Chosan Reservoir operation in Korea, in December 1950.

Aside from the very interesting reading offered by this book, I feel that it cannot help stirring up a quiet pride in the breast of every American parent whose boy has participated in our wars. These boys asked for so little and gave so much.

Lt. General Field Harris, u.s.m.c., ret.

ESCAPE FROM

Corregidor

1. Takeoff

The four engines of our B-17 wind up with a thundering roar as we lumber down the runway on Hamilton Field, California. Pencils, books, maps and everything loose slide to the back of the table, and the force of the acceleration takes hold of my body as the plane lunges forward. Runway lights flash past faster and faster, until at last I feel light and breathing becomes easier. We are off the ground; and through the plastic nose of our plane, I can see the lights of the bay, the boats and the bridges of San Francisco. I press my face to the cold window to drink up these last precious glimpses of the U.S.A. It is October 16, 1941, and we are on our way to a two-year tour with the Air Corps in the Philippine Islands. It will be a long time before we see this again. We may never see it again.

Little do I know that I am starting on a strange trip around the world, perhaps unlike that experienced by any other person . . . that I will be captured by the enemy . . . that I will escape and be captured again . . . that I will be accused of being a deserter and returned to the U.S.A. with a name not even my own . . . or that I will have to fly from San Francisco again before I can take an active part in the war.

Seconds after the anti-aircraft searchlights salute us high above the long string of lights which I recognize as the Golden Gate Bridge, we plunge into a wall of total blackness. With the darkness comes torrential rain and turbulence; the aircraft begins to pitch and toss, and loose gear falls to the floor.

I feel a little weak in the stomach as I realize that it is my responsibility to navigate this giant bomber with its crew seven thousand miles across the Pacific. As I sit back and wait for the weather to clear so I can take a celestial observation to establish our position, I wonder what "Old Charlie" would think of me now.

It was Charles J. Lunn, chief navigator for Pan-American Airways at Miami, who had taught us what we knew about navigation less than a year ago. At night Charlie used to take us to the top of the San Sebastian Hotel and point out all the important stars in the heavens. He called out names for them that sounded like something out of Grandma's almanac; but after a few weeks, Arcturus and Betelgeuse became as common to us as Smith and Jones.

"Don't write that down," he would say. "You've got to get it up here in your head. Your notes and papers won't do you any good when you're out over the ocean some night. You've got to know this stuff."

When we were more advanced in our navigation training, Charlie used to take us on flights down to Havana or out over the Bahamas in the Pan-American flying boats which had been converted into classrooms, with individual tables and equipment for each cadet.

When we were graduated, we gave Charlie a two-hundred-dollar watch to show our feelings of appreciation for what he had done for us; and with big tears in his eyes he sent fifty of us off to the Army like a proud father sending his sons into the world to make their way. "You guys are going to be captains and majors in the Army Air Corps some day, and some day you'll have the responsibility of navigating bombers across the Atlantic and Pacific."

Charlie's predictions had come true, and on this night of October 16, 1941, twenty-six of Charlie's boys, including Seamon, Jones, Horowitz, Oliver, Berkowitz, Warner, McAuliff, Schreiber and me, were individually navigating the first flight of B-17's from the United States to Clark Field in the Philippine Islands. It was the 19th Bombardment Group under the command of Colonel Eugene Eubank.

The blackness of the night as we departed from San Francisco Bay turned out to be just one of many thunderstorms we flew through as our plane made its way to Hawaii, Midway Island, Wake Island, Port Moresby in New Guinea, and Port Darwin in Australia.

In Australia we were met by a Captain Colin Kelly who had flown down from the Philippine Islands to brief us on the long flight from Port Darwin to Clark Field.

Though the flight from Australia to Luzon had been by individual navigation, by prearranged plan our squadron rendezvoused near Batangas on the south shore of Luzon, and we flew in formation at a low altitude across the island of Corregidor, the mouth of Manila Bay, Bataan Peninsula, and on across the plains to Clark Field. From the nose of the B-17 I looked with eager eyes at the scenery below as it flashed past, for this was a new and interesting land. Clark Field lay in the western portion of a vast plain, stretching from Lingayen Gulf at the north to the swamps of Manila Bay on the south, and bordered on the eastern and western sides by mountain ranges. Directly to the east of the field, a volcano-shaped mountain marked the approximate center of the great plain as it rose abruptly out of the flat country that lay all around it. As we circled for landing we could see the golf course spread out west of the field, a swimming pool, and a number of large frame houses just to the west of the field. We were eager to get on the ground and to learn what our new home in the Orient had to offer. From the air everything looked clean, fresh, and green, and we were certain that Clark Field in Pampanga Province, Luzon Island, would be a wonderful place to spend the next few months.

On the ground, we were unimpressed with the fact that we had just completed the greatest mass flight in aviation history. We were more interested in getting settled in our new oriental home. Clark Field was a pleasant place and fairly well suited to our purposes, as it had been an air base for many years, although it was too small to accommodate our bombardment group and the other squadrons which were stationed there before we arrived.

Within a few days about seventeen of our bombers were flown to Del Monte, about five hundred miles to the south on the island of Mindanão. We were quartered in old Fort Stotsenburg to the west of the field, where we occupied quarters which had previously been used by service families before they had been sent back to the United States. By setting up our cots on the porch and in the living room we found that fifteen or twenty of us could live comfortably in a big old wooden frame house previously occupied by only one family.

In spite of our somewhat crowded conditions, we soon learned to appreciate the luxury of military service in the Orient. It took us no time at all to find that life was impossible without a battery of servants to wash our clothes, make our bunks, keep our shoes polished, and fetch tall cool drinks at our beck and call. All these services were available to us for a few cents a day. We could swim, play golf, or hike to the various little villages near the field. On these walks we observed beautiful groups of multi-colored birds. There were parakeets, canaries, and parrots, all very much at home in the heavy tropical vegetation to the west side of Fort Stotsenburg. There were tall palm trees, banana trees with their wide green leaves, and all kinds of crisp green vegetation.

The villagers were a friendly sort of people with

nothing more important to do than to visit with us and to be of service to us in any way possible. For the most part they worked as servants, cooks, and waiters at Clark Field and Fort Stotsenburg.

Back at the field, we learned that we would have a few days of leave to go to Manila and rest up from the long flight we had just taken. There was much excitement around the old house after news came of our leave. A fellow by the name of Warner Croxton and I decided to make the trip together.

"They say there's a place in Manila where you can store your winter stuff. Think I'll take a few things in," Croxton said as we prepared for our trip.

"That's not a bad idea. Crowded as things are here, it would be a good idea to put some of these things in storage," I answered.

After packing our bags and getting shaved and showered, we made our way to the train station at the south side of Fort Stotsenburg. The train was crowded with American and Filipino soldiers and a large number of Filipino civilians. As we bumped along from Stotsenburg to Angeles and San Fernando, Croxton nudged me and asked, "Do you see what I see?"

I turned slowly. Across the aisle, a young mother was breast-feeding a very small baby which she held in her arms. The child—she was hardly more than that—was clad only in a dress which barely reached to her waist.

"They say that's common here in the tropics. Out in the Bondoc a lot of the kids don't wear anything at all," I answered.

Croxton grinned. "No, I mean the cigarette."

I looked across the aisle again. While the mother fed the baby she was also smoking a long brown cigarette with the fire end in her mouth.

"That's a hell of a way to smoke a cigarette," I said. "Think I'd rather chew betel nut."

"Me too," answered Croxton.

We continued to watch the young mother as our train made its way along toward Manila. She did not puff on the cigarette very often; but from time to time she would take it from her lips and flip the ashes on the floor.

Croxton raised his eyebrows. "Watch her. Pretty soon she will throw that baby on the floor and go screaming for a bucket of water."

But nothing happened; she continued to smoke the cigarette, and the baby slept until we were almost to Manila.

"Bet we'll find out about a lot of new customs here that we never heard of before," Croxton observed. "Last night I was reading a book by Florence Horn called *Orphans of the Pacific*, which tells a lot about the customs here in the islands. There's this one tribe of natives up in the northern part of the island who feed a starved dog on uncooked rice; then after a few hours, when the rice is partly digested, they cut the dog open and eat the rice themselves."

"Sounds like a dirty trick to pull on a starved dog," I answered. "But I'll bet that's not as good as a baloot."

"What's that?"

"They tell me they take an egg and bury it for several months. Then when they dig it up, it's a baloot and very delicious."

"No, thanks," he replied. "Think I'll just stick to steak and potatoes for mine. But I guess these people don't care too much for that kind of food. One of the fellows was telling me that although they have steaks and pork chops in the refrigerator all the time, their houseboys are continually asking for money to get fish heads and rice for themselves."

The little train came to a jolting halt, and we found we were in the Manila station. It seemed that everyone in Manila was a taxi driver, for taxis were everywhere, and little brown men were everywhere to meet the hundreds of people who flooded off the train.

"Taxi, Joe. Taxi, Joe. Take your bags for you, sir?" they shouted, waving and pointing to their cabs. The taxis ranged in size from tiny little autos to stately, ancient touring cars. We chose one of the latter; and the instant our choice was indicated, we found ourselves seated and our bags loaded, and ourselves off with a jerk. The driver's rubber airhorn honked wildly as we plowed recklessly into the crowded street ahead of us.

There were more horse-drawn carriages (called carromatas) than autos on the crowded, dirty streets, and the thousands of undersized taxis seemed literally to pump themselves along with their horns. The horn seemed to be by far the most important part of the vehicle as the taxi driver pushed madly across town, honk! honk! honking! his way along. Whenever the traffic caused him to stop, he would continue to honk his horn and make nasty remarks to the nearest driver of a horse-drawn rig.

The city was dirty and ugly; and it smelled bad. The streets were crowded with little people scurrying in all directions, some barefooted and dressed in sleeveless sport shirts and shorts, while others wore white suits and expensive-looking dresses.

"Where's the Manila Hotel?" I shouted to the driver when he stopped at an intersection.

"On over," he answered, still honking his horn and waiting for the "go" sign.

After a while we came to a river with a sign on the bridge which told us it was the Pasig River. On the other side we drove out onto a wide boulevard lined with huge, stately trees. In the distance we could see many beautiful buildings. It was apparent that we had left the old part of the city and that now we were in the new, modern section of Manila. To our right we saw a green golf course, and beyond it a long wall which we later learned was the Walled City.

Inside the wall was the ancient city of Manila, built around the old Spanish fort of Santiago. In a very few minutes we pulled up to the magnificent Manila Hotel. Our driver unloaded us, and we paid him the two pesos which he asked. Later we learned that the reasonable rate for that distance was twenty-five centavos. We had paid the equivalent of one dollar in American money for a ride that should have cost us about twelve and one-half cents; but we had learned our first lesson in Filipino—the first in a long list of lessons which finally cost us everything but our very lives. Our first look at Manila had been worth a dollar, but our lesson was worth far more than that.

After we were checked in at the hotel we learned that we were situated on the eastern end of Manila Bay. From high in the hotel we looked out across the bay to see the reflection of a red sun sinking into the distant horizon. In the foreground were ships of all descriptions lying at anchor with their flags waving high in the evening breeze and their many lights blinking signals to the shore. Rising out of the water far in the west were black mounds which were the island of Corregidor and the peninsula of Bataan.

As we drank in the splendor of the approaching twilight, Croxton said, "Sometime when we get more settled, we ought to go out and look over the island of Corregidor."

"Yes, it seemed like an interesting place from the quick look I had at it as we flew over. Like to see it myself," I replied. "Any idea on where we might go tonight?"

"Well, I have the address of a fellow here I used to know back at the Point. Name's Bud Watkins. He's in subs here."

"A West Pointer in submarines? How did that happen?"

"No, he was at Annapolis when I was at the Point." Croxton rummaged through his luggage until he came out with a little notebook. "Here it is. St. Louis Apartments. That shouldn't be too hard to find."

"All right. Let's get a cab and go there. Maybe he can tell us where this place is where we can store our clothes."

In a few moments we were down on the street and hailing a cab for the St. Louis Apartments; but we didn't climb in until we had firmly established the fare as being twenty-five centavos.

At the apartment house we found the name on the mailbox and rapped on the door with the appropriate number. In response to our knock a big, husky fellow swung open the door and greeted his old friend Croxton with the usual, "Well, you old son-of-a-gun. What the hell are you doing here?"

Croxton told of our flight and introduced me to Watkins.

"Honey, come here," Watkins shouted into the other room. "Come see who's here. My old friend Croxton."

A very glamorous girl, the likes of whom we hadn't seen since we left the United States, appeared from the next room. "Ellie, these are Lieutenants Croxton and Whitcomb. . . ."

The four of us visited for a while until it became apparent that Bud and Ellie had a previous engagement for dinner at the Army-Navy Club. Croxton accepted the invitation to join them but I, being curious to have a good look at Manila, headed out alone to see the bright lights of the city.

Manila was a great and wondrous city on that Saturday night in early November, 1941, as I strolled along the Escolta and up Rizal. I was exploring the place, for it would be home during the next two years while we were stationed in the Philippines. Parts of the city were dirty, and parts of it smelled bad. On the other hand, there were modern theaters, hotels, and night clubs, and I found one fine spot where it would be nice to bring a party later on—a night club

21

with good food and a good orchestra on top of the Avenue Hotel, six or seven stories above the heart of Manila.

Along the dark streets carromata drivers were more anxious to take a lone passenger on a joy ride than to take him sight-seeing. "You want a very beautiful girl, Joe?" they would ask over and over. "She is very beautiful and very clean. Only two pesos." But the girls were neither beautiful nor clean. The houses of prostitution were nothing more than Filipino homes with mother, father, and all the rest of the relatives sitting around the living room where the bargain was made for girls as young as fourteen or fifteen years of age. Then there was a younger member of the family peddling his wares.

"You need medicine, Joe—only fifty centavos. You take this medicine, you will not get seek," he would insist. But the boys did get sick, and it was rumored about Manila that the V.D. rate for the men on a two-year tour reached 130 percent, which meant that the average soldier should expect to have the "scourge" one and one-third times during his stay in the islands.

Several blocks away, I found a different element of Philippine society attending a cabaret, severely chaperoned by proud mothers who managed to stay awake until three o'clock in the morning. By custom, everybody departed from the dance together. It was socially improper for anyone to leave before the end of the dance.

On the big ballroom floor smartly dressed Filipinos danced and swayed with natural grace, while along the sidelines the chaperones cared for babies too young to be left at home. Along one side of the ballroom were rows of wooden benches where tiny tots with no more clothing than a short dress which reached the midriff, like the one we had seen on the train, were snoozing peacefully; others, demanding more attention, were being breast-fed by their patient, sleepy mothers.

On the streets in the early hours of the morning, the pride of Uncle Sam's Navy could frequently be seen sitting in the driver's seat of a carromata racing down the boulevard, the Filipino driver holding on for dear life in the passenger's seat.

Yes, Manila was a great and wonderful city, and it was certain we would have great times here after we were settled and better acquainted. Manila was called the "Pearl of the Orient," and now we knew why. During the next couple of days Croxton and I put our clothing in storage with a concern called Joe Bush's, strolled through the hundreds of little shops within the old Walled City, and basked in the luxury of the Manila Hotel. All too quickly it was time for us to board the train and make our way back to Clark Field.

Back at Clark Field we were reminded of something we had forgotten for the past three days—that our air group had been sent to the Philippines on an exceedingly serious mission—that the possibility of war between the United States and Japan was becoming more acute day by day. Although every one of us had a strong feeling that we would soon be flying combat missions against the Japanese, not one of us worried for a second over the danger we were facing. Actually, no one knew the danger or could even imagine it, for we knew nothing of the horrors of war. We never dreamed of seeing our beautiful Flying Fortresses spinning to earth in flames or disintegrating in mid-air, carrying our buddies to sudden death. Nor did we dream of seeing our planes returning from missions riddled with thousands of bullet holes and with the crew members wounded and dying. These were pictures of air warfare that we were fortunately unable to foresee or imagine.

In spite of our inability to foresee the peril that lay ahead, we found ourselves living in a new and exciting atmosphere. After our first day back from Manila we were ordered to wear our forty-five's, a bulky gas mask on our left sides, and a steel helmet. This last was the old-fashioned World War I type that our doughboys had worn in France. It would take some time for us to get used to this new life. Never before in history, to our knowledge, had such a large group of men been taken from their homes and families and transplanted into a foreign civilization almost halfway around the world in so short a time. Men who only a few days ago had been mowing their lawns, playing softball, and enjoying the peaceful life of Albuquerque, found themselves the vanguard of the American forces in the Pacific. Instead of polo shirts and slacks they wore khaki trousers, steel helmets, gas masks and forty-fives. The transformation from a semi-civilian status had been too rapid for them, and only the most pessimistic could possibly have appreciated the gravity of the situation.

The feeling of American superiority had a strong hold on each of us. Since childhood we had been taught that American machines, American planes, American equipment, and American men were superior in quality to all others on the face of the earth. With few exceptions, our autos traveled faster, our planes flew higher and faster, and our athletes excelled in more sports than those of any other country in the world. Why, then, should any of us doubt that we would be able to crush the Japanese in a very short time if they were foolish enough to attack us?

We had been told that the Japs, by the very nature of their physical makeup, were poor pilots. Their vision and balance were poor, and their aircraft were vastly inferior to our own. On the other hand, our B-17's could fly so high that they were beyond the reach of the Jap's anti-aircraft and planes, and with our secret bombsight we could pinpoint targets and destroy them with miraculous accuracy.

So we sat through November, 1941, poised in our best battle dress and ready for anything. Many trenches had been dug about the area of our squadrons, and huge revetments were made for the B-17's which were scattered about the small field. Hundreds and hundreds of big, ugly two-thousand-pound bombs were dispersed about Clark Field. All bomber crews remained on the alert, ready to be in the air within two hours' notice. Fighter crews were, of course, ready to take to the air on an instant's warning, and a few remained above the field from early morning until after sunset every day. The bomber crews had been moved from the old family-type barracks to new sawali barracks which had been built on the edge of Clark Field near the runway. We were advised of an air warning network of telephone and teletype communications from all remote points of the island to Clark Field. In addition to this, our bomber squadrons were assigned sectors far out to sea in all directions from the field for daily reconnaissance flights.

I was assigned to Colonel Eubank's headquarters squadron, and on December 6, we combed an area from the northern tip of Luzon Island to a point within ten or fifteen miles from the southern end of the island of Formosa, the strongly fortified Japanese island. It was an exceedingly monotonous journey as we swept back and forth across the sector, and the only excitement on the whole trip was when we cleared our machine guns. Mine was a thirty-caliber which could be fired out of any one of a number of holes in the big plastic nose of the plane.

Back in the radio compartment the radio operator was having trouble with the twin fifty-caliber guns he was supposed to operate out of the top of the ship. As I watched him, he seemed to have difficulty manipulating the guns.

"What's the matter, Sergeant?" I asked. "Having trouble?"

"Yeah, this son-of-a-bitch doesn't want to fire."

"Are you pretty good with it?"

"Danged if I know. Never fired one before." With that he aimed the guns out into the low gray skies and tried again. A thundering roar filled the compartment as the twin fifties spat a short burst into the sky above. The startled look on the big Sergeant's face gave way to a broad grin. "That's a son-of-a-bitch."

Those were the only shots the Sergeant ever fired, for a few days later he was dead.

Two mornings later, on December 8, we were up, dressed, and on our way to breakfast at about seven. As I stepped out the door of our sawali barracks it was apparent that the day would be perfect, as all the days had been since we arrived in the Philippines. About fifty yards away and off to the right stood the big wooden frame building which Colonel Eubank had taken over as headquarters for the 19th Bombardment Group. That was where I worked when I was on duty and not flying. I took care of the maps and general navigation equipment for the squadrons, and Croxton operated his communications section in a little building to the rear of the headquarters building. Straight ahead of me to the east there was the usual amount of activity on the field, with the fighters that had been flying the early morning patrols coming in, and those going out on reconnaissance missions taking off. To my left, officers were pouring out of the east doors of the barracks or walking toward the mess hall, about a block to the north. There was the usual amount of chatter and friendly conversation as little groups proceeded along the sidewalk in the shade of the huge trees which lined the walk from the headquarters building to the mess hall.

I had almost reached the sidewalk when I heard a voice which I recognized as that of Jim Dey, a bombardier. "Hey, Whit, wait up." I turned and waited.

"Did you hear about the Japs attacking Pearl Harbor?"

"Yeah, sure, we heard about that yesterday," someone beside me volunteered. "Don't you have anything more up to date than that?"

"No kidding," Jim answered seriously. "A bunch of Jap planes bombed hell out of Pearl Harbor and Hickam Field."

Jim Dey was a fellow with a great imagination. He

was light-hearted and gay and seemed to have very few worries in the world. But now he sounded dead serious.

"I can't imagine it, with all the stuff we've got at Hickam. A Jap wouldn't have a chance," the fellow on my right objected as we moved closer to the mess hall.

"But they're telling it for the truth," Jim insisted.

"Boy, I can imagine what would happen to any Japs who tried such a thing," I added. "I got a friend there named Lucas that I knew back at Indiana University. He told me our Navy had a constant watch on the Japanese Navy and knew the positions of all their ships all of the time. He was on the alert almost constantly, himself, sleeping over in the hangar and ready to take off on a minute's notice."

But as we drew nearer the mess hall, we could hear more and more talk about Pearl Harbor and the Japanese attack.

The mess hall was crowded, as usual; and, as usual, the little Filipinos in their white coats were serving water glasses full of ice-cold pineapple juice, tomato juice, or orange juice, followed by generous portions of fruit, French toast, eggs, ham, and whatever we desired. Some of the people at our table had heard the rumor of the attack. Others had not. In general, we concluded that it was just a rumor and changed the subject to something else. It did not make sense to us that the Japanese should attack Pearl Harbor and leave Clark Field unharmed. With the B-17's and equipment we had at Clark, we felt certain that even the Japanese would not be foolish enough to commit such a blunder. Also, if it was true, why had we not received official word of it? Why were we not on our way to bomb Formosa, that heavily fortified Japanese island? No, it could not be true.

Some of the fellows at the other end of the table were talking about their trip to Baguio, a resort city a hundred and twenty-five kilometers to the north of us, where they had collected all kinds of souvenirs.

"Baguio is the place to go if you want to have a real good time."

"Yes, it's supposed to be the cleanest and most beautiful city in the islands."

Then a navigator named Berkowitz spoke up thoughtfully. "Say, if the Japs did attack Pearl Harbor, that means we're at war with the Japs. We are soldiers in the U.S. Army. Now, if we're at war with the Japs, it looks like somebody oughta tell us about it so we could start doing whatever soldiers are supposed to do in war."

"I'd rather be doing what I was doing last night," said a fighter pilot sitting nearby. "There I was with these two lovely brown-skinned gals, not one, but two . . ." he stopped suddenly, as his eyes met those of the chaplain sitting across from him. An uneasy silence fell upon the group, and the chaplain smiled politely.

After a good hearty breakfast we strolled back toward the headquarters building; but everyone around me stopped suddenly as a radio from a nearby building blared out the excited voice of news commentator Don Bell, the Lowell Thomas of the Philippines: "Japanese aircraft have attacked Pearl Harbor. There is no report of the damage at this time. Further information will be broadcast as soon as it is available."

Then the rumor was true! Pearl Harbor had been attacked! But why did we have no official word of it?

I walked faster and faster until I reached group headquarters. There I found the various officers and men going about their duties in the usual fashion. Out across the field there was no unusual activity. A few planes were landing, and a few planes were taking off, as usual. It was all so ordinary that it was almost mysterious.

I went to the back porch of the building and

opened a new bunch of maps which had just arrived. Finally, at about ten o'clock, I walked to the front of the building and found Colonel Eubank talking to a group of officers and men.

"Here it is," he announced. "I have just received official word that a Japanese force attacked Pearl Harbor this morning at seven fifty-five. We will continue to be on the alert and wait for orders."

Lieutenant Ed Green, my pilot, who was standing in the group near me, turned and said, "Whitcomb, go out to the ship and check the cameras. If there is no film, you can get some from the supply tent."

"All right, sir. I'll check with you just as soon as I get back here," I replied.

Things were beginning to happen. Now, at least, there was something to do, something to occupy the time while we waited. Perhaps we would get orders to take off at any moment. I drove a jeep back down the street, past the mess hall and around the edge of the field, until I came up to the B-17 with the number 87 on her tail. The ground crew, radio operator, and engineer were going about their usual duties as I climbed the ladder into the belly of the plane to check the cameras. They were empty, so I proceeded back to the tent about twenty-five yards behind the plane to get the necessary film. I asked the corporal inside the tent, "Can I get some film here for our camera in 87?"

"Yes, we got it, but you'll have to wait till the sergeant gets back so you can sign for it," he replied. As we finished digging out the film, the sergeant walked into the tent and made out the necessary papers for me to sign.

When I turned to head back to the aircraft, I suddenly realized it had vanished. I shouted at a soldier nearby, "Hey! What happened to that ship?"

He came running toward me, swinging his arms. "Took off," he shouted excitedly. "You should have seen 'em. P-40's, P-35's, and B-17's, all taking off at once. Dangdest thing I ever saw. Must be going on a raid. That '17—was it yours?" I nodded, looking into the sky. "It took off with only three fans turning," he said. "Never saw anything like it."

Without a word I jumped into my jeep and headed back to headquarters. As I ran through the door, I bumped into Croxton. "What the hell's happening?" I demanded.

"We had word that a raid was coming in, and everything was ordered off the field."

"Where's Ed Green?"

"He took off out of here like a bat out of hell. Guess he's out flying around somewhere now," Croxton said. He added wistfully, "We can't seem to get orders to bomb Formosa."

"Why?" I asked abruptly.

"Nobody seems to know."

It seemed inconceivable that it had been several hours since the Japs had attacked Pearl Harbor, and yet we had neither bombed nor been bombed. Now they were talking of our going to Formosa to take pictures. What did they want to know now that they didn't already know? We all knew that Formosa was alive with Japanese fighter planes and that there were a number of Japanese submarine bases around the island. But now there was a war going on, and it was as if the Japs did not know even the existence of Clark Field with its hornet's nest of fighters and big heavy bombers. We could bomb and destroy any number of their bases in Formosa, only three hours away. Why did we not bomb them? Were we waiting for them to bomb us first?

It was about an hour before the first planes started coming back in. We were as much in the dark as we had been when we first heard the rumor, early that morning. With nothing more important to do, I left headquarters and walked back down the sidewalk to the mess hall. The sun was high in the heavens, the day was bright and clear, and everything at Clark

Field appeared perfectly normal. I ate a hurried lunch and rushed back to headquarters to see if there were any new developments. There I found Colonel Eubank with his squadron commanders and operations officers in a meeting in his office. I edged closer to the door to see what I could learn. When Lieutenant Green stepped out, I asked, "Are we going to get to bomb?"

"Still no orders to bomb, but we may get some photos . . ."

"Here they come," Lieutenant Pat McIntyre screamed from the back of the building. Without a word I rushed to the back steps and made a wild dive for the trench about twenty feet away. The air was charged with a loud crackling sound like that of dry boards being broken. Then, as I hit the bottom of the trench, there was a terrible explosion followed by another, another, and another. The earth rocked and rolled, and huge weights fell on me, one after another, until I felt I was crushed. Everything went black, but the rumbling and roaring continued for a long time. I struggled to move, to get my gas mask on, but it was no use. I twisted and squirmed until I realized my face was buried in the dirty Luzon sand. It was in my mouth, nose, and ears.

After a long time the roaring and rumbling subsided, and I found that I was on the bottom of the trench and that a large number of other persons had tried to get into the same trench. When I was finally able to stand up I wiped the sand out of my eyes and ran over to the end of the headquarters building to see what had happened. There, across the field, we could see our beautiful silver Flying Fortresses burning and exploding right before our eyes as we stood completely powerless to do anything about it.

It had been a terrible raid. Fifty-seven high-flying Japanese bombers had approached Clark Field from the northwest and laid down a pattern of bombs starting with the mess hall, where I had just finished lunch, and spreading diagonally across the field to the southeast. A number of officers had been killed by a direct hit on the mess hall, and other officers and men were killed on the field and along the flight line.

Colonel Eubank stood silently, his hands on his hips and his jaw dropped, as his eyes swept across the field of devastation. There stood the commander of one of the most potent bombardment groups of the United States forces, with several decades of military service behind him, defeated on the first day of the war. For months he had trained his 19th Bombardment Group at March Field, California, and at Albuquerque; then he had led the greatest mass flight in the history of the world, from the United States to Clark Field, to become the first and only bombardment groups in the Pacific on the opening day of the war. Now we all stood silently as at a funeral; but through the big black cloud of smoke, which was by now blotting out the sun, we could hear the rat-tat-tat of approaching machine gun fire.

Like rabbits, we pounced back into the trenches as a wave of strafing planes swept across the field, spraying their deadly machine gun fire as they went. Then we watched, while again and again the little fighters came down to treetop level, spraying first one target and then another and darting back up into the black cloud of smoke.

Through all this, a lone figure stood on top of a mound near my trench, still looking across the field. "You'd better take cover, sir," I ventured; but the Colonel heard no more than if he had been made of stone.

After a long time the strafing ceased as abruptly as it had started, and we climbed out to have another look at the wreckage. Across the field there did not seem to be a plane that had not been hit. Our fighters had been knocked down as they tried to take off. Crews standing by their planes were destroyed along

33

with the ships. Four bodies were found beside our own ship, number 87, charred beyond recognition; but I knew one was that of the radio operator who had never fired a machine gun before.

Among the many others lost was my old roommate, "Tex" Gary, who only a few days before had spent a whole afternoon laboriously constructing a will in which he bequeathed all of his worldly possessions to his mother back in Texas. Berkowitz, who at breakfast had wanted someone to tell him there was a war so he could start doing "whatever soldiers are supposed to do in war," got a shrapnel wound and lost his leg.

Yes, we were at war with Japan. There could be no doubt about it now, but what had happened? What had happened to the air warning net about the island which was to give us two hours' notice before any enemy reached Clark Field? What had happened to our fighters and our anti-aircraft which would keep enemy planes so high they could not bomb with any degree of accuracy? What had happened to the orders we should have received to unleash our many bombers against the enemy installations at Formosa? No one knew the answers to these questions, except that things did not work the way they were supposed to work. The very first warning that any of us had on Clark Field came from those who saw the fifty-seven high-flying bombers. Very few of our fighters ever got off the ground, and our anti-aircraft had accounted for only three or four of the enemy planes.

It had all happened so quickly that none of us could realize what had happened or what it meant to us. It was too much for the mind to comprehend. One thing was certain. We would have to get a new supply of planes from the United States immediately, for the few bombers which had been sent to the base at Mindanão were not enough.

We knew little of the extent of the damage to our forces at Pearl Harbor, five thousand miles to the east of us, nor could we believe that it would be impossible to get new planes from the United States immediately. What is more, not one of us would have believed that this was the beginning of the end for us; that thousands of us would be spending long years behind barbed wire to be starved, beaten, humiliated almost beyond human endurance, and brutally murdered; or that only a handful of us would ever see home again.

The question as to why our bombers were not sent on a mission before they were destroyed on the ground has never been satisfactorily answered. Even the armchair strategists could never properly explain it, if they overlooked the human elements of negligence and jealousy. It cannot be denied that our generals and leaders committed one of the greatest errors possible to military men—that of letting themselves be taken by surprise. That error can be exceeded only by treason.

The world has received minute details of the catastrophe at Pearl Harbor, but few know what actually happened at Clark Field. In both instances the Japanese made what we Americans choose to call a sneak attack. From the Japanese standpoint, both attacks were well planned and highly successful.

There can be no doubt that the policy of the United States of America with reference to the oriental nations gave the Japanese leaders perfect material for propaganda to arouse feelings of bitter hatred against the United States. The Japanese purpose was to defeat the United States for reasons which they themselves considered adequate; how they did it was incidental. The Japanese reasons for starting the war are set out in the Imperial Rescript, which stated that Japan was "insuring the stability of East Asia and contributing to world peace."

When the planes had stopped burning, a stillness fell over Clark Field that we had never felt before. A few hours ago the field had been a beehive of activity, with dozens of planes taking off and landing and ground crews hustling about the hangars; now it was just another field in the great Luzon plain. But it had been christened on this first day of war with the red blood of hundreds of American soldiers and the molten metal and ashes of our new B-17's. The big black cloud of smoke from the burning oil dump had vanished, and as the bright sun descended toward the mountains in the west, the sky was clear and quiet. As night spread over the vast plain, it covered the grim wreckage, and it seemed that the world was at peace again. But we knew that tomorrow was another day, and the bombers and fighters would be back again strafing. Our only hope lay in the thought that some of our bombers would fly up from the southern islands and that we would get to fly some missions to Formosa.

It was almost completely dark when I walked into the headquarters building, which was now more like a haunted house than like the headquarters of a great bomber outfit. I walked through the building from the back to the front porch without finding a soul. Blackness blotted out all of Clark Field, and all that could be seen to the east was the outline of Mount Arayat towering majestically above the Luzon plain. As I stared into the blackness before me, I heard a noise in the back part of the building. "Who is it?" I shouted. "Croxton and Seamon," came the answer. "Got any matches?"

"I've got some back on the porch," I answered. "Where's everybody gone?"

"Out to the bondocs," Croxton replied. "I've got some maps of Formosa here, but only a few. Think we'd better trace off enough so we'll have at least seventeen in case the other ships get up here tomorrow."

Croxton lit a candle, and we set out on the tedious task of reproducing maps of the island of Formosa with all the airdromes, Navy stations and submarine locations.

"Where'd these maps come from?" I inquired, never having seen them before.

"They are secret maps which Intelligence was able to get."

During the several hours that we worked, we strained our ears for the possible sound of enemy planes, but there were no sounds of any kind to be heard.

"I'm going to have to have some help in my communications section. Would you like to help me out?" Croxton inquired.

"Sure, but I don't know a damned thing about it."

"You'll do all right," Croxton said.

It was late in the night when we finally traced off our last map and walked across the street to our barracks. We found the barracks completely deserted, so each took a blanket and headed off into the fields to the north and west of the air base.

"Who's that?" a voice whispered when we were about a quarter of a mile from the barracks.

"Why, hello, Drack! It's me," I answered, recognizing the voice of Drachenberg, a photographic officer from Rosenberg, Texas.

"Think they'll be back tonight?" he asked.

"Christ! I hope not! Don't know what they could do to us that they haven't already done. We may get up to Formosa tomorrow if those planes from Mindanão come in. We've been over to headquarters tracing off maps of Formosa with all their air bases. They've really got a slew of 'em," I replied.

"Man, oh man, what a day! I don't want any more of that," he said seriously. "Do you know where the target range is? Dey said he was going up there, but it's so damned dark I can't find anything."

"I'm not sure, but that would be a good place in case they come back tonight. Let's have a look." With that, the four of us proceeded to the north into the darkness of the meadow.

After we had walked a short distance, Seamon whispered, "What's that?" I turned in time to see a flare arching into the sky not far to the south and west of us.

"Looks like someone sending signals," observed Croxton. "We'd better stop here and wait a while." The four of us spread out our blankets on the ground and lay down in the meadow. No one spoke as we listened and waited.

Thoughts raced through my mind. I wondered whether a spy had sent up that signal. Croxton had said down at headquarters that the island was full of spies, and that the Filipinos were more favorable to the Japanese than to us. He had also said that the reason we had no warning of the Jap attack was that the air warning system had been sabotaged. Telephone and teletype had been systematically cut so that no warning ever reached Clark Field.

So this was war, the first night of a war! Only this morning we had heard the fantastic rumor of the Jap attack on Pearl Harbor. We had all laughed and scoffed at it; later, when we learned that it was true, we began to wonder why we had not taken some action. But nothing had happened; we had waited and waited until the Japs came and destroyed our planes. Now we lay on blankets out in the middle of an open field seven thousand miles from home, with gas masks, helmets, and forty-five caliber pistols. What would happen to us next?

As these thoughts ran through my mind, I noticed that it was beginning to get light. "Let's get back down to the field and see what's going on," I suggested, for I knew none of the others was sleeping. We all picked up our blankets and walked back across the field toward headquarters. The dawn was cold and gray, and we were all weary from lack of sleep and food. On the road behind the headquarters building we found Colonel Eubank and Major Welsh, our operations officer. There seemed to be no point in asking questions, for we felt that they were as much perplexed as the rest of us. When the Major saw us he nodded toward the Colonel and said, "He hasn't slept a wink."

The Colonel walked toward us and stated, "We'll have to be getting some new planes in from the States right away."

"Any report from Mindanão?" Croxton asked.

"We don't have any report of any bombing there yet," replied the Colonel.

There seemed nothing more to say, so the four of us turned and walked away. "Let's get rid of these blankets and see if we can find some chow," Croxton suggested. In the barracks we learned that a field kitchen had been set up in a thicket about a quarter of a mile south of the headquarters building.

We found the kitchen out in the bushes, were furnished with mess kits and utensils, and had our first meal in the open field. After that we split up and each went his own way.

The following days were filled with confusion. We established our headquarters farther to the south in a thicket. There we air crew members learned about bivouac areas, command posts, message centers, etc. We also learned a lot about the soil of Pampanga Province as we rooted deeper and deeper into our foxholes with each successive air raid. By this time the enemy planes had complete command of the situation. They sometimes flew so low that we could look up into the bomb bays when they opened the doors to drop the bombs. It was terrifying beyond words to realize that just one of those bombs could put an end to everything. It was like being a wild animal, pursued by a deadly hunter.

In connection with his communications section, Croxton was in charge of a large truck-trailer affair containing a powerful radio receiver and transmitter and a room with a table where telegraphers, radio operators, and cryptographers could work in comfort. Since we had no planes, I had no duties as headquarters squadron navigator, so I devoted my time to helping Croxton code and decode secret messages. We used code books and various code devices which were more complicated to me than were the messages we sent. The whole affair from the beginning of the war until Christmas was like a nightmare—a maze of utter confusion. It was like an I.Q. test lasting twenty-four hours a day, seven days a week.

Planes did fly in from Mindanão to Clark Field, but only for the purpose of refueling or taking away some of our personnel and equipment. Generally, the same crews remained on the planes, and there was no chance for any of us to do any flying.

We contacted our planes in flight from the southern base of Del Monte on Mindanão to Clark Field, or on missions against the enemy. We were also in constant contact with the ground stations at headquarters in Manila and the ground station at Del Monte. From these sources we learned that large forces of enemy troops were landing on our island and moving in toward us from all directions, that Air Force units were being evacuated by air to the southern island bases, and that no relief was anticipated in the immediate future. Grave as the situation was, we found little time to worry over what would happen to us or what we would do next, for the long hours of going over the code books in the hot trailer, trying to construct an intelligent message from a garbled mess, took all our strength. Croxton and I both remained on duty twenty-four hours a day, sleeping rolled up in a blanket just outside the door of the trailer whenever there was a lull in our work.

One morning, as I lay rolled up in my blanket near the trailer, I was awakened by a sound like that of planes coming in on an attack, but increasing in intensity until it became a violent, ululating roar. I jumped up and ran to the edge of the thicket and saw a thin spiral of smoke running from the clouds to the east of us down toward the foot of Mount Arayat. The roar ended in a dull explosion, and we knew that a plane had been knocked out of the sky. What we did not know was that it was one of our own remaining B-17's with our friend, Colin Kelly, plunging to his death. He was returning from a mission on which he had got one or more good hits on a Japanese battleship when, as he started to let down over Clark Field, a couple of Zeros jumped him and shot him down. All of the crew members bailed out, and Kelly made the attempt but failed.

Our situation became more grave day after day, as we learned of the loss of more and more planes. Our big blow came when returning fighter pilots reported that they had spotted a convoy of eighty-five warships in Lingayen Gulf, some miles to the north of us. The message was brought to us by Boyd (Buzz) Wagner, one of the first aces of World War II, who had led the remnants of his P-40 fighter squadron in over the convoy as it was unloading troops. He told us how he had got a hit on one of the ships and seen it disintegrate below him. But his efforts to stop the landing were about as effective as shooting at a tank with a pop gun. Buzz told us that one good squadron of dive bombers could have destroyed the entire convoy. But we did not have one good squadron of dive bombers, and thousands of Japs swarmed ashore on the beaches of Lingayen Gulf just sixty miles to the north of us.

If there was any one thing more certain than anything else, it was that the invading Japanese would soon be overrunning Clark Field. How long would it take them to travel sixty miles? We had no way to stop them and nowhere to go.

3. Sweating it out

The worrisome hours had grown into days and the days into weeks since the Japs had first bombed Clark Field. And for anyone who might have been interested, it was the twenty-third day of December, 1941. There was no talk of Christmas and there was no talk of home, for neither could have any meaning for us. Our new oriental home, which only three weeks before had been such a tropical paradise where we lived in luxury such as we had never known before, had been bombed and blasted out of existence. We no longer had houseboys at our beck and call to wash our clothes, prepare our food, shine our shoes, or bring us a drink of water. We ate on the ground out of mess kits. We slept on the ground rolled up in blankets, and when we wanted a drink we filled our canteens with warm, chlorinated water from a lister bag—when we could find one. We had been bombed and strafed so many times we had lost count, and the sound of approaching planes became agonizing to our ears.

I was sitting in the doorway of the communications trailer when Croxton suddenly appeared before me. "Let's get the station torn down," he ordered. "We're getting ready to move out."

"Where're we going?" I inquired.

"I can't tell you."

"What do you mean, you can't tell me? You mean you can't tell me or you won't tell me?"

"I can't tell you."

This was good news, and the men moved rapidly as they started to dismantle the antenna, which was supported by long guy wires.

"Hold it a minute! That's our call. Someone's trying to get us," the Sergeant called out.

"Better take it. Might be something important," Croxton ordered.

I dug out my code book, and as the Sergeant wrote the symbols, I excitedly decoded the message: "ZY to MY, CARRIER PIGEONS ARRIVED SAFELY."

"That does it. Let's get this thing down and get the hell out of here," Croxton cried.

The sun was sinking behind the mountains to the west of Clark Field as our outfit started to roll to meet the main body of our convoy on the road south of the landing strip. I had been handling secret messages all day, but not one message had given the slightest clue as to where we were going. Certainly the carrier pigeon message had thrown no light on the problem. To my knowledge, Croxton was the only one who knew our destination, and I was not certain that he knew where we were going. One thing was sure, we were headed in a southeasterly direction on the road toward Manila at a very low rate of speed. We passed many foot soldiers loaded down with their gear, traveling in the opposite direction, but we had no way of knowing where they were going either. We passed the little town of Angeles, and it was completely dark when we reached San Fernando. Then, instead of taking the road toward Manila, we turned to the right and headed for the west. Our speed picked up, and we clipped along at thirty-five and forty miles an hour, passing truck after truck which had stalled or run off the road and upset. From time to time the caravan slowed down, and later there were long stops with nobody knowing where we were or the reason for stopping. At about two o'clock in the morning orders came down the line for us to pull off the road and find a place to park where we would not be observed by enemy aircraft in the morning. We parked the truck-trailer in a clump of high bushes, rolled up in our blankets, and slept on the ground for a couple of hours, until the light of day awakened us and showed us our new home—the jungles of Bataan.

Bataan was a beautiful place as dawn broke on that day before Christmas. The jungles around us were green and dense, but out across the blue water of Manila Bay to the east we could see the skyline of Manila. To the southeast two radio towers on the distant coast marked the Cavite Navy Yard, and across the channel to the south was the mighty fortress of Corregidor, guarding the mouth of Manila Bay as it opened into the wide China Sea to the west. We knew that Bataan Peninsula was about sixteen miles long and about seven miles wide. We were on the southern tip of the peninsula, and we had left the landing forces of the enemy far to the north of us. This gave us a feeling of security which we had not enjoyed since we first learned of the Japanese landings on the island.

Bataan had been chosen as the place where we were to maintain a defensive stand until reinforcements of planes and men arrived from the United States. It was comforting to be within three or four miles of Corregidor, which had guns that could blow a ship out of the water eighteen miles at sea—Corregidor, with a system of mine fields controlled from a central switchboard so that it could blast any ship which dared to venture near—Corregidor, the most heavily fortified island in the world, with stores of food and ammunition sufficient to last for five years.

After acquainting ourselves with the scenery about us, we set up our radio station to keep guard for any messages that might concern us. The air was dead on our frequency for the entire day. It was as if the war had ended and left us stranded in the jungle. There were no air raids, and we saw no enemy planes.

Toward evening, as we were whiling away the time in the radio trailer, I looked up to see the lanky figure of Jim Dey standing in the doorway. He beckoned me to come outside.

"Whit, the whole damned outfit is shoving off tonight," he whispered.

"Shoving off?" I queried. "Where're we going?"

"Del Monte Pineapple Plantation on Mindanão," was the reply.

"Golly, that's good news. Maybe we can get back to flying. They ought to be getting some new planes in from the States one of these days," I answered. Then, after thinking for a second, "I haven't had any word of it, and it'll take at least half an hour to get this station knocked down."

"Don't worry about that, pal," he replied. "You're not going any place. This boat is reserved for air crew members. You and Croxton are signal slingers now, and you're going to keep your ether tickler up here and keep in contact with us Air Corps boys when we get lonely flying around these parts." He turned to leave, then added, "Don't worry, Whit. I'll drop you a nice juicy pineapple on my way over sometime."

"Wait a minute, Jim," I pleaded. "Do you mean that just because I volunteered to do this work while you guys sat on your fat A's, I'm getting rewarded by having to stay here? Where did you get that bit of cheerful information?"

"Major Miller told me. He said he would be up here right away, so I thought I'd drop by and prepare you for the shock."

"Thanks a lot, old fellow. See you later."

"It's not as bad as it sounds. They say the boat will come back and pick up the rest of the squadron later."

With that Jim strode away through the bushes. I really hated to see him go. He could make fun of the darkest situation, and we had great need for that type of talent.

Seconds after Jim had left me, Major Charles Miller, who was to be our squadron commander, walked up. He called the men of the communications section together and said, "Men, we're going to be separated from the rest of the 19th Group for a short time. A portion of the squadron is being transported to a southern base. As soon as the ship returns we will all be evacuated. In the meantime I have selected a new spot for the communications section, about three kilometers down the road and then about two kilometers inland into the foothills. Colonel Daly will be in command there."

With that we started tearing down the station, and in a short time we were on the move again. It was almost completely dark as we observed the more fortunate members of our squadron making their way down to the ship to sail for Mindanáo. I rode in a jeep with the guide, and when we turned off the main road and headed back into the foothills, it became obvious that no motor vehicle had ever traversed this trail before. In the pitch-black of the night we inched our way along, little by little, fording streams at one time and then hugging close to a narrow trail on the side of a hill. Some of the men in the other vehicles became restless with the slow progress and preceded us up the trail on foot.

Suddenly a dark figure appeared beside our jeep and shouted excitedly, "Hey, Lieutenant, somebody ran past us up ahead. They won't answer our challenge. Shall I fire on 'em?"

With that a tall figure rushed past the side of the jeep shouting, "All right, you! Come out or I'll shoot!" As if in answer to the challenge, two figures which appeared to be cows, or more likely carabao, went running through the bushes.

"Don't shoot till you see the whites of their eyes," somebody laughed, and everybody joined in.

"Just can't take any chances," said a voice which I

46

recognized as Jim Dey's. It was he who had challenged the carabao.

"Hey, Jim, thought you were taking a cruise," I gibed.

Walking along beside the jeep, he answered, "No, they decided it wouldn't be safe to leave you boys up here with all these Japs running loose, so they left me here to look after you."

"Well, whatever your reason, I'm damned glad you're here." I was honestly glad that Jim was still with us. He was one of those rare individuals who seemed to get a kick out of a dangerous situation. I never did understand why Jim had not finished pilot training until he told me he had the distinction of being one of the few people in the Air Corps who had successfully landed a plane upside down and backwards at the same time. To substantiate his boast, he had clippings from the Washington papers which he had cut out while recuperating in Walter Reed Hospital.

At last we came to a stream which was wider than the others. After removing some large boulders, we managed to get our jeep and other vehicles across. On the other side we found ourselves in a huge flat area surrounded by big trees. There, our guide said, was the location of our new camp. We had reached our destination, and before bedding down for the night, we set up the radio station in order that we might keep a monitor on our frequency.

With the dawn of the new day we found ourselves deep in the heart of the Bataan jungle. The remnants of our headquarters squadron and the 93rd Squadron moved in with us, and we had a sizable camp in a mango grove which gave us protection from the hot Philippine sun and would also hide us from Japanese reconnaissance planes.

During the last few days of the old year and the first few weeks of the new year, we worked constantly. Croxton was assigned to a higher headquarters several kilometers down the road, and I was left in charge of the communications section. In addition to the radio station, I had charge of setting up a telephone system connecting our headquarters with Bataan Field to the east. At the point nearest to the bay from us, where we had turned off the main road to get to our camp, an outfit known to us as the Navy Engineers scraped off the rice paddies and built an air strip which we called Cabcaben Field. Later I set up the telephone switchboard and a radio transmitter and receiver on the ridge above the field for a control tower.

As our little air strip in the rice paddies began to take shape, our officers and men built and camouflaged revetments for the dozens of fighter planes and bombers which would be coming to us soon. Ours was, no doubt, one of the very first of the hundreds of tactical air strips which later grew up all over the Pacific wherever there was an island that could be used. Bataan Strip, about three kilometers to the east of us, was already in use by the few fighters which had flown down from Clark Field when we evacuated the place; and another strip was being built at Mariveles, on farther to the west. But our Cabcaben Field had one unique feature no other tactical air base possessed—we had no airplanes.

One evening, when I was walking back to camp from our air strip, I stopped by Jim Dey's bunk to catch up on the latest rumors, for every day the rumors of reinforcements increased in number and in interest. Jim was not there, but as I turned, I saw him standing in the middle of a stream on a big boulder, stark naked, singing at the top of his voice and strutting as if he were leading a victory parade down Market Street in San Francisco:

"The men will cheer, the boys will shout,
The ladies they will all turn out,

And we'll all feel gay
When Johnny comes marching home!"

I watched and listened until he had finished, and then shouted to him, "And what, my dear MacArthur, is the occasion for all this merriment?"

"Christ, Whit, haven't you heard the news? A big convoy is coming through the San Bernardino Straits right this minute. Aircraft carriers, battle wagons, the whole works. It's only a matter of hours until . . ." Then he started in again:

"The old church bell will peal with joy,
Hurrah! Hurrah!
To welcome home our darling boy,
Hurrah! Hurrah!
The lads and lassies gay,
With roses they will strew the way,
And we'll all feel gay
When Johnny comes marching home!"

Another voice sounded up from nearby. "Hello, Whit, we got an honest rumor." I turned to see an old friend whom I had not seen since we arrived on Bataan.

"Why it's old Renka, you old son-of-a-gun. John Ivan Renka, where did you come from? Thought you had sailed south."

"No, I've been over with the 200th Coast Artillery boys, helping them identify friendly and enemy planes. We never saw anything but Jap planes, so the colonel said I might as well come on back to the outfit."

"Where did this latest rumor come from?" I asked.

"Jim picked it up down at the Navy base at Mariveles today. The Navy is betting two to one that there will be planes in within twenty-four hours."

"Sounds good to me," I answered, "but what I learned today wasn't so good. You know that ship that was supposed to come back and take us to Del Monte?" They both stood with open mouths as I went

49

on, "Well, she was unloading at the dock there in Mindanão, and a lonely Jap patrol plane spotted her, dropped an egg, and sent her to the bottom."

"No!" exclaimed Renka. "Where did you get that?"

"Major Miller had me send a query about the ship because she was due back several weeks ago, and that's the answer I got back," I answered.

"Did they all get off?" asked Jim.

"Yeah, except one signal officer was killed and Elmer Brown, that young West Pointer, got hurt when he dived into the water."

"Well, I'll be damned." Renka shook his head. "That means we're really stuck here, doesn't it?"

"Yes, but of course if there's anything to that rumor Dey . . ."

"What do you mean if there's anything to that rumor?" interrupted Dey. "That came straight from the Navy."

"We've had rumors from the Navy before, from the chaplain and from Corregidor, but we're still here. I'm going to believe that there's reinforcements on the way when I see 'em coming," I answered. Then I added, "I'm OD tonight. Think I'll get an early chow and get back down to the strip. I'll let you know if I hear anything good."

I headed for the mess area, wondering whether there might not be some truth to the new rumors. The mess area consisted of our field kitchen and a few wooden tables which had been built near the edge of the stream and around the foot of a small hill which separated it from the rest of the camp area. The chow was the same as it had been for days on end—rice and canned tomatoes—but before going to the chow line it was necessary to take the usual dose of liquid quinine, doled out by a sergeant, as if that were the price one had to pay for the meal.

After a quick meal I walked the long trail from our camp to Cabcaben Field on the edge of the bay. It was twilight, and everything was peaceful when I stopped in at the dugout where we had the telephone switchboard. The operator was taking routine calls and had nothing of interest to relate. There were several groups of men sitting around in the bamboo thicket, discussing the various rumors of the day. The phone rang in the little bamboo shack we called "operations," and I wandered over to listen to the conversation. Before I reached the shack the operations officer burst out of the door and said quietly to me, "Planes coming in sometime tonight."

"How many and where from?"

"I don't know," he answered, "but we're going to be ready for 'em."

"That confirms the rumor Jim Dey got from the Navy today."

"Lord, I hope so," was his answer. "I better get my crews together. We're all set for 'em."

After a while the excitement of the news died down, and the ground crews sat around in the dark bamboo thicket waiting for the big moment which we had thought would never come.

I listened to one of the groups engaged in a serious conversation.

One voice was saying, "Then that means the Japs have captured everything north of New Guinea and west of Midway in about three months."

"Yeah, damned funny how easy they took Singapore, and it supposed to be such a strong base," another said.

"Well, they won't take old Corregidor so easy. I'd like to see that old baby open up on a Jap fleet," spoke another.

"It's a wonder there's anything left of the place, the way they been bombing her the last few days. They say the Japs are using it as a practice range to train crews before they send them south."

"Bet old 'Dugout Doug' is so deep down in one of them tunnels you'd have to use a diver's suit to reach him."

"No, I heard that whenever the air raid siren sounds, he orders his private car and drives around the island to watch the bombs fall. Says he gets a thrill out of it." Everyone laughed at that.

"Then how did he get the name 'Dugout Doug?'"

"I don't know, but you'd better not be heard calling him that. They say it's a court-martial offense and that it actually came out on orders on the Rock."

"Speaking of MacArthur," a new voice joined in, "I thought I'd fall off the control tower this afternoon laughing at that crazy Smith. He put on an imitation of a San Francisco newscast. Started it with 'Ladies and Gents, KGEI now brings you fifteen minutes of the latest war news from the Pacific. MacArthur, MacArthur, MacArthur, MacArthur, etc. And now to repeat the headline news—MacArthur, MacArthur, MacArthur. Ladies and Gentlemen, for the past fifteen minutes you have been listening to news from the war in the Pacific. KGEI nows signs off!'"

Everyone laughed at this, and then there was a long silence as if everyone were listening and thinking. The night was quiet except for the spasmodic rumble of artillery fire up at the front, which sounded the same as it had for the past few weeks. The infantry had set up a line of defense about eight miles from us, and it had been holding well.

Presently another voice spoke out, asking the same question I had heard dozens of times before. "What in hell are we doing out here in this God-forsaken place anyway? So we defend the Philippines. So what? What if the Japs should get the place, then what? I can't see that it makes a damned bit of difference to any of us Americans except a few who own sugar plantations, pineapple plantations and mines out here. Now if I were defending San Francisco Bay, that'd be a different story. Boy, could I fight then!"

As if the name San Francisco had suddenly awakened him, another said, "San Francisco, San Francisco, what a beautiful name! Boy oh boy, my one prayer in life is that some day I can walk up to one of them beautiful bars on both of my two good feet, slap both my two good hands with five fingers on each hand down on the counter, look the bartender in the face with my own two eyes and say, "Give me a double shot of Seagram's with some of that good old San Francisco water—minus chlorine—for a chaser."

"Amen, brother!" shouted another. "I'd even be satisfied with an old warm beer for a chaser if I had . . ." He stopped abruptly, as the murmur of an airplane engine came through the darkness.

We ran to the edge of the strip, our hearts beating faster and faster as we listened—not a word was spoken. The roar grew louder and louder. Then we heard a plane warming up on Bataan Field to the east of us. Sounded like a plane taking off from there. It was probably going out to lead the expected planes in.

Suddenly a plane came into sight, approaching our strip from the bay to the south. He flashed his lights, and our field lights came on, tiny points which faintly outlined the strip. The plane was making a straight-in approach. What would it be, a P-38, a P-39, or a P-47? We waited breathlessly as the dark shadow descended toward the runway. He was on the ground, and before he stopped rolling another light flashed out over the bay. It was another plane. Help had arrived. We were safe. Excitement filled the air, for we knew we would soon be flying missions.

Like clockwork our ground crews took the first plane as soon as the engines were cut and rolled it into the revetment. "What kind of a plane is it?" "Looks like an old P-40," "Yes, it's a P-40." By now three were on the ground, and the fourth light had just flashed over the bay. Three pilots stood there watching number four come in. They were young kids, laughing and carefree. How I envied them! If

53

only I were a pursuit pilot, I could be flying one of those planes myself. What a thrill it would be to fly again, looking down, instead of looking up into the open belly of a Jap bomber from a foxhole.

"Down! Bake, down!" one cried. "Nope, he'll have to make another pass at it." The plane roared over our heads and banked around to the left. We followed the reddish-blue light of his exhaust as he circled low above us. Then suddenly there was a cough in the engine, a red flash lit up the sky west of the field, and seconds later a loud explosion reached our ears.

The succeeding silence was broken by one of the three kids. Lieutenant Sam Grashio called, "Somebody call General George and tell him Baker has crashed!"

I rushed to a telephone and called General Harold E. George, head of the Fifth Intercepter Command, at his headquarters. "Who was it?" he asked.

"Baker, sir."

One word, "God," and the receiver clicked on the other end. I knew the news would be received gravely by the General, because he took a personal interest in each of his boys. He was proud of them, and they were proud of him.

Baker's P-40 was demolished and strewn over five hundred feet of jungle. He was found staggering among the trees, talking to himself, when men from the nearby antiaircraft unit reached the scene.

We had received our reinforcements. Three beat-up P-40's from Bataan Field, three kilometers away!

After the great disappoinment of that night, Dey's rumor of an approaching convoy was enhanced by more and more rumors. Our sources were the Navy, the chaplain, the Marines, and an officer from Corregidor. All were good, all were reasonable, and all had one thing in common—they were figments of some brave soul's imagination. Wishful hoping. Despite the fact that rumor after rumor of everything under the sun was proving false day after day, we all had faith and hope so strong that we embraced each new rumor as if it were the first we had ever heard.

I set up a radio receiver in our camp area under the mango trees so that everyone could hear the latest news from station KGEI in San Francisco at six every evening. For the first few nights everybody in camp turned out to hear the news—to hear how help was on the way—how our Navy had destroyed the Jap Navy in the Marshall and Gilbert Islands—how the United States would produce thousands of tanks and planes this year and thousands of tanks and planes next year—how the Rainbow Division, veterans of World War I, at a big banquet in New York had wished they were on Bataan—how a vast armada of Jap planes had hammered at Bataan and Corregidor throughout the day and night. We knew this last part of the news was true without any doubt.

That was the news day after day until the Japs finally located the frequency and jammed it so that all we could hear was ". . . thousands this year—thousands next year—Jap planes—etc." The crowd of listeners dwindled. After a few weeks only a handful of hollow-eyed, ragged soldiers hung on, trying to glean a word of hope from the mixture of static and confusion. It was heart-rending to see them turn away evening after evening and walk back to their areas without a word.

The camp became infested with malaria and dysentery, and the number of cases increased steadily until half the men in camp were unable to perform their duties. As a result, it became necesary to lengthen the hours on guard duty, switchboard operation, and work on the airfield. Matters became even worse when half the men in our camp were ordered to front-line duty with the infantry eight miles to the north of us. Later, an order came through for another one hundred men, but it was cancelled because of the large amount of sickness in our camp.

Through the latter part of February and the early part of March, the routine at Cabcaben Field was much the same day after day. The *Voice of Freedom,* Corregidor's radio station, continued to play *The Star-Spangled Banner* and give out with morale-boosting programs from the tunnel deep under Malinta Hill. Among other things, they told of the new game the troops on Bataan were playing to relieve the monotony of the long hours of waiting. They called the game "Slap the Jap off the Map," and it was played by throwing bread at one another. The ostensible purpose of the program was to make the Japs believe that we really had bread to throw away. Actually, we were slowly starving, and we did not think the news broadcasts were funny. By that time our field rations had been cut in half and then cut in half again so that we were always hungry.

More and more we found ourselves walking into the hills in search of food and berries. Some of the fellows learned of a root which, when boiled for a long time, closely resembled potatoes. At chow one evening Jim Dey called me aside and handed me what looked like a piece of squirrel. Without questioning, I took a bite—or rather, tried to take a bite.

"What's this?" I asked. "Petrified squirrel?"

"No, boy, that's the real stuff. Monkey."

"Monkey? Where did you capture him?" I tried another bite.

"Didn't capture him," Jim grinned. "Turned himself in. Said the other monkeys had accused him of looking like a Jap."

"Tastes good, but it's too tough to chew." I tried again, but found the morsel I held in my hand more like leather than like meat.

"You've gotta get used to this because we're going to have plenty of this from now on. There's a whole family living up on the ridge, and we're going back and get some more tonight."

"How do you get 'em?" I asked.

"Well, you cut a hole in a piece of bamboo just big enough for the monkey to get his hand through. Then you put some rice inside, and when the monkey gets his hand full of rice, he can't get it out. He'll stay there all night because he's not smart enough to let loose of the rice," Jim explained.

"Sounds good if you can get the monkey to cooperate," I said. When I looked into the stew pot and saw what looked like the body of a very small baby, I lost my appetite for monkey and everything else for a moment.

Almost every day Jim had some new concoction to supplement the meager rations we got at the mess area. One of his tastiest dishes was iguana stew, made from the giant lizards which looked more like prehistoric monsters than anything we had ever seen. Jim's genius at procuring rations did not go unnoticed, and old Colonel "Mo" Daly, although he did not always approve of the tactics used, rewarded him by designating him our supply officer.

This recognition by "Old Ironsides," as we sometimes called Colonel Daly, seemed to stimulate Jim's genius. When the pilots complained that Cabcaben Field was too dusty and that in warming up their engines they blew dustclouds high enough to be seen by the Japs, Jim brought them a small fire engine which he had somehow procured from Corregidor. When there was a shortage of salt and spices for the mess hall, Jim turned up from somewhere with a generous supply.

One evening word spread over camp that we were to have steak for dinner and that it would not be carabao or horse meat such as we had received from time to time. It was unbelievable, for we had never had steak on Bataan before. But come chow time, there it was—a fine piece of juicy steak for each of us. When I asked Major Miller the reason for the fine meal, he said, "Dey says everybody gets steak today."

That seemed to be a satisfactory answer to everyone except me.

"Where in the world did you ever get that fine steak?" I asked Jim when he came through the chow line.

"That Corporal Jack Gould is a prize." Jim looked at me with a twinkle in his eyes. "When the sergeant at the supply dump told me that quarter of beef was for the generals' mess, I just winked at Gould and led the sergeant away to another part of the dump for some more supplies. When we got back to where the steak had been, it was gone, Gould was gone, and the truck was gone. I started to hitchhike back to camp, but when I got down to the main road, there was Gould, grinning from ear to ear, with that quarter of beef in the back end of the truck. Gould said he figured those generals had eaten steak since he had, and that he wanted to get another taste of it before he died."

"He's a fine soldier, and if he doesn't get court-martialed for this, I suggest we put him in for a promotion," I said.

Without further conversation we finished our delicious meal and walked back to the camp area.

The next morning at dawn I heard wild cheering from the center of the camp area. Shouting like that could mean only one thing—good news—so I threw my clothes on and ran to learn what had happened. The first fellow I met announced, "There's a hell of a big convoy steaming into Manila Bay, and that ain't no rumor 'cause I saw it with my own eyes."

By this time there was a general mass movement from the camp area up the hillside. The trail was steep, and it was almost a quarter of a mile to the top of the hill where we could see out over the water. Many men with more enthusiasm than strength fell by the wayside and had to rest before continuing up the trail, but everyone got a boost about halfway up the hill. One man who had been to the top passed us on his way to camp with, "They're American ships. I saw them myself. It's a big convoy coming around Corregidor."

What a day! That was the day we had been waiting for so long. The rumors had come true, and our hopes and prayers had been realized. As I drew nearer to the top of the ridge, I could see some ships. The sun was shining and there was not a cloud in the sky as we finally reached the top of the ridge and looked out across Manila Bay. It was true. It was no longer a rumor. There, before our eyes, we saw a number of big ships rounding the eastern tip of Corregidor from the south and west.

At last the time had come when we would see a turning point in the war with the Japs. We would have food, airplanes, mail from home, and relief from all the worries that had plagued us over the past few months. Each time another big ship appeared around the point, another wild cheer rang out over the hill-side and into the valley below. Nothing so completely wonderful had ever happened to any of us before, and not one person was hiding the emotion he felt.

There was no aerial opposition to the convoy, and it looked as if the whole fleet had sneaked in without being noticed by the Japanese. Although the ships were some four miles away, there was no question that they were big transports and that they were American.

As soon as I had feasted my eyes upon the sight and satisfied myself that I was really awake and not just dreaming, I started back down the ridge to find Dey and Renka. But when I located Dey in the camp area, he did not display the enthusiasm I expected. "The old man wants to see you in his tent right away," he informed me.

"It's a real convoy, and I just saw it with my own eyes," I assured him as I ran toward Colonel Daly's tent.

Inside his tent, the Colonel greeted me with a

stone-cold face. "Whitcomb, what's the matter with those telephone operators of yours—sending false messages? You must impress them with the fact . . ."

"Sir, I have just been to the top of the ridge and saw those ships coming in myself. There were . . ."

"What you saw were the ships that have been lying south of Corregidor since the beginning of the war. They are simply being moved around to the north side so they will be out of range of the Jap artillery fire from the Cavite shore."

Much embarrassed and deeply disappointed, I answered, "Yes, sir. I will tell them."

"See that it does not happen again," he ordered as I left the tent.

The letdown that followed this episode left us lower than we had ever been before. We wondered how much longer it would continue. How would it all end? We refused to consider the possibility that it would not end well—that the great convoy we had hoped and prayed for so long would never arrive.

Strange, the conclusions a rational mind can reach when hope is gone. A man gambling his last dollar does not consider how he will face the world with empty pockets, but instead he looks upon that last dollar as a winner. He convinces himself that it is a winner until he loses it. So help would come to Bataan—it could not be otherwise.

It was natural that we considered Bataan to be the very heart of the war in the Pacific. If Bataan could be reinforced, we could easily sweep on northward to the China coast and ultimately crush the Japanese from there by air. After that, the entire Allied effort could be diverted to the European Theater. That seemed entirely sensible and feasible to us. Nothing less than total defeat could ever convince us that any other plan ever existed.

That night, after we had seen the big convoy steaming around the tip of Corregidor, I could not sleep. Jim and I talked late into the night.

"But that doesn't mean there is no convoy on its way. It's been more than three months now since the war started, and there ought to be something here any day now," Jim mused.

"Yes, but if the Japs make another landing behind our lines, and it's successful, the convoy may be too late."

"Of course, there is also the possibility that the sub will come back and get us."

"What sub?" I had heard nothing about a submarine.

"Eight or ten of our B-17 pilots went out last night on their way to Java," was the answer.

"Say, that's good news. Who all went?"

"Oh, 'Pinkie' Hovette, Croxton, Shed, Carpenter, Pease—that's about all I can think of."

"Well, I hope that's the beginning of a movement to get air crews out of here so we can go to work."

"You know, I get nervous when I'm on the ground too long at a time," Jim said thoughtfully, "especially when there's a bunch of Japs just over the hill arguing over who's gonna get old Jim Dey's scalp. You know, I'm gettin' so I don't even enjoy my rice any more. Must be worry."

"Probably worry," I agreed, "or it might even be the rice. Had you noticed that the worms in the rice we're getting lately aren't as fat as they used to be?"

"Yeah, they're probably worried too," he sighed.

Then all was quiet. There had been a little firing at the front lines, but it had died down completely, and only the noises of the jungle broke the peaceful silence that hovered over Bataan.

As I lay there, I wondered what new hope would be born tomorrow. What dream would send our hopes sky-high, only to be blasted to pieces again? At dawn the eager beavers would be over Cabcaben Field again with those old-fashioned planes with the fixed landing gear. They would come diving in through the puffs of anti-aircraft fire and into a vast spray of flying red embers of machine gun tracers, drop their bombs, and fly back to Manila apparently untouched. Minutes later the second shift would pay its respects to our mighty force of three P-40's at Cabcaben Field. My thoughts raced on. Funny how they bombed us day after day and week after week and never put a single scartch on any one of our three ships. Not to be discouraged, though, they would come back a couple of times before noon. After the first show was over, I'd go down the hill to chow. At breakfast in our outdoor dining hall, the boys from the Second Observation Squadron would relate what they had heard and seen on duty during the night up the coast.

After breakfast we would see what the night crews on the switchboards and radio had to report—any good news—any radio messages to go out—how many more unable to report for duty. Then there would be infantry training—how to fire plus how to take cover and how to approach your objective. Many of the men had never so much as fired an Army rifle, and I was one of them.

After that there might be a telephone line to string to the new anti-aircraft outfit on the ridge to the west, toward Hospital Number Two.

Yes, tomorrow would be just like yesterday, the day

before, and the day before that. Wonder what the folks back in Indiana are doing. No word from them for about four months. They'd probably get a laugh if they could see this cot I made out of bamboo and this square mosquito net with a piece of canvas tied across the top of it. Seems like Indiana is in another world from this, and we have been here on Bataan for a lifetime.

The stars are bright tonight! Wonder if the people at home ever look up at these stars. Surely Mother would sit and look at them by the hour if she could only realize that they were the same stars shining down on Bataan tonight.

And Dad—I had stood in the kitchen at home only six months ago and told him that we might go to war against the Japanese and that we would surely defeat them in about six months.

It seemed I had hardly slept a wink when I heard a familar voice with a familar song:

> "How ya gonna keep 'em
> Down on the farm
> After they've seen Bataan?"

That could be no one but Drachenberg, who was then assigned to our motor pool about two kilometers to the west of us. As I started to raise up off my bunk, he looked down at me. "What's happened to you, my boy? You look like I felt yesterday when those 'Sons of the Sun' dropped their bombs on the motor pool."

"Don't know, Drack," I answered. "Maybe the old malaria bug has caught up with me. I don't think I slept a wink last night."

"Yep, looks like you've got it. Just take it easy for a few weeks and you'll be like new. I'd rather have malaria six times than go through another bombing like yesterday."

"We thought they'd land somewhere near you. They were almost directly over our heads when they unloaded, and it looked like they were going to get us. Anybody hurt?"

"Hell, no, but you should have seen old 'Buckshot' Burgess—never saw him so excited in my life."

"Did he get any shots in with his fifty-calibers?" I asked.

"No, he took that fifty-caliber machine gun off his jeep last week because he never got a chance to shoot at anything. About the only damage done was that some washing we had out got ripped to shreds. Well, I gotta get goin'," he added in his soft Texas drawl. He turned and headed down the trail singing:

> "How ya gonna keep 'em
> Down on the farm . . ."

In the middle of the morning the camp doctor came by and determined that I had malaria, and had me transferred to the makeshift infirmary on the other side of the camp. Friends stopped in to cheer me up with stories of how six of our P-40's from Bataan Field had hovered over a small training plane piloted by Captain Jesse Villiamor while he took pictures of Jap landing preparations at Cavite Navy Yard, and how it ended in one of the most spectacular dog-fights of the war. Six Jap planes had been shot down in the skirmish. Others told how Captain Ed Dyess, who had recently brought back the remnants of his squadron to our camp from Agnaloma Point where they had repulsed a Jap landing, was carrying five-hundred-pound bombs under his P-40. Dyess, with a couple of others, had sunk several ships in Subic Bay on the far northwest side of Bataan Peninsula. Two of our P-40's had been wrecked while landing, and Cabcaben Field had only one operational aircraft.

One morning I saw an altar with a cross and a priest with outstretched hands, and several dozen weary men kneeling on the ground before the altar, across the area under the big mango tree. I knew they were praying to the Lord to save them and to save us, and I wished that I could pray. But I had not prayed since I was a kid in Sunday School. Once I had received a Bible from my Sunday School teacher for a year's perfect attendance. What had happened to the faith I had then? I felt that it would be cowardly for me to pray when I had not even been to church for several years. As I lay there on the hospital cot, I felt I had no one to turn to. My thoughts were no more than empty hopes and wishes.

I saw the congregation rise, and the men strolled away across the area, each feeling better for having prayed and believing that his prayers would be answered. How I envied them!

When a man is healthy he can stand and defy the world and fight to defend himself, but when he loses the use of his body through illness, he realizes how powerless he is and wishes he had something to look to for help. As the body becomes weaker, things which were of paramount importance before seem inconsequential. The war seemed a long way off, although the artillery fire sounded closer and more intense. Even word that General MacArthur had issued a stirring plea to stick to our guns because "help is on the way" meant little to us.

But a few days later word that the good general was on his way to Australia did have some meaning. It seemed a fitting climax to whatever enthusiasm we might have built up by his "help is on the way" message. This followed the usual pattern of a big build-up followed by a tremendous letdown. The hordes of Japanese over the hill would continue to press us, and ultimately there would be a landing on the sector of the beach that we defended. That was our war. It was only a tiny part of the big picture, but the stage was set. MacArthur's presence or absence meant little to us, since few of us had ever so much as seen him.

In the infirmary I lost all count of time, but it must

have been a couple of weeks before I began to regain my strength. The liquid quinine tasted bitter again, and the taste of kerosene-carbon-tetrachloride solution in which the thermometers were immersed became almost unbearable. These were signs of recovery, and soon I was up on my feet and back to duty.

The artillery fire over the hill had actually moved nearer to us, and our outfit was having nightly alerts. That meant that we would hurry to the beach with our machine guns and rifles and assume the positions that had been assigned to us in case of a Japanese invasion on the south coast of the peninsula. During my illness one of Dyess' communications officers had been assigned to my job, and I was assigned the duty of liaison officer between our sector and the headquarters of General Francisco down the beach to the west of Cabcaben Field.

Just after dark on the night of April 7, I drove a jeep westward toward the General's headquarters to check in. I knew the exact strength and disposition of the units in our sector and was supposed to keep the division headquarters advised of our position. When the invasion came and it became necessary to change the defensive plan, it would be my duty to communicate any pertinent information to my own sector commander.

The Filipino adjutant to whom I reported exclaimed, "Ah, you are Air Corps. Perhaps the other liaison officer is your comrade?"

"I doubt it," I answered, "as I am the only one from Cabcaben Field. Where is he now?"

"I think he is sleeping in the reconnaissance car out there," he answered, pointing into the darkness of the trail over which I had just traveled.

At the reconnaissance car I found a sleeping form, shook him, and as I started to ask who he was and to which outfit he belonged, he sat up and asked in a startled voice, "What is it? What is it?"

"Why, Drachenberg," I exclaimed, overjoyed to hear the familiar voice. "What are you doing here?"

"I'm liaison from our sector," he answered. "Anything new at Cabcaben Field?"

"Not a thing so far as I know, except that they really gave 'em hell up front today."

"Yeah, they say the Japs are really putting on a big push up front. Looks like if help doesn't get here pretty quick they'll be pushing us right off into Manila Bay. Think they'll try a landing tonight?" Drachenberg asked anxiously.

"I just don't know what to think. They've been telling us it would happen every night for the past week. I don't know what's holding them up."

"Boy oh boy! Did you see 'em knock those two high-flying babies down the other day? What a sight!"

"Yeah, I saw 'em. You should have seen the fellows when that one spun in like a maple leaf with just one wing. The fellows cheered more than at any time since we thought we saw the convoy coming in. Well, several seconds after the plane hit the water a terrific roaring sound, like a hundred-plane attack, sent everyone diving for the foxholes. Imagine our feelings when we realized that the sound was only the noise of that plane we had just seen fall into the bay."

"We've all been pretty jittery over at the motor pool ourselves," he replied. "Wonder why nobody bailed out of that plane. Do you suppose it's true that the Japs don't carry 'chutes?"

"Don't know, but I had a funny feeling when I caught myself feeling sorry for the Japs in that plane. I've thought of finding myself in that same position a thousand times, and I suppose those boys have brothers, sisters, girl friends, and mothers back home just like us, don't they?"

"Yes, no doubt they do, but they're not going to be thinking about our girl friends and relatives when they get a shot at us."

"No, and it doesn't look like that's going to be very long from now," I replied.

"No, it doesn't seem like it will be very long now, the way they're pushing our lines back," he said seriously.

"That aerial attack yesterday up along the coast was the most ferocious I've ever seen. Those damned fighter planes were having a field day, ripping up and down the road. Wish we had just one good squadron. We could take care of them."

"A couple of fellows came through our area last night. No rifles or anything. Said the front lines were going to pieces, and they got separated from their outfit. Damned funny how we all just sit here, knowing those bastards are going to be here within a matter of hours unless that convoy comes in," he went on.

"But what in Christ's name could we have done that we haven't done?"

"Brother, I wish I knew. Well, it's getting light. Think I'll be getting back to Cabcaben Field and see what's going on there."

It was dawn, and we had talked all night. After checking out with the adjutant, I bade Drachenberg goodby and headed my jeep back toward Cabcaben Field.

The day was much like the other hundred days we had seen on Bataan. I did not sleep, for sleep seemed unnecessary. Throughout the day more and more men from outfits up front came straggling through our camp, each telling the same story. Each had been separated from his unit during the attack in which most of his outfit had been wiped out. Toward evening a full colonel came walking through our area from the hills to the north. His outfit had become disorganized, and he had but one aim—to get away from the Japs who had broken our lines.

The artillery and aerial attacks seemed twice as heavy as they had been on the day before, and at evening time twenty-seven heavy bombers passed over our area just above the treetops. A few bombs could have wiped out our entire outfit; however, no bombs fell.

That evening I went to division headquarters early, for it seemed certain that if the landing were ever to come, it would come then. I was looking forward to talking with Drachenberg again and seeing what he had learned in the course of the day. As I turned off the main road I saw before me what had been the division headquarters, but there was not a soul in sight. Headquarters had moved out. Had they gone to the front or to the west? I had no way of knowing, so I started back toward Cabcaben Field.

On the road leading back to the camp from the main road I stopped to pick up a soldier walking toward our camp.

"Where're you headed?" I asked.

His voice was shaky and tired. "I don't know, sir. My outfit's gone."

"Gone? Where did they go?"

He looked at me with a hollow-eyed, vacant stare, his mouth partly opened, and answered, "I don't know. When I went back they were gone. I haven't had anything to eat since yesterday."

He seemed badly shaken and frightened as he went on, "Oh, God, it was terrible! They bombed and shelled us all day along the road. I kept moving past men who had been wounded. They kept crying for help. Christ! I couldn't help them."

"What's the name of your outfit?" I asked, trying to divert him from the thoughts of what he had just seen.

"My outfit? My outfit—I don't know." He hesitated and then started again, "They kept begging and begging for help but I couldn't help them. They cried for water. I gave 'em all I had and I . . ."

"I know you couldn't help," I interrupted, "but if

69

you can think of the name of your outfit, maybe I can help you find them. Where were they headed?"

"If we moved from there we were going to an airfield," he said.

As we neared camp the road was clogged with tanks, trucks, and all kinds of heavy equipment. It was reassuring to see the equipment, but it also meant that they had been forced to withdraw to this position.

As we passed one group, assembled near a field kitchen which had just been set up, my passenger exclaimed. "There's Cheb! There's Cheb!" I stopped, and he jumped out and started asking about the various fellows in his outfit. I could tell by their conversation that their losses had been heavy. Then I hastened to get back to our camp area to see what I might find there.

The area under the mango trees was crowded with weary-looking soldiers. On the western side of the grove I found Jim Dey, much excited. "Whit, get ready! We're moving to Kilometer Post Number 184 down by Mariveles. Our lines were shattered today, and we're going to get the hell out of here while the gettin's good."

I approached a group of officers just as Major Miller was giving them instructions. "We will leave here as soon as you can get your things together. Verity, Graham, Evans, Whitcomb, Jones, and I will take about twenty men each. Lead them through the back trail to the motor pool the way I showed you. Then follow the highway from there to Mariveles. The motor pool should have trucks enough to carry all of us."

A loud report resounded throughout the valley as if to punctuate the Major's instructions. "That's the 155's. They've moved up on the ridge behind us. It's time we were moving," he added as another thunderous roar burst out.

The trail across the hills to the motor pool was

difficult to follow even in the day time, and I knew it would not be easy to find our way through the black jungle at night. We hurried to our bunks and gathered up the personal effects we knew we could carry, and then went back to the grove to get the twenty men we were to guide through the two kilometers of black tropical jungle.

The hike to the motor pool was a tedious business because we could not see where we were going, and it was necessary to feel our way along. From time to time we found ourselves off the trail and in underbrush so thick that we could hardly move. At one point about halfway along the trail the group led by Lieutenant Jones wandered off the trail to the north into a valley. From the top of the ridge we could hear them screaming for help, and I had to work my way back down the hill and guide them back to the trail. The walk, which should have taken us about forty-five minutes to one hour, was accomplished in a period of three or four hours. It was late at night when we finally straggled in to the motor pool area, and we were very much relieved by the thought that the rest of our trip would be by truck.

The satisfaction we felt at reaching the motor pool was short-lived, for it took us a very few moments to find that the area had already been evacuated. The area was pitted with huge bomb craters, and the only trucks we found were those which had been put out of commission by air raids, so the only thing for us to do was to make our way back to the road and continue toward Kilometer Post Number 184 on foot. Again we assembled our individual groups and walked in single file toward the main road to the south. It was a very short distance, and in a few moments we broke out of the jungle onto the road. There we were greeted by a sight that made our blood turn cold in our veins.

The entire road was packed with vehicles of all kinds, each one overflowing with combat-weary soldiers. Both sides of the road were choked with soldiers unable to find a place on a vehicle.

I was so surprised and stunned by the sight that I was unable to speak for a few moments. Then, in a voice that I hardly recognized as my own, I suggested, "It's too far for us to try to walk to Kilometer 184. Let's wait for rides if we can find them and then meet at Kilometer 184 whenever we can get there."

By this time there were only about sixty of us in the three groups which had been led through the back trail by Lieutenants Jones and Evans and myself. We had no way of knowing what had happened to Major Miller and the other groups, whether they had gone on ahead or whether they were still fighting their way through the dark jungle behind us. Sometimes the traffic on the road was fast, and sometimes it crept along at a snail's pace. Then, at other times, there would be long halts in the procession to the west. Gradually, we were able to find rides for one, two, or three of our members until, after a long time, only Lieutenant Evans and I were left to catch a ride. Evans was a tall thin B-17 pilot from Enid, Oklahoma, and he was as much stunned and surprised at the spectacle of the large mass movement along the road as I was. Finally we caught a ride on a truck loaded with personnel from Hospital Number Two, including a couple of Army nurses.

"Where're you headed?" we asked.

"To the docks at Mariveles. Then to Corregidor. Where're you going?"

"We're going to Kilometer Post Number 184 to meet the rest of our outfit," Evans answered.

The traffic continued to move on as before, sometimes at a good gait, then, at other times, at a very slow speed or completely stopped. After moving along in this fashion for about an hour, we came to a stop that lasted longer than any of the others. It was in the vicinity of Army Hospital Number One. There were tremendous explosions up ahead, and we guessed that a road was being shelled to the west of us.

"Looks like we're getting some interference up ahead, doesn't it? Don't suppose we're being cut off?" someone asked.

"No," another responded. "That looks like maybe the ammunition dump's going up. It's along here somewhere."

Soon the whole forest and sky ahead of us were lit up like an exploding inferno with all the colors of the rainbow shooting through the trees and into the heavens. The noise was deafening, and the odor of burnt powder filled the air. No Fourth of July spectacle was ever half as impressive as the show before us. We sat in awed silence while the inferno ahead increased in fury until it seemed the whole world was about to explode. It seemed a fitting climax to our campaign in the Philippine Islands. We had been bombed out of Clark Field, starved and driven from Cabcaben Field, and now, with the Japs pushing us from the east, we were up against a wall of fire to the west. After a long time the explosions subsided, and we moved forward again and on through the wall of fire.

By the time we reached the Mariveles docks the curtain of night began to lift, and a cold gray dawn spread over Bataan. The truck stopped at the turnoff, and we started to unload.

"Better come along to Corregidor with us," one of the nurses invited.

"Sure like to," I answered, "but we have to go up to meet the rest of our outfit north of Mariveles."

"What're you going to do there?" one asked.

"Looks like we'll set up a last-ditch stand and hold on until reinforcements arrive," I said.

"Good luck to you," another shouted as Evans and I climbed off the truck and started walking along the road.

"Better walk where we can take cover when the planes come over," Evans suggested.

"We'll get another ride and be there in no time at all," I answered.

We had walked only a short distance when a truck stopped and picked us up. We moved fast from then on, since there were very few vehicles on the road going in that direction from Mariveles.

"Looks like everyone else is going to Corregidor," Evans observed.

"I expect we'll find a lot of them up at 184 when we get there," I said.

As we raced along the highway we passed a number of vehicles coming from the opposite direction. Then we noticed some trucks which had big white sheets held up by the passengers. Farther along the road we saw the drivers of some of the trucks holding white rags tied on the ends of sticks. At last our truck pulled to a stop, and I saw a small cement post along the side of the road which was marked "KM 184." We unloaded and walked into a big open field where there was a large number of persons assembled. As we left the road and started into the field, two colonels met us. One said, "General King drove to the Japanese lines this morning to surrender his forces on Bataan. Nothing has been heard from him since; however, the troops will be prepared for an orderly surrender to the Japanese when they arrive."

Then it struck us suddenly. The white flags we had seen were the white flags of surrender, and we had not recognized them. It was as if we were being guided into a trap by our own people.

Evans looked at me seriously and asked, "Do you suppose they knew that we were coming here to surrender when they ordered us to Kilometer 184 last night?"

"I don't know. But I don't like it."

By this time we were nearer to the middle of the field, and there another officer had an order for us.

"Put your forty-five in this pile and your ammunition in that pile over there." As Evans followed the officer's instructions, I walked on toward the edge of the field as if I had not understood him. There I sat down and slipped off my gun belt with my forty-five and the ammunition and pushed them under a little bush before I walked back to join the group.

I walked back to the center of the area where there was a big pile of rifles and pistols and another pile of ammunition, and searched the area to see if I could find Major Miller. After a while I found Jim Dey sitting on the running board of a truck staring at the ground. "Hey, Dey, what do you make of it?"

"Don't know," he replied, shifting his eyes up without moving his head.

"Where's Major Miller?"

"He's about two kilometers down the road. There's another group over there on the Mariveles cutoff."

As we talked we heard the drone of planes, and looked to see three small Japanese aircraft winging leisurely overhead. "Seems funny not to have to duck into a foxhole when they come over," I observed.

"Yeah, but don't be too sure. I wouldn't trust those sons-of-bitches." As the words left Jim's lips we saw two tiny silver streaks drop from the plane that had been over us just a moment before. With that, everyone in the area instinctively ran for cover.

"Let's get the hell out of here, Whit!" Jim cried.

"I'm all for it, but where can we go from here?"

"Don't know, but wherever it is, it will be as safe as this is."

At that instant Renka walked up and stopped in front of us with his hands on his hips, without saying a word.

"We're getting the hell out of here, Renka," Jim whispered. "Get yourself a forty-five and come along."

"I have mine hidden over here," I said. "Meet you at the main road as soon as we can get there."

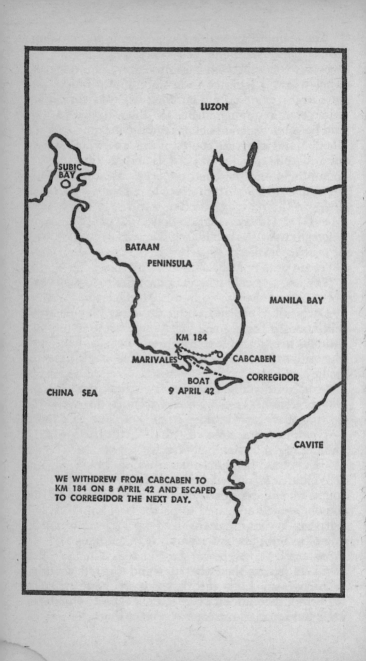

The moment we reached our decision to escape our whole perspective changed. Though we had no idea where we were going, we had one purpose in mind. That was to get down to the shore, get a boat, and get away from land before the Japanese soldiers came streaming over the hills to take us. No longer did we have to remain in one place to be bombed and shelled and starved. We were free to move, and we moved quickly.

By the time I reached the road I found Jim and Renka waiting in an old reconnaissance car they had found. Without a word we turned and drove toward Mariveles Harbor. There were still a number of vehicles on the road with white flags, and as we streaked across the Mariveles air strip we observed a large group of Filipinos hovered at one end of the strip with big white flags, waiting to surrender. When we reached the other end of the field, I turned in time to see a Jap plane drop bombs into the mass of Filipinos we had just passed. Planes were diving and strafing the town of Mariveles as we raced through the streets toward the harbor. At one point, when a plane headed directly toward us, we abandoned the car and took refuge in a vacated machine gun position. When he had passed we jumped back in the car and hurried to the harbor.

"There must be a rowboat here somewhere," Renka said as we beat our way around the harbor.

"Looks like some up ahead," I answered.

We hurried around the harbor to our left. There we found several different types of boats and picked out the one which appeared to be the best suited to our purpose. We dragged the boat down to the water's edge, pushed it in, and shoved off from shore.

"Where'll it be, boys? Australia or China?" Jim asked as he grabbed the oars and started rowing.

"Anywhere. Let's just get out of here," Renka answered, then added, "Better stick close to the shore until we reach the point out there, 'cause if one of those babies sees us," he pointed to the three planes to the west, "we'll be dead ducks."

We rowed and rowed with all our strength, for just over the ridge to the east we could hear intense small arms fire. It was still a considerable distance to the point where we would be out in the open water, and it seemed that we were hardly moving.

Suddenly Jim dropped the oars and stood up in the boat, waving his arms, and screamed, "Hey there! Hey there!" Startled at this, we looked ahead to see a motor launch about 150 yards ahead of us. There were several persons on her, and they were about to shove off. When our screaming and whistling failed to attract their attention, Jim jumped overboard wearing his six shooter and wrist watch as well as all his clothes, and swam to shore. He then ran up the coastline shouting and waving his arms until he attracted the attention of one of the men on the boat, who waved to us to hurry up.

By the time we reached the boat they had their engine running, and we moved out without any delay. "He's going to Corregidor." Jim pointed to the little island seven miles to the southeast of us.

"You'll have to get over on this side 'cause she's got a hole in her right side," the soldier said, pointing to a gaping hole just at the water line on the starboard side of the boat, where water was splashing in. Jim and I climbed up on top of the cabin just as two Filipinos, carrying a sack, climbed into the boat.

"What's in the sack?" Jim inquired.

"Pineapple, sir," the little Filipino said, pulling the sack closer to his chest.

"Pineapple!" Jim and I repeated in unison. Jim reached over and pulled the sack open so that he could see several cans of pineapple inside. "How much for the bag?" Jim asked, pulling twenty pesos from his pocket.

"How much you give me?"

"I've got twenty pesos," Jim offered.

"No," answered the Filipino. "Not nearly enough." I pulled out all the money I had in my pocket, which totaled seven pesos, and handed them to Jim.

"Twenty-seven pesos," Jim offered.

"No, no. Not nearly enough." With that Jim shoved the twenty-seven pesos down inside the Filipino's shirt with one hand and grabbed the bag with the other hand. He took out one can, handed it to the vendor, and tossed the bag to me.

"Whit, I promised you some pineapple a long time ago. Hope you don't mind it being in cans."

Down inside the boat someone found a tool with which we could open the cans, and we all had pineapple. It was the most delicious food any of us had had for a long time.

Thus, on April 9, 1942, we were gorging ourselves on pineapple as we raced away from Mariveles Harbor, away from the small arms fire and the jungles of Bataan. Bataan—where we had lived on hopes from day to day, and where our hopes had been shattered until we were afraid of hope itself. Bataan—where we had starved for 105 days for food, for word from home, and for all the good things of life. Bataan—where our friends had prayed and died for a cause which they never understood but which they sincerely hoped was right. Bataan—where the friends we had left were about to begin the most infamous trek of our century—the Bataan Death March.

Before us lay Corregidor, the most heavily fortified island in the world. Before us lay a new hope.

5. Getaway

There was a flight of twenty-seven high-flying Jap bombers coming in from the east just as we approached the North Mine Dock.

"Goose that thing up a little down there," Jim shouted down into the cabin. "Bombers coming in from toward Manila!"

"We've been running her full throttle all the way," someone yelled back.

Our position was terrifying, and we glued our eyes to the bombers as our little boat came full speed into shore. We abandoned our boat hastily and scattered over the wreckage of the dock area to find cover in a small stone building, just seconds before the bombs rocked the island about us. When the bombers had passed we made our way on up the hill to Malinta Tunnel, where we would be secure in case the bombers made a return visit.

Inside the tunnel we greeted friends we had not seen for a long time and found some other people who had made their way over from Bataan during the course of the night just past. We also found many officers and men in freshly washed and starched uniforms, living as comfortably as if the war had never caused them the slightest inconvenience.

The main portion of the tunnel appeared to be about twenty feet high, thirty feet wide, and about an eighth of a mile long. From this, large passages or halls, fingering out in both directions, gave it more the appearance of a large building with numerous corridors than that of a tunnel. Malinta Tunnel was very clean, and we felt that it would be a comfortable place to stay while we were waiting for reinforcements to arrive. We congratulated ourselves upon successfully reaching this haven of security.

No one could have convinced any of us that our experiences on Corregidor would make the events of the past three months on Bataan seem like a Sunday School picnic.

As we were chatting with our friends and telling of our escape from Bataan, someone advised us that we should check with Colonel Laughinghouse, who was the senior Air Corps officer in the tunnel.

"Where is he?" I asked.

"I think I can find him, if you will come with me," came the answer. "There is some talk that air crew members are going to be taken out of here very soon."

We found ourselves in the presence of a slightly-built gentleman with gray hair, silver eagles on his shoulders, and command pilot's wings on his chest. He looked from one to another of us. "You are the ones who just arrived from Bataan?"

"Yes, sir," we replied in unison.

"You were fortunate to get here, because we are arranging to get air crew members sent to Australia by submarine."

"Swell!" replied Dey. "How soon do you think that'll be?"

"Not long. They need air crew members, and it is just a matter of waiting until the subs come in for you."

That was good news. Things were breaking just right for us, and it would be only a matter of time until we were back with the old gang in the 19th Bombardment Group. Then we would be able to do some bombing ourselves, and get away from the one-sided war where we were always on the receiving end of the bombs.

While we are waiting for the submarines to come

in, I'll take your names and put them on my list. In the meantime, you will be assigned to the Marines until you are notified," the Colonel added.

"I'm James Dey, and I'm a bombardier," Dey volunteered.

The Colonel looked at me. "Edgar Whitcomb, navigator," I said.

"And I'm John Ivan Renka, a B-17 pilot," Renka added.

"Well, looks like we've about got a bomber crew right here," the Colonel commented. "You will report to the colonel of the Fourth Marines over in the Communications Tunnel."

We left the Colonel and made our way through the tunnel and into one of the long corridors, where we finally located the Marine colonel. The Marines, being a very efficient organization, would not permit even an Air Corps officer to sit around idle while waiting for transportation. In a short time each of us found himself assigned to a different outfit, in different parts of the island, on beach defense outside the tunnel.

By nightfall I found myself sitting out on a lonely corner of the island known as Monkey Point. It was the southeast end of the island, and there were no huge guns pointing out at the sea, no cement and steel revetments for protection, and no supply of food that would last for five years. I found that I had been put in charge of an antiquated British seventy-five-millimeter rifle, the likes of which I had never seen except in parades put on by veterans of World War I back home. The thing had big wooden wheels, but it was mounted in such a position that it could be fired only between the eastern tip of Corregidor and Fort Hughes, a small island to the southeast, in the direction of Cavite. The only comfort I found in my position was when I learned of three or four similar guns located in the long tail of the island, which pointed out toward Manila. Those guns were under the command of several fine young Marine officers.

My gun crew consisted of nine Filipinos and one third lieutenant. He was a very young boy who had just been graduated from the Military Academy of the Philippines, and it soon became obvious to me that he resented my taking over his command.

That was Corregidor, the impregnable fortress of the Pacific, bristling with steel and concrete emplacements. Half a dozen hours before, we had stepped onto the island congratulating ourselves for having reached safety at last. We had been elated by the news that we would be able to join our outfit in Australia. Then, in an instant of time, we found ourselves assigned to beach defense in a position more precarious than we had ever experienced on Bataan. The first night on Corregidor I slept on the ground beside my gun position, but I felt more as if I were sleeping on a powder keg that had the fuse lit and was just about to blow up.

When the dawn arrived the place took on a more cheerful appearance. The bright sun came up over Manila Bay, and I looked out across at the skyline of Manila and the radio towers of Cavite Navy Yard to the east. To the north the black jungles of Bataan were silent, and I wondered what had happened to the thousands of persons we had left behind.

A gentle breeze stirred the leaves of the trees along the edge of the cliff in front of me, and I stood up to have a better look at the island. As I looked down the road which ran to the west of my position, I could not believe my eyes when I saw a blond boy walking in my direction. It was Drachenberg. I ran toward him shouting, "Drack! How did you get here?" Without waiting for him to answer I went on, "Thought they had got you on Bataan."

"When we got to Mariveles just before daylight, they told us General King was surrendering Bataan and that everybody was supposed to get on the barge

83

for Corregidor," he explained. "Now they got me down on the beach in charge of three machine gun positions on the south shore."

I told him how Dey, Renka, and I had made our way over, and that we were on the list to go to Australia in a submarine. As we talked an artillery shell whistled through the air, and I fell flat on my face in a ditch to protect myself.

"Don't worry about them. The ones you hear whistle are never going to hit you," he laughed.

"Don't laugh. I know I've got buck fever, but any time I hear those things sound off I'm going to hit the dirt."

"Don't mind me laughing, but the way you hit the dirt you really looked funny," he explained. "Where did you sleep last night?"

"On the ground up by the gun position, and it was hard as hell."

"There's on old house down the road about a block that has been badly bombed, and I saw some good mattresses in there. Let's go down and have a look," he suggested.

We walked down to the house and found an excellent innerspring mattress, which we carried back up the hill immediately behind my gun position. Then we dug deep trenches on each side of it, so that in case of enemy shelling or air raids we could roll off the mattress and into the trench.

During the first few days on Corregidor the shelling from the Bataan shore was spasmodic. However, it increased from day to day, until after a few days the little island was being subjected to long periods of intensive artillery shellings. The attacks lasted from two to four hours at a time without letting up, concentrating first on one portion of the island and then on another. At night the Bataan coastline was lit up like Broadway from the flashes of the big guns. In addition to the shellings, flight after flight of bombers and fighters swept over the island night and day.

Life on Corregidor was like living on a bull's-eye during target practice. It became unsafe to venture very far from a sheltered position.

We heard no more talk that a submarine would come and take air crew members off the island, and we did not enjoy the many rumors that help was on the way, like those we had heard on Bataan. Our problem became one of survival—a problem of remaining in a safe place to keep from getting killed.

We had no mess hall, but a chow truck came past our area once a day, sometime between seven and eleven o'clock at night. Then our rations would be no more than a mess kit full of cold potatoes, canned tomatoes and a couple of pieces of bread. The best part of the food was the bread, which seemed almost like cake to us after all the rice we had eaten. We ordinarily saved it for breakfast the next morning, when a Marine sergeant would brew up some of the most terrible coffee anyone ever drank. There were few complaints about the cold chow, since we were glad to eat anything we could get our hands on.

In the morning, when we drank our coffee and ate our bread on the edge of the cliff, an old, one-eyed grandpappy monkey would come swinging from limb to limb through the trees below us, followed by eight or ten younger monkeys. He would chatter and do all kinds of tricks for us until someone threw him a little hunk of bread. Then he would scamper away through the trees with the young ones following him again. Then, ordinarily, we would not see any of the monkeys again until about breakfast time the next morning.

On occasion a Marine captain named Bromeyer would stop by and visit with Drachenberg and me while we waited for the chow truck in the evening. One evening just before dark, when we were waiting for the captain to appear, a Marine corporal sauntered up the road toward us. "I'm going down to the shore battery to see why none of them guys on the gun crew came up today," he announced. He stood facing the north shore and looked out across the bomb-pitted air strip with a worried look on his face.

"They're probably waiting until it gets a little darker," I suggested.

"Don't know, sir. Looks like some of 'em would have come up before now. That was an awfully bad shelling we got this afternoon," he answered, squatting on his haunches and looking into space. But when he glanced back over his shoulder and saw Captain Bromeyer approaching from the southwest with mess kit in hand, the corporal stood erect.

"Did you . . ." the Captain started to ask.

"No, I can't. I can't go," the Marine interrupted.

"That's all right," said Bromeyer in a steady voice, raising his hand as if to silence the corporal.

"But I just can't go, sir," the Marine cried. "My father was shell-shocked in the last war. I can't go. I can't go," he sobbed. Big tears were rolling down the boy's face. Captain Bromeyer patted him on the shoulder and then, without a word, headed out to the north across the air strip.

The boy was much shaken and very much frightened, for he knew, as we knew, that at any instant the big guns of Bataan might open up and that anyone out on the open air field would have little chance of surviving.

We waited after Captain Bromeyer had gone, counting the moments until he could get across the air strip to where he could take cover in case the barrage did let loose. Nothing happened as we sat waiting in the dark, and soon the corporal left us to return to his area. My one thought was that if I ever found myself in his position, I hoped those around me would understand as Captain Bromeyer had understood. After a while I heard footsteps, and looked up to see Captain Bromeyer in front of me. He paused for a second to announce, "All dead," and walked on down the road.

"How many were there?" Drachenberg asked after the Captain had left.

"Eight or ten, I suppose. That's the usual gun crew." After a pause I went on, "Wonder what the Japs are trying to prove? Everything that can be bombed and shelled on this island has been bombed and shelled ten times. From a tactical standpoint this end of the island was neutralized a long time ago. Now the only thing they accomplish is the knocking out of an occasional gun position and the killing of a few men in their foxholes by direct hits. Wonder what they're waiting for before they make their landing."

"Beats me," came the answer. "My one hope is that none of those shells has got the name of Dayton Drachenberg on it."

"Amen, brother! You can say that again. Sometimes during the shellings, when each blast seems to get a little closer, I think the next one has my name on it. The law of averages is going to catch up with us sooner or later. When that one comes with your name on it, your war will be ended—no more worries, no fear, no starvation, no more struggling to carry on. It could be this very instant, and you would be gone. To the few fellows who know you, word would be passed about that you had 'got it' during the shelling. To the headquarters boys down in the tunnel it would be sixteen dead today instead of fifteen."

"Now, Whit, don't get carried away with this thing. Those Japs probably don't even know how to spell Whitcomb," he gibed.

"Oh, I don't know. They'll probably learn how to spell Whitcomb as quickly as they'll learn how to spell Drachenberg," I answered. "Say, it doesn't look like Captain Bromeyer is going to eat with us."

"I think he feels pretty bad about losing that gun crew. He knew they were in a dangerous position, but there was just nothing that could be done about it," Drachenberg said. "I sure wouldn't want to be stationed over on the north side of the island myself."

"Neither would I. A fellow wouldn't have a chance. Sometimes I begin to wonder whether we have a chance anyway."

As we talked we heard the chow truck coming up over the hill. When it stopped fifteen to twenty Marines swarmed in to get their daily rations. It was pitch dark and the only noises to be heard were the ladles striking against the mess kits and other containers as the mess sergeant doled out the cold tomatoes and potatoes. When the mess truck moved on, we made our way back to my gun position and sat on the edge of the innerspring mattress with our feet dangling into the trench as we ate our supper.

There was the usual amount of shelling during the night, and with each series of blasts we would roll off the mattress into the trench and hug the bottom until the shelling was over. At dawn the next morning, after we had drunk our coffee and Drachenberg had gone back to his gun positions, I ran my gun team through a drill on the old British seventy-five. Each of the Filipino scouts knew his duty and practiced it with great precision. I was little more than a spectator as they threw the practice shells into the gun, slammed the breech block, took aim on an imaginary target, and fired an imaginary shot. It was satisfying to know that the seventy-five millimeter gun was manned by competent and devoted soldiers. Except for the third lieutenant, the average military service of the other members was about twenty-five years each. I knew they could do the job that had to be done in case of an invasion. But I also knew that if the invasion came in our small sector, there would be only two or three such guns pointed in the right direction, and that if it came in any other sector our gun would be worthless. Therefore, our entire effort would be about as damaging to the enemy, if he came in a large invasion fleet, as if we had a pocket full of rocks to throw at him. We were the defenders of Corregidor —Corregidor, that bastion of steel and cement with ammunition and supplies enough to last for five years. Its giant guns, which disappeared into the hillside after firing, were all pointed in the direction of the China Sea to the west, and its vast mine fields protected only the entrance to the harbor. They would be of no value in case of an invasion from the eastern end of the island.

After the gun drill Filipino Scout Private First Class Domicos, a short, stocky man of about forty-five, beckoned me aside. "Sir, I would like for you to read," he requested as he pushed forward a white sheet of paper.

I read, "My most darling Magnalina, etc."

The message, in the most flowery language I had ever read, stated that he was sorry he had not written sooner but that he would do better from now on. He stated that life on the rock was very dull and only bearable because of the memories of the moments they had spent together. Although the letter appeared to be in perfectly proper English, there were adjectives and terms completely unfamiliar to me.

"Who wrote this?"

"I, sir."

"Where did you ever learn to write like that?" I inquired.

"Oh, sir, I used the dictionary," he answered matter-of-factly.

"Where is Magnalina?"

"*Maneea.*"

"You don't really expect to send that letter to her, do you?" I inquired.

"Yes, of course."

"But how do you expect to get it across the channel?" I was completely puzzled.

"Sometimes small boats go across at night to the other shore."

"Who are they, and when do they make these trips?" I looked at him again.

"Oh, just a Filipino who takes messages back and

forth," he answered as if there were nothing particularly unusual about it.

"But you said the other day that your wife lived in Baguio, didn't you?" I asked.

"Sir, thees is my common-law wife."

"You mean you have more than one wife?"

With that the private said, "Excuse me please, sir," and turned and ran back to his foxhole. In a couple of seconds he returned with two pictures in his hands.

"Sir, thees is my wife, and thees is my common-law wife," he explained.

"But don't you get into a lot of trouble that way?"

"Oh, not too much, sir. One time before the war started I went to *Maneea* to meet thees before she was my common-law wife; but thees met me at the boat." He pushed forward the picture in his right hand. "But I told thees that thees was my seester," he added, pushing forth first one picture and then the other.

"But wasn't there trouble?"

"No, sir. We took thees home, and thees became my common-law wife," he answered with a twinkle in his eyes.

"Which one will you go back to when you return?" I inquired further.

"Oh, sir, I shall not return. I shall die fighting for my country."

I knew this was not just idle talk, for certain of the Filipinos, particularly the scouts, were romanticists, some of them as fanatical as any Jap ever dared to be.

Private First Class Domicos had been in the Philippine Scouts for twenty-nine years and was almost ready for retirement, which came after thirty years of service. If he succeeded in living through the war he would return to his home town and become what the Filipinos called a pensionado. As such he would be a highly respected and honored citizen in his community, enjoying a larger income and more prestige than of any of his neighbors.

After our visit Domicos took his pictures and his beautiful letter and returned to his foxhole on the other side of the gun position. I sat pondering over our conversation until I heard a shout from Drachenberg, returning from his gun positions. "Whit, down at the Navy Tunnel it came on the radio that a bunch of American bombers bombed Tokyo a few days ago."

"That's really great. How did they do it?"

Drachenberg explained how a squadron of B-25's had taken off from the decks of Navy carriers and flown a bombing mission over Tokyo.

"If they can bomb Tokyo I wonder why they never send any American planes to the Philippines? I haven't seen an American plane for so long I'm afraid I'm going to forget what they look like."

"You'll be seeing them in big numbers one of these days, when that convoy comes in here," Drack stated hopefully.

"I'm not too sure about that convoy. If they're bombing Tokyo, it's possible that they have decided to bypass the Philippines. We might just be sitting here till the war's over," I suggested.

"There's a story going around down at the Navy that two seaplanes took off last night loaded with American Army nurses and headed for Australia," Drachenberg said. "Seems like everything is going out and nothing is coming in."

"There seems to be a possibility then that they will be taking air crew members out at last," I said.

We visited for most of the day, there being little else to do. During the course of the day there were several air attacks, and the shellings from the Bataan coast were incessant. During these long periods of shellings and bombings we would hug the bottom of our foxholes and pray that the shell with our name on it would not arrive. During the course of the shellings it was not uncommon to have a hot, jagged piece of shrapnel fall into the foxhole. We had been shelled so long over the past few weeks that we could have filled a coal bucket with the shrapnel that was lying on the ground around our area. In addition to the shellings, the island underwent an average of about ten raids a day from the high-flying bombers.

We visited—and waited.

6. Invasion

We had been waiting for the invasion by the Japanese night after night, so when we looked down across the air strip to the north one night to see the red and green flares arching above the shore line, it came as no great surprise to us. We had just climbed out of our foxholes after a savage shelling and walked over to the road to wait for the chow truck. It was about eight-thirty at night, and when the shout rose, "Here they come," we could have been no more ready or less ready to meet them had they waited another ten years.

The Jap landing forces had approached the island under cover of the artillery barrage. When the firing ceased, they rolled onto the coast as easily as if they had been on maneuvers, for our power to resist had long since been destroyed. It was only a matter of minutes until we could hear the sound of small arms fire, which sounded much like an American twenty-two caliber rifle, as the enemy closed in upon us.

Although the initial landing had been from the north and was out of range of the sector of our fire, we stuck to our guns throughout the long night with the thought that another invasion might be attempted in our area. The night was an eternity, with wild firing of small arms all about our gun position. When dawn finally came, we threw the breechblock over the cliff into the deep water to prevent the enemy from making use of our own gun against us. Then we proceeded to the top of the ridge to the north and made an effort to establish a line of defense. After calling in everyone we could find, we managed to establish a firm line from our gun position for about a quarter of a mile to the west toward Malinta Tunnel. It was a mixed-up conglomeration of fighting talent, with sailors, Marines, Filipinos and a large number of soldiers from the 803rd Aviation Engineers. I spent most of my time running up and down the line ordering them to scatter out and take a protected position. For one reason or another, they gathered in small groups and peppered away at anything they could see moving on the north slope of the hill. As I approached one group, a tall, skinny lad who was firing one volley after another shouted, "Why, this is just like shooting rabbits in Kentucky!"

Officers were few and far between, but I finally found Captain Bromeyer, who had organized a line on farther to the west. He told me that he had a number of wounded, but had no stretcher bearers to help them back away from the lines.

"I haven't seen any stretcher bearers except a couple who took some men back down toward the Navy Tunnel. But they didn't come back. What we need are hand grenades. You don't know where I could get some, do you? There is a machine gun over the ridge and we can't seem to silence him with rifle fire."

"Why don't you go down to the Navy Tunnel and get some stretcher bearers and see if they don't have some grenades?" he suggested.

"All right, I'll meet you back here as soon as I can get back."

I left him and headed down the hill to the south toward the Navy Tunnel. There I found more men inside the tunnel than we had up on the ridge trying to defend the line. After a considerable amount of scurrying, I enlisted the aid of three sets of stertcher bearers, found a box of grenades, and got some food to take back to the men on the ridge. As we started to leave, someone called to me. I turned to see Drachenberg coming in from his gun position. "Drack, come on up on the ridge where you can get in some shots. These damned Japs can't hit a thing."

We ran a zigzag course back up the hill, as we had on the way down, because there was at least one Jap lodged somewhere in the trees to the rear of our line. As we ran, dirt splattered up here and there from the rifle shots aimed in our direction. At the top of the ridge I pulled the pins on a couple of hand grenades and threw them quickly in the direction of the enemy machine gun.

We had no idea of the progress of the battle. All we knew was that over the hill the Japanese were firing at us, and that we were firing back at them. In the early part of the morning a number of Japs had been flushed out of the trees in which they had spent the night, but later on it became a mere exchange of volleys. It was not one-sided and we were taking our share of the losses. The gunner on our only thirty caliber machine gun received a hit in the muscle of his left arm. A few seconds later a rifle shot hit the machine gun and put it out of commission. A rifle shot drilled Private Domicos through the lower part of his throat and went out between his shoulders in back.

As a group of us gathered together just below the crest of the hill to discuss the possibilities before us, one said, "I'm an officer, but these fellows won't pay any attention to me when I give them orders."

"Where is your insignia?" I asked, noticing that he was wearing only a pair of coveralls.

"Back in my foxhole. Didn't have a chance to get anything before we left there," he replied. I took off my brass second lieutenant's bar and handed it to him.

We were asking one another questions in an effort to find out what was going on on the island, but one of us knew as little about the big picture as the other.

Just about the time we had reached this conclusion there was a sudden explosion at our feet, and we were blown to the ground. With no idea of what had happened, I jumped to my feet and saw that Drachenberg was about fifteen feet down the hill. When I got to him I found a hole in the top of his helmet the size of a silver dollar, and blood spurting out of his head and his side. The boy to whom I had just given the brass bar was also injured. We immediately found stretcher bearers and took them back down the hill to the Navy Tunnel.

The accuracy of the Jap mortars was surprising; more surprising was the coordination between the artillery on Bataan and the forces that had landed on the island. Now and then flares would go up, and the artillery would open up and shell a sector into which the Japs had not yet moved. While the shelling went on, the dive bombers continued to fly in so low that we could see the faces of the pilots in the planes.

It was about eleven o'clock when word spread down the line that General Wainwright would surrender Corregidor Island to the Japanese at noon. With that information we withdrew to the vicinity of the Navy Tunnel, where we could stand off any attack until that time.

A little after twelve o'clock noon on May 7, 1942, a couple of Japs came over the hill toward us. They came cautiously at first, then more briskly as they drew nearer. A white sheet hanging outside the entrance to the tunnel indicated to them that we were surrendering. Presently one called, "All men coming out holding up hands!" With that, about three hundred men filed out of the huge tunnel and onto the road, holding their hands above their heads. We were then formed into a column of fours and marched across the air field to the north shore of the island. On the way the Jap leader deviated from a direct course, apparently in order to pass the corpse of a young Filipino soldier lying with his hands tied behind his back and a big gash in the back of his head. The Jap pointed to him to make sure that we did not miss seeing him. That was apparently an object lesson to show us what could happen if any one of us got out of line.

On the north shore road the men were searched and relieved of their watches, pens, rings, money, and anything else of value. I had previously attached my watch and my fountain pen to my dog tags, and when I was searched they were not found.

After we had been searched we were marched over the shell-torn road to the southeast entrance of Malinta Tunnel. On the way we passed several hundred wounded Japs stretched out on the ground in their makeshift field hospital. We also passed some of our friends who had been taken prisoners at other places. Among them was Domicos, with the hole through his throat, and several other members of my gun crew. Already the Japs were strapping a harness-type affair on some of the men who were to be used in carrying cargo for them. We continued our march to the middle part of the island. It was about dark when our captors brought us to a halt. The orders that followed were, "Sit down," and "Sleep." The first order was easy to obey, but the second order, "Sleep," came more difficult, because at the time the order was given we were standing on a railroad track.

Thus the first night we spent as prisoners of the Japanese we slept, or tried to sleep, on the crossties of a railroad track. But our feelings were deadened to the point where it made very little difference to us where we were or what was happening to us. I knew none of the fellows about me, and none of them knew me. I had no idea what had happened to Dey or to Renka, or whether Drachenberg was still among the living. I knew only that I had reached the bitter end of a long, long road. Common sense should have told me that from the date the Japs first knocked out our bombardment group at Clark Field, we were fighting a losing battle. If not then, I should have recognized it when we were blasted off Bataan. With the realization that the fighting and struggling were all over, my mind and body were filled with a sort of peace. It was a dismal and disheartening feeling; but nevertheless it was peace of a kind. So, crowded together so closely that we could not lie down, we found further peace in the sleep that overcame us.

At dawn the next morning the arrogant little Japs in charge of us marched us back to the eastern end of the island over the same road we had taken to reach the place where we slept. Back at the air field, we were put to work with hoes, rakes, shovels, and other small garden tools, leveling off the bomb-pitted landing strip. We worked like slaves in the boiling hot sun until about noon, when a can of American C rations was given to each prisoner.

I knew that the tunnel where we had taken Drachenberg was just over the hill, and when I had an opportunity to get on a water detail, I hurried into the tunnel to locate him. By that time the tunnel was full of Americans who had been injured in the fight. At last I found Drachenberg at the same place where I had left him the day before. At first I thought he was unconscious, but he opened his eyes and looked at me when I shook his cot. Just then I heard a voice shouting something in Japanese. I turned in time to see a Jap soldier entering the room, waving an American forty-five caliber pistol. He went from one patient to another, grabbing up anything he could find. I stood dumbfounded as I watched this spectacle, for most of the people he was robbing were seriously injured, and the weapon he carried was completely unnecessary. When he came to me, he jammed the barrel of the gun into my chest and started to reach for my pockets, but as the gun hit me, it rattled my dog tags under my shirt. Immediately he ripped open the front of my shirt with his free hand and tore my wrist watch and Parker 51 pen from my neck. Then he slapped me across the chest with the gun and turned to Drachenberg. The bold bandit held the forty-five in Drachenberg's face while he twisted a gold class ring off his finger and pulled the gold watch from his wrist. With his pockets full of loot, the Jap vanished out through the other door.

I turned and looked down at Drachenberg, and realized that he little understood what had just happened. At that moment the ring and the wrist watch were of no more value to him than the old steel helmet with a hole in the top of it lying beside his bunk.

"How're you getting along, Drack?" I whispered.

"Not too good," was the response. "They said I would be taken to Malinta Tunnel."

"I sure hope so, because you need a doctor." As I said this I noticed a pair of coveralls beside the empty bunk next to Drachenberg. They were badly spotted with dried blood and bore a single brass second lieutenant's bar. I knew they had belonged to the lieutenant to whom I had given the bar the day before. Looking at Drack, I asked, "Where's the lieutenant who was in this bunk next to you?"

"He died," came the answer.

"Anything I can do for you?" I asked Drachenberg.

"I need help bad. Do anything you can to get me a doctor or to get me to Malinta Tunnel," he whispered faintly.

"I'll do anything I can, but I don't know what that would be," I told him. "I'd better be getting back to the air strip. I'm on a water detail, and if I don't get back up there, someone will be looking for me." I said good-by to Drachenberg with the feeling that I would never see him alive again, and made my way into the main part of the tunnel to fill up my water container.

The bright Philippine sun was bearing down hard as I struggled back up the trail with my container of water. On the trail I almost stepped on the body of a dead Marine lying face down across the trail. There was not a sign of a wound on the back of the bloated form, and it was apparent that he had been dead even before the Japanese had invaded the island. As I looked down at him, I observed under the big, round fingers of his outstretched hand a red-backed book. In spite of the penetrating stench that hit me in the face, I leaned over to see what he had been reading. What I saw was unbelievable. The title of the book was *Jump-Off Island*. As I looked I pronounced the words aloud. "Jump-Off Island," and wondered what the story was about. Could it possibly have been about a young American Marine from California, Texas, or Arkansas who had joined the United States forces to "see the world"?

Somewhere a mother, a wife, or a sweetheart was wondering about this boy and praying that he would be taken care of. Now he had found his peace. For him there were no more air raids, shellings, strafings, starvation, or struggle. For him there would be no prison camp, no torture, no humiliation. Corregidor had been his "Jump-Off Island."

"Hello! Hello!" Someone was calling, and I turned to see two smartly dressed Japanese officers approaching me. Both were short and stocky, and each wore a Samurai sword hanging at his side. "What you do?" one asked.

"I carry water," I answered, raising my water container and pointing to the air field.

"Go! Go!" commanded the spokesman as he directed me toward the other prisoners.

Back at the air field we worked until sundown and again were lined up in a column of fours and ordered to sit down and sleep. This time it was not yet dark, and we were not as completely exhausted as we had been the night before. Three little Japanese guards were in charge of our outfit. Two of them sat in a small Japanese truck in front of us, and the other stood at the other end of our line, all with rifles and fixed bayonets. Some of the soldiers from our group engaged the Japanese guards on the truck in conversation. "Where do we go when we get through with this work?" one of our soldiers asked.

"Some place to do more work."

"Do we stay on this island?" another asked.

"The war will soon be over and you can go home," came the reply from the same Jap who had spoken before.

"But will our treatment be according to International Law and the Geneva Rules?" a member of our group inquired.

"Japanese law is International Law," was the response. That was the general attitude of our captors. They were exuberant beyond words at the victory they were enjoying. Some were haughty, some were contemptuous, and some conducted themselves in a reasonable manner, but underlying the attitude and actions of each there seemed to be the feeling that he had done something he never really expected to do. Perhaps none of them had ever visualized the moment when he would be lord and master over a large number of American soldiers.

At that moment it was more important to us that we had each eaten a full can of C rations, had a good drink of water, and had a comfortable place to sleep on the ground of the air strip under the peaceful Filipino skies.

At dawn we were ordered back to work on the air field, and within a few hours the job of leveling the bomb craters was finished. Then we stood at the edge of the field and watched the first Jap plane ever to set its wheels down on Corregidor winging in across the bay. It was a sad occasion for the boys of the 803rd Aviation Engineers, who had worked frantically night and day for weeks to keep the tiny air strip in shape for any rescue planes that might come to Corregidor. But for the rest of us it meant that we had finished the job and that we would be moving to another place. Where we would go and what we would do was unimportant. The important thing was that we would be going to some place new.

There had been several hundreds of us in the group working on the air field, and after the little Jap plane sat down on the field we were again lined up in a column of fours and ordered to march. Our march took us again past the south entrance to Malinta Tunnel, then to the southeast to a spot about halfway between Malinta Tunnel and Monkey Point, where my gun position had been located. There was no warning of where we were going or what was about to happen to us, but as we broke over a hill to the south, I could see we were being herded into an area where several thousand Americans and Filipinos were waiting. It was a large crescent-shaped area near the level of the sea, bounded on the south by the South Channel to Manila Bay and with steep slopes to the west, north, and east. Before I entered the main gate another American stopped me and marked a 0-200 on the back of my shirt with black pencil. That was to be my prison number. From there I wandered through the vast crowd, searching for a familiar face. There were soldiers, sailors, Marines, Filipinos, with every rank from private through colonel, and not one person I had ever seen before.

The area included about what would have been two city blocks, and it was so crowded with people that it appeared there would be standing room only. Toward the east end were two big hangar-type buildings which came to be known as the 92nd Garage area. The two buildings, being near the shore, looked as if they had been seaplane hangars at one time. As I approached the northwest corner of the northernmost of the two buildings I came face to face with Jim Dey and John Renka. We were not glad to see each other because we were not glad to be there in the first place. "Come over here and stay with us," Dey invited. "We're in with some of the Marines here."

"Have you heard anything? Do you have any idea how long we will be here or where we are going?" I inquired.

They both shook their heads. Jim pointed to the area at the side of the building where a number of Marines were sitting. "This is Gunner Farrell," Jim introduced one of the group. "Meet Ed Whitcomb, who came over from Bataan with Renka and me. This is Jack Mann, Al Manning, and Bill Harris." Jim pointed from one to the other. I sat down in the shade of the big building and made myself better acquainted with the group as we continued discussing what was likely to happen to us. But before I had got settled, a call came out for volunteers to go on a work detail. Several of us volunteered to work and soon found ourselves in a group of three or four hundred, making our way back up over the hill to carry supplies for the Japs. On our first trip we carried tons of canned food from the island's cold storage plant to a Japanese ship at the docks.

When the work was done and we were back in camp, I learned that no provision was being made by the Japanese to feed us, and that the only food we could expect was what we were able to steal and pilfer while we were on work details. Various members of our group had come back with small bags of cornmeal, rice, and cans of food which they had hidden inside their shirts while working. Gunner Farrell assembled the provisions and prepared various concoctions for us on an open fire. For utensils he used old tin cans, pieces of flat tin, and anything else available. By nightfall of the first day there were hundreds of little fires throughout our area, with

103

other groups like our own sitting around a fire and dividing up whatever food was available.

When night came and everyone lay down to rest, we found that the area was so crowded it was almost impossible to move from one section of the camp to another.

We were dazed and stunned and completely powerless to do anything about our position. The darkness of the night blotted out the miserable situation about us, and the only comfort we found was the comfort we could wring out of sleeping on the hard ground.

We found that one day in the prison camp was like another, except that as the days went by each became more miserable than the one before. The hot May sun boiled down on us throughout the day, and flies were like demons as they swarmed over our perspiring bodies. Everyone broke out with blisters which were called "Guam blisters." These broke out first in the upper part of the body around the neck and shoulders and grew into clusters under the arms and between the legs. Everyone had them.

The latrines for the camp of eleven thousand men were big holes four feet wide, fifteen feet long, and ten feet deep. Because of the size of the camp it was necessary to have five or six such latrines open at one time. Everyone in camp was plagued with dysentery; no one escaped it. Day and night there was a continuous line to and from the latrines along paths so crowded with human bodies that it was difficult to avoid stumbling over the arms and legs of the sleepers. Many too weak to make the numerous trips back and forth lay in the vicinity of the latrine area. One man fell into one of the pits and nearly died before he was rescued.

Such were the conditions we endured day after day in the Japanese prison camp.

As an escape from these conditions, we volunteered for work details as frequently as they were available, or lolled in the filthy water along the beach adjoining the camp where evidence of human excretion was everywhere.

People began to die in increasing numbers, and it looked as if we would all die if things continued as they were.

7. Ordeal by water

The main topics of conversation in our little group were the possibility of an exchange of prisoners and the possibility of escaping from the Japanese. It was the consensus that we would be transported to the mainland, and then the opportunity for escape would increase.

Lieutenant William Harris, one of the Marine officers, and I talked some of swimming to the mainland. One day, as we sat on the beach and looked across to the Cavite shore to the south, I suggested, "It would be a long haul across there. They say it's about eight miles to the shore across the South Channel."

"Yeah, if a fellow were going to swim from Corregidor it would be a lot shorter across the North Channel. It's only a couple to three miles there."

It seemed completely out of the question to think of swimming the distance, but it did offer one possibility for escape.

"I'll tell you one thing, Bill. I am going to watch for my chance to get away from this place and the first time I get a chance I'm leaving," I said.

"I feel the same way," he agreed. We took another long look at the eight miles of water that separated us from the mainland, and made our way back through the congested area to our group. When I was able to find Jim Dey and Renka, I whispered, "What do you think of the chances for swimming to the mainland?"

"I don't think I could make it," Jim said thoughtfully. "I've been sick with malaria most of the time since we arrived on Corregidor, and I just don't think I could swim that far now."

Renka looked at me seriously and said, "I am going to escape the first opportunity I get. I know you have the same thing in mind, but if you ever leave without me, I will consider it a very unfriendly act."

"I'd like to escape with you because we've come a long way together, but I'm telling you right now that I am going to take the first chance I get to get out of this place," I answered.

We talked on and on about various things, but the idea of escape was uppermost in everybody's mind. I thought of it night and day.

That night, while I was trying to sleep, a dark form knelt beside me and whispered, "Let's get out of here tonight." It was Bill.

"What do you mean, tonight? How can we get out of here tonight?"

"We can make our way up over that ridge if we take it slow. I've been watching it every night, and there is no activity at all after midnight."

"I'm afraid of it, Bill," I whispered. "You know damned well they're watching that hill like hawks." There were several machine gun nests planted about half-way up the hill, and I was certain that there were guards on the alert for anyone who might try to get past.

"Come on, Ed. Do you want to put up with another day in this hell?" he pleaded.

"No, Bill, I don't. But I don't think it's safe to try that hill at night, and I'm not going." With that Bill left me, and I finally went to sleep.

The next day was hell, just as Bill had said it would be. Instead of going on a work detail as I had previously done, I went to the aid station and offered to help carry a litter up to Malinta Tunnel. The aid station was nothing more than a small marked-off area where those sicker than the rest were kept until they could be moved to the hospital in Malinta Tunnel.

My one thought was to try to get to the hospital area in the tunnel and locate Drachenberg, if he were still alive. As I stood waiting to be called to help carry one of the stretchers, I watched a man lying on the floor of the aid station as he breathed his last. It happended quietly and peacefully, and no one else noticed it. At that moment I felt that death was very near. It could happen to me, or Dey, or Renka, or any of the others if they remained in camp much longer under these conditions.

After a long wait, a Jap finally beckoned to me to take the end of a stretcher and help carry a sick soldier up to Malinta Tunnel Hospital. Our burden was not heavy at first, but as we made our way up over the hill toward the tunnel, he became as heavy as if he were made of lead. As I struggled on and on up the hill I gained a new strength because I reached a determination. It was then I decided that I would attempt to swim back to the mainland to get away from the prison camp. Inside Malinta Tunnel, after we had deposited our litter patient in a ward, I wandered farther into the tunnel to inquire about Drachenberg.

At one desk I asked, "Do you happen to know anything about a Lieutenant Drachenberg who was injured during the fighting on the east end of the island?"

"One moment and I will see," the male orderly started to look at his records. "You don't mean that Air Corps fellow who was paralyzed, do you?"

"That may be the one. Do you know where he is?"

"Yes, if it's the same one I can take you to him."

With that the orderly led me through the corridors one after another until I looked across a row of beds and saw Drachenberg flat on his back. Before we reached him the orderly whispered, "He has about eleven inches of his spine paralyzed and cannot move his body from the waist down." That should have been bad news to me but the sight of Drachenberg alive and inside the tunnel on a bed was very encouraging.

"Hello, Drachenberg. How're you doing?" I greeted him.

"Not so good," was the answer. "They're starving us to death."

"Well, if you're getting anything to eat, you're better off than we are. Say, look here!" I said, as I saw a pretty nurse coming toward him. "Why, it's Ann Williams." I had known Ann at Clark Field and Bataan before we had come to Corregidor.

"Are you in the hospital now?" she asked.

"No, just came in to see Drack; looks like you're taking pretty good care of him." I added, "I have something I want to tell you, don't repeat it to anyone." They both looked at me, wondering what kind of a secret anyone could possibly have at a time like this. "I have decided to try to escape from Corregidor by swimming the North Channel back to Bataan," I whispered to them.

As the words left my mouth I felt foolish, for I knew it sounded ridiculous.

"That's a long distance to swim," was the only observation Drachenberg could make.

Still feeling a little foolish, I bade them good-by and took my leave from Malinta Tunnel and headed back down to the camp area.

Back in camp that night, Bill and I again walked over to the water's edge. "What do you think about giving it a try tonight? I'm sure it's safe," he said.

"No, Bill. I won't go at night because I don't think we could get up over that hill without being shot," I answered, but went on, "Why don't we get out of here tomorrow with a work detail and hide until dark, and then swim from the north coast back to Bataan?"

"I'm awfully tempted to give it a try tonight by myself if you won't go along," he threatened. "If we could get over to Bataan, I'm sure we could get a boat to sail across to China. The Japs hold a very small

109

part of the coastline there. We could get through and back to Chungking and join the American forces there."

"We've been all over that before. Our big obstacle now is on that ridge right above us. Let's get out of this camp tomorrow and give it a try. If it doesn't work that way, then I'll go over the hill with you tomorrow night."

"Okay, it's a deal, but I still think we should try to make it tonight. I just hate to think of spending another day in this place," Bill argued.

The next day was May 22, 1942, and I was happier than I had been at any time since we reached Corregidor. While my fellow prisoners went about their daily routines, I was filled with excitement, for that was the day when Bill and I would make our escape from the island and from the prison camp. Neither Bill nor I made any mention to our fellow prisoners of our intention to make the swim, but about noon Bill walked over to the other side of the camp area to visit with his uncle, a lieutenant commander in the Navy. Whether or not Bill told his uncle about his intention I never knew. In a while he was back with me, and we left our buddies and walked toward the main gate to wait for assignment on a work detail.

It was about two o'clock in the afternoon when a group of about sixty officers and men filed out of the sentry gate and made its way toward the top of the ridge to the north. Bill and I were with this group, which was headed out on a trip to gather wood for the fires back in camp. Wood was easy to find, for the trees and buildings that had been standing on Corregidor had been shattered to kindling wood by the incessant artillery fire from Bataan and the bombs from hundreds of planes that had blasted the island over the past few months. In spite of the fact that there was plenty of wood available, the men scattered over the hillside, searching as if it were hard to find. Actually, they were searching for items that might be useful back in camp—a piece of tin to cook on, an old spoon, a tin can to drink from, or just anything that could be found.

Bill and I, while going through the pretense of gathering wood, wandered far to the north of the group, which was scattered far and wide over the ridge. The Jap guard was paying little attention to our activities.

"Over this way," Bill directed as we edged farther and farther away from the group. "There's a good place down here where we can take cover until dark." He knew this part of the island, for it was in the area to which he had been assigned since his arrival on Corregidor a few weeks before. Nevertheless, the scenery had been so vastly changed in the last few hours of the battle that he was unable to locate the foxhole that had been so familiar to him at one time. I turned to look back at the guard, and saw that he was facing in the opposite direction from us; then, when I turned to Bill again, he was nowhere to be seen.

"Hey, Bill. Where are you?" I shouted in surprise.

"Here," he answered, and as I looked down I found myself about to step into the hole where he was hiding.

"Quick! And be sure no one sees you."

After another quick look toward the guard, I dropped into the hole beside Bill. It was a greater drop than I had expected, and when I looked about me I found that I was in an underground room about six feet deep, four feet wide, and ten feet long, with a small entrance at either end, just large enough for one person to climb through.

"This is the place some of the fellows dug out a few weeks ago. We should be safe here until dark. Better pull that bush back over the entrance," he said.

The sun was still high in the western sky, and we knew that we had more than five hours to wait for darkness. The first step in our journey had been easy,

111

and we were jubilant at our prospects for an easy escape. The inside of the cave was cool and comfortable, with no flies to torment us, and yet we could not relax. Time and again Bill and I walked to one of the entrances, stood on tiptoes, and peered out in all directions to see what we could see. After a while the wood-gatherers disappeared from the hillside, and there was nothing to be seen but the shattered ruins of the once-mighty fortress.

In the corner I found several small bottles, and upon examining them discovered that one was about half-full of quinine tablets. Into another small bottle I squeezed thirty paper dollars and sixty pesos in Philippine currency, which I had managed to keep from the Japanese, then put them in the hip pocket of my trousers with my silver wings and dog tags. We both tore our trousers legs off high above the knees, thus converting them from Army khakies to swimming shorts. Again and again we looked out over the hillside, but the scenery was always the same. At long last the sun began to sink behind the hill to the west of us; but even after that it seemed like hours before darkness descended upon Corregidor.

Although I had stood looking out across the island for several hours, waiting for the night to come, I felt a sudden apprehension when I realized that it was finally dark. The time we had been waiting for had arrived, and now it seemed that it had all happened very quickly. It seemed that it had been only a short time since we dropped into the pit, but the time had come for us to make our way down over the steep north shore and start swimming. In the sky to the east small black clouds raced across the face of the moon; but on the ground there was a quietness that was frightening. It did not seem right that at that time, one of the most important and probably the most dangerous in our lives, everything should have been so peaceful and quiet. Both of us would have been more at ease if there had been bombing and shelling; but instead, as we looked out across the island in the twilight, we saw a Corregidor that neither of us had ever seen before. There was a strange tension in the air, much like the quiet before the storm, as we tramped down over the hillside looking in every direction at once, lest a Japanese guard put a sudden end to our trip.

It was about 8:30 p.m. when we lowered ourselves into the water to start swimming. There I stopped for a moment to kiss the old Rock good-by. As I hesitated before shoving off, a lot of thoughts ran through my mind. I thought of how we had made our way across the same channel in a small boat, fleeing from Bataan six long weeks before, with planes all over the sky, dive-bombing and strafing everything that moved; the new hope we had felt when we first set foot upon the fortress; the hours upon hours of sitting in a foxhole with bombs and shells falling all about and fragments of hot shrapnel whizzing in; the boost to the morale when we heard of the Doolittle raid on Tokyo; the empty words of encouragement from the San Francisco radio; Drachenberg, with a hole in his helmet and his head, and with shrapnel in his guts when the mortar shell had dropped between us; how we had resented not being able to fight back. We had a lot of catching up to do. "Good-by, Corregidor."

"What's the matter, Ed? Something wrong?"

"No, just saying good-by."

It was only two or three miles across from Corregidor back to Bataan at the closest point, and it should have been possible to swim the distance in a few hours if things went well. Both Bill and I had a lot of confidence in our swimming because we had been practicing every day, just off the shore from the prison camp on the opposite side of the island. We took off our shoes, socks, and shirts, and lowered ourselves into the water. There was not a sign of life up or down the shore as far as we could see.

The water was cool, and it felt good to the body.

113

We thought it would offer a kind of protection against being seen; but as I started to swim my arms glowed as if they were painted with some brilliant silver color. I looked at Bill and could see the outline of his body with a fluorescent glow as he swam.

"What makes that glow?" I whispered.

"It's the minerals in the water. I doubt if we can be seen very far away," was the response. But even with that assurance I swam so that I made a minimum of disturbance in the water, and kept looking back toward the shore for any possible signs of life.

After about half an hour we appeared to be a considerable distance from the shore; however, the dark outline of the Bataan coast ahead seemed very little closer to us.

"How're you going?" Bill asked.

"Fine. This is great. The way I feel, I could swim all night."

"I think we ought to swim for that light, the brighter one of the two," Bill suggested.

"I've been watching it, and I believe we're getting closer to it all the time. At least it's looking brighter to me," I said.

Off to our right and in a northeasterly direction a big black cloud seemed to hang over Manila Bay. The cloud seemed to grow darker as we swam. As I looked at it, Bill said, "Hope that big cloud over there stays where it is until we get to Bataan."

"Oh, I don't think we have anything to worry about. At the rate we're traveling, we should be there before the cloud gets here even if it is coming in our direction."

"Sure, look back there. We're really leaving old Corregidor in our past," Bill assured me. After that we swam for a long time without talking. It seemed too good to be true that we were on our way to freedom. All we had to do was to keep swimming toward that little light on the Bataan coast. Several times I convinced myself that we were closer to it and that it

114

looked much brighter; but then again it would look just as dim as it had looked when we had first started our swim.

After a long while it started to sprinkle lightly, and the water was not as smooth as it had been before. "Looks like we're in for a little shower," Bill observed.

"Yes, I felt some drops, and it looks like that cloud is beginning to reach us." As if in answer to my statement, it started raining a little harder.

"Still see the light?" he asked.

"Sometimes it seems to fade out for a while, but then it comes back again. I'm sure we're still headed in the right direction," I answered.

Again we lapsed into silence and settled down to the business of swimming. There could be no question that we were getting closer to the shore. I thought of what a wonderful thing that would be. We could walk to Cabcaben Field and find some of the Filipinos and get something to eat. Then we could sleep in the jungles, far away from all the things we had been doing during the past few weeks. As I swam along I cupped my hand to my lips to catch a few drops of fresh water that was coming down more heavily. I managed to get a few drops before a big wave swept over me and choked me as it forced salt water into my throat and nose. I coughed and tried to get my breath. I called for Bill to hold up for a minute. Then I realized I had not been in contact with Bill for a long time. I looked all about me, only to find that the waves had grown higher, and it was impossible to see more than a few feet in any direction.

"Hey, Bill!" I screamed at the top of my voice. No answer. "Hey, Bill! Where are you?" I shouted it again and again, trying to raise as high in the water as I could to look about me. The wind was blowing, rain was coming down in torrents, and the waves were breaking over my head even though I did everything possible to keep it above the water. The terrible thought struck me that something had happened to

Bill. He was lost, and I was alone in the middle of the North Channel. I tread water and shouted until I was certain that he would never answer. Then I realized for the first time what a foolish idea this swim had been, and I understood why the others back in camp had ridiculed the idea of swimming to the mainland to escape.

I remembered how some of them had said, "Let's wait until we get to the mainland before we try to escape." I remembered some of their discussions about the strong current in the channel and about the sharks. I also remembered Bill when he had said, "You don't want to spend another day in this hell, do you?" That was why we had been so impatient. That was why we had been willing to take the chance, because we felt that we would surely die if we remained there.

Again I tried, "Bill, for Christ's sake, where are you? Answer me!" Then I thought I heard a sound above the roar of the water.

"That you, Bill? Answer again. I think I heard you," I shouted, trying desperately to swim in the direction from which the sound came. I suddenly realized I was making no progress. Although I was trying hard, I was bobbing like a cork in the big waves. Then I heard, "Ed!"

"Yeah, Bill. I hear you! I hear you!" I shouted, and I thought I saw a dark figure ahead. "For Christ's sake, Bill, let's don't get lost again," I pleaded.

"We'd better check with each other and talk to each other more," he suggested. "Wonder where we are. Haven't seen the light for some time."

"Neither have I," I answered. "I've been looking for you."

We talked, bobbing up and down with one big wave after another. There was no use in trying to swim, for we could make no headway, and we had not the slightest idea in which direction to proceed. We had been in the water at least three or four hours and should have been near the Bataan coast; but the sky was black and the sea was black. There was nothing for us to do but tread water, wait until the storm subsided, and keep from getting separated.

It was a long time before the rain began to slacken, and even before it had stopped completely, we were again able to see a tiny light shining in the distance.

"There it is," Bill said, and we both started swimming again with new enthusiasm.

Bill said, in a very discouraged voice, "I'm afraid it's a star, Ed. Looks too high in the sky to be a light."

It was still rather faint, but I strained my eyes harder and harder. "It may be. No, wait a minute; it is a light, and it's not very far away. I think I can see the shore right over there."

"Yeah, that's it!" Bill saw it too.

Our luck had changed. At the time when we had been bobbing up and down in the big waves of the channel thinking we were hopelessly lost, we were just off the shore of Bataan. We were very near the shore, and all we had to do was to get in to land without being seen by the Japs. That light was probably an enemy encampment.

Through the mist something big loomed up ahead of me. "Looks like a big wall up there, Bill."

"Wall, nothing," Bill whispered in alarm. "That's a ship. Let's get out of here before they see us."

We turned and swam in the other direction for a considerable distance before we stopped and looked back. By that time the atmosphere had cleared, and we were able to make out the outline of a large transport near a dock.

"Can you make that out?" I asked, because it did not look familiar to me.

"Looks like the North Mine Dock to me," Bill said meekly.

"Couldn't be," I replied, but even as I spoke, I recognized the pier and big Malinta Hill behind it. "Well, I'll be damned. Let's get away from here."

There was no question that it was the North Mine

Dock of Corregidor, and we were only about a hundred yards from shore and not more than half a mile from the place where we had started swimming several hours before. The storm and the current had played tricks on us and swept us back down the coast. After several hours of swimming and battling the waves we were no nearer to Bataan than we had been when we started. We could see no signs of life on the ship, but we kept swimming away from it.

"Think we can still make it before daylight?" I asked.

"Don't know. It's worth a try. There's no turning back now. Better to try anything than to go back to Corregidor," came the answer.

Bill was right. Anything was better than that—even the bottom of the sea. By now the water was smooth again, and swimming was easy. The night cleared up beautifully; and after a while the clouds above began to break up so that we could again see the stars. We could easily see each other, so we swam on for a long time without a word between us. There was nothing to say. We had a long swim before us.

Swimming sidestroke, I would reach out with my right hand far in front of me, pull an arm full of water back past my body; then kick. Then there was a small stroke with the left hand while the right reached out again. It was pull, kick, pull, kick, on and on, mechanically, like walking hour after hour. For a long time it seemed that we were suspended there between the two shores, getting neither nearer to Bataan nor farther away from Corregidor.

What if it gets light and we're still out here swimming?" and without waiting for an answer to my question, I went on, "We might possibly make it to shore without being seen, even in the daytime."

How long those thoughts ran through my mind, I had no idea. It was like a dream, being somewhere and not being able to get away; but I was suddenly brought out of my bad dream when something hit my leg. Then it hit me again. Was it a shark? "Bill!" I screamed.

"What is it?" he asked in alarm.

"Nothing," I answered shortly. I could see no point in telling him and having him as frightened as I was at that moment. I imagined I saw fins cutting the water in circles about me, and at any moment I expected to be hit again. The next time I was it, it was only a light touch.

Then Bill spoke up. "I think little fish are trying to eat me alive."

That was it! It was little fish. They were swimming along, trying to nibble at my arms and legs. After a while they left us, and all was calm again.

By this time it was clear that we were getting closer and closer to shore; then old Venus came peeking up over the eastern horizon like the red light that pops up on the instrument panel of a plane, saying, "Fuel pressure is getting low." Old Venus seemed to be a warning light to us. We started swimming faster and faster, for it was beginning to get light.

Off to our right we were able to make out an object which we were unable to identify.

"Is that a ship?" I asked.

"Seems to be standing still, whatever it is." We strained our eyes at the object until it took the form of a large seagoing barge.

"It's not too far away," I observed.

"No, I don't think so. Maybe we had better go over and spend the day on her rather than try to make it to shore," Bill suggested. We changed our course slightly to the right in order to bring ourselves closer to the barge. We were both very tired and eager to get some rest. But before we were halfway to the barge, we were able to make out the trees on the shoreline more distinctly, and we could see that it was only a short distance from us. Without a word we turned and headed for the shore, which offered much better security for us than the Japanese barge.

Some twenty feet before we reached the shore we came upon a lot of large rocks, and like two sea monsters emerging from the water, we struggled our way across the rocks and onto the shore. The place appeared to be completely deserted.

It was not until we were on solid ground that we realized how completely exhausted we were. In the cold gray dawn of Bataan I turned and had one last look across the channel, back to Corregidor. Then we both dropped exhausted into a clump of bushes.

When we awoke, the sun was low in the western sky. We were free!

8. Jungle interlude

It was about five o'clock in the evening when we got up from the wet ground and started moving about. If anyone ever felt lost, we did then, and yet we were happy with our success in getting away from Corregidor. Across the choppy water of the North Channel lay that black ghost of an island, quiet and still as if she had died when the white flag of surrender was raised over her more than two weeks before. No longer were her big guns thundering defiance, nor were her anti-aircraft guns barking at the enemy planes that came at her night and day. Corregidor was dead, but we were two lives who had slipped away from that veil of darkness.

Ahead of us lay the treacherous jungles of the Japanese-occupied Bataan Peninsula.

"I haven't the slightest idea where we are, except that I feel certain we are somewhere west of Cabcaben Field," I told Bill. "If we can find the field, I'm sure we can find some Filipinos who will give us food." I knew of a little fisherman's hut at the edge of the Cabcaben Field where we used to shoot craps with some of the natives.

"We'd better start walking. I'm hungry as a bear," Bill said.

Dressed in nothing more than our khaki shorts, we headed eastward along the coast. There were good trails and roads everywhere, and from time to time we passed through areas that had been used for camps by the Japanese, Filipinos, or Americans. We could tell by the debris scattered about the area who had used it last. We scoured each place for clothing that might fit us, and after a time we were able to find shoes, long trousers, and khaki shirts which fit each of us fairly well. We also scoured each place for food; however, the only thing we were able to find was a little pile of onions. We squatted on our haunches, picked the little onions out of the dirt, and feasted on them. Then we put the remainder in our pockets for later.

The twilight of Bataan was very peaceful as we hiked along through the giant trees. A rustle in the leaves up ahead of us startled us until we both saw a young deer running toward us through the forest.

"Say, I'd like to have a hunk of that in a skillet about now," Bill said.

"That would be wonderful, but it shouldn't be too long now until we find that fisherman's hut. This place has changed so much that I still don't recognize any part of it," I answered.

We passed a number of trenches and saw barbed-wire barricades which the Japanese had placed along the shore. Pointing to them, I said, "They were sure wasting their time with that stuff."

"If we don't get there pretty soon, it's going to be dark, and we may not be able to find it," Bill observed.

"It should be anywhere along here now." As the words left my mouth, I recognized a grove of coconut trees ahead of us which I was certain was the place we were looking for.

"There it is. I'm sure that's it," I said.

"Why don't you go ahead, and I'll remain back a ways just in case anything happens. We won't be taken by surprise," Bill suggested.

"That's a good idea," I answered. "But I'm sure these people are our friends and will help us any way they can."

It was dark as I approached the little hut and

called, "Tao poo." That was the greeting Filipinos use, which they told me meant, "We are people." There was no response, and I repeated, louder, "Tao poo, tao poo."

With that the old man stuck his head cautiously out of the door. "What do you want?"

I approached closer. "Do you remember me? I was one of the soldiers here at the field before the Americans left."

He looked at me more closely. "There were so many, and it was so long ago," shaking his head to indicate that he was not certain he remembered me. "The Japanese patrol comes by here about this time every evening. You had better go some place else."

"But I have a comrade with me, and we are hungry and need food. Could you fix us some rice?"

"My wife is in bed, and my two daughters are sick with malaria. She will fix you some rice, but better you hide over there until it is ready." He pointed to a grove a little distance away.

"All right. We will wait until you call us," I said, and headed back to where Bill was waiting for me.

Bill was sitting on a log waiting patiently when I reached him. "They were all asleep. The wife is going to fix us some rice, but the old man says we had better stay out here and wait because the Jap patrol comes along about this time of night."

We waited and listened for what seemed to be a long time. Bill broke the long silence with "Do you still have that quinine?" I remembered transferring it to my new trousers, and reached into my hip pocket and handed the bottle to him. "We'd better take a few tablets in order to ward off malaria," he suggested.

"Not a bad idea." By that time I heard a hissing sound from the direction of the Filipino hut and knew it was the signal of the old man for us to come forward. The steaming rice was laid out on two big banana leaves, and we carried it back to our hiding place, where we devoured it in a hurry. The old man

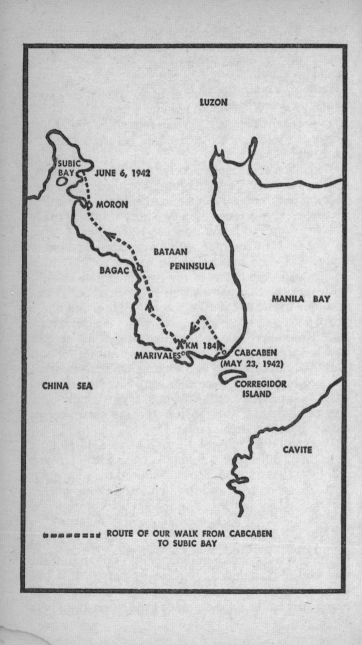

ROUTE OF OUR WALK FROM CABCABEN TO SUBIC BAY

went with us and talked to us while we ate. "It is very difficult for us. We would like to help you more, but if the Japanese caught us, our entire family would be killed."

With a mouth full of rice, Bill answered, "We understand that perfectly and do not want to cause you any trouble. As soon as we eat we shall be on our way."

"Take this bolo. You will need it in the jungle," the old man offered, pulling his knife from its sheath on his side. "Also, there is more rice which you can take along for later."

"We won't need any more rice now," I answered. My stomach was so full that I felt I would not need more food for a week.

"But it is ready, and you can have it," he insisted.

"Thank you very much, and thank you for everything you have done for us. We won't need it," Bill agreed. "We'd better be getting on our way."

We took our leave of the old man and headed for the ridge west of Cabcaben Field which I knew so well.

On the way we passed through an area I recognized as the old Army Hospital Nnmber Two, on the opposite side of the ridge from Cabcaben Field. It was there I had known Army nurses Alice Hahn, Ann Williams, Evelyn Whitlow, Harriet Lee, and a large number of others. There was also the spot where we had prayed on Easter Sunday, just a few days before the fall of Bataan. It had been an out-of-doors hospital, with cots and mosquito nets spread out under the trees of the jungle. We left the hospital area and started our climb to the ridge. After walking a long time, we reached the point where we had seen the "mighty convoy with reinforcements" sail around the east end of Corregidor a few weeks before. If it had been daylight, we could have seen down into our old camp area on the opposite side of the ridge. But it was not daylight; it was terribly dark, and the trail ahead of us was black.

As we walked along the top of the ridge I saw some terrible sights. I saw the remains of the battle of Bataan, soldiers, Marines in all kinds of positions, some dead, some alive, and all scattered over the hillside in the distance. It was like pictures of ancient battles I had seen years before, and it was all so vivid that I was almost certain it was real, but my better judgment told me that I was suffering from hallucinations. My imagination was on a real spree.

"Bill, I've been seeing some of the damnedest things, but I know they're not real."

"That's funny, because my imagination has been running away with me, too. Must be that quinine we took back there."

"Must be. But I never saw anything like that before."

We walked and walked into the black jungle until it seemed we should have been reaching the top of the mountain. The trail was continually running out, and it was so dark that we had a hard time making progress. Finally, we found ourselves entangled in a thicket so dense that, regardless of which way we attempted to go, we found ourselves unable to move. After probing first in one direction and then in another, we finally gave it up and decided to sleep until daylight.

With the light of a new day, Sunday, May 24, it was an easy matter to find our way out into an open meadow where we could see that it was still a long distance to the top of the mountain to the north.

In the meadow on the hillside I saw a sight that caused me to break away from Bill and run. The trees ahead looked like cashews, and if it were true, we would have a feast on the delicious fruit. Bill followed, not knowing the reason for my excitement. Looking into the trees, I found a small fruit about the size and shape of a green pepper with a small pod on the bottom of it which bore the cashew nut. We had become familiar with this tree when we were foraging for food over the hillsides during our stay on Bataan. I handed the first one to Bill, for he had never eaten them before. "Delicious!" he exclaimed as he bit into the fruit. We found more and were delighted with our first breakfast on Bataan. The sun was shining, the atmosphere was cool and pleasant, and we were on our way. Our decision to walk across the mountains had been a good one. In a few days we would cover the seventeen-mile distance to Subic Bay, where we could find a boat to sail to China.

Our early morning breakfast over, we continued on our march toward the top of Mount Mariveles. It was a long, hard walk, but not always uphill. Sometimes we reached a crest, and it was necessary to cross a valley before we continued our climb. At about two o'clock in the afternoon we reached a part of the mountain where an avalanche had caused a big bare spot on the side of Mount Mariveles hundreds of years before. The area, some fifty feet wide and perhaps a couple of hundred feet high, was covered with huge boulders, and there were very few trees. We had seen this streak on the side of the mountain from the foothills of Bataan and from the island of Corregidor many times.

We stopped to rest on a big boulder, and for a long time looked out across the bay to Manila to the east and to Corregidor to the south of us. The only signs of life we saw were the Japanese minesweepers plying back and forth across the channels between the islands.

As I reflected on the days on Bataan and Corregidor, they seemed like something that had happened years before, or more like something I had dreamed. We sat in this quiet and peaceful spot, which seemed far closer to heaven than to the hell we had experienced over the past months. The scene before us seemed like something from a movie, and we were as detached from it as if we had been watching it on a movie screen.

We knew that on the peaceful-looking island in front of us were "Fightin'" Jim, Renka, Drachenberg and eleven thousand more souls being parboiled in that little corner of hell where we had left them. I wondered if they had any idea of what had happened to us. Certainly at that moment they had no way of knowing that we were sitting on top of the world. Our future was ahead of us, and we had only to start walking.

The going from there on became much more difficult, and unlike the proverbial bear, we did not see the other side of the mountain when we got to the top. Instead, there were more mountains and ridges and peaks. On and on we went, up and over one ridge after another until darkness came at last. In In our eagerness to reach our destination we continued on, feeling our way over the roughest terrain imaginable. Sometimes we were scaling a hill that seemed almost straight up, and other times we were feeling our way along the edge of a cliff. At some time in the night it began to rain—a cold rain that chilled us through—and we found shelter on the leeward side of a big boulder and slept till dawn.

The next day, after several hours of climbing over one ridge after another, I suggested, "It looks to me as if we are walking three miles to cover one mile, and it would be better if we followed one of these ridges back to the foothills instead of trying to go over the tops of all these hills."

"I've been thinking the same thing. At least we might be able to find a Filipino house and get some food," was Bill's reply. It was then Monday noon, and we had eaten nothing since Sunday morning.

It was much easier walking as we followed the top of a ridge which took us in a southwesterly direction, and by nightfall we were well into the foothills. Our big thrill came when Bill cried out, "These are banana trees all around us!" Bill started to climb a tree, and I gave him a boost. When he had a hold of the stock he swung out, and his weight pulled the thing to the ground. We grabbed first one and then another of the bananas, but they were all green.

"Let's get over here on the ridge where they get more sun. There'll be some ripes ones there." But it was the same everywhere; they were all green.

"The only thing to do is to eat a couple of these and then wait till morning. Maybe we can find some ripe ones then," I suggested. With that we both started peeling the hard, green bananas. By taking a small bite at a time and chewing it for a long time, I was able to down one after several minutes. It was about the size of a piece of chalk and tasted about as good. Bill, with a better appetite than I for green bananas, ate three.

"I feel a little stronger than I did before I ate them," Bill said. We found a comfortable place to lie down in the middle of the banana field and slept until dawn. With the light of day we continued our search for a ripe banana, but it was all in vain. For breakfast we each ate a couple more green bananas, which seemed harder and more bitter than those we had eaten the night before.

We found a road at the edge of the banana field which we recognized as the Mariveles-Bagac Pike. A signpost told us that it was only ten kilometers to Mariveles, and I knew that we were but a short distance north of the spot where we were supposed to have surrendered to the Japanese six weeks before, Kilometer Post 184.

We knew it was virtual suicide to walk along the road in the daytime, but we were starved for food, and we were willing to take the chance. Climbing through the mountains for the past two days had sapped our energy until walking, even along the road, became a struggle for us.

Less than a mile up the road toward Bagac we

came upon another deserted camp area. From the debris about the area it appeared that it had been a Filipino Army camp, later used by the Japs. There were knapsacks, blankets, shelter halves, and everything imaginable scattered around the area. There was also a huge stack of American rifles with a stack of ammunition alongside, as if the place had been used for a surrender area like Kilometer Post 184.

"Here's where I get myself a rifle and some ammunition," Bill said.

"I don't think I want one. It's hard enough walking without lugging something like that along."

"If any Japs try to capture us, I'm going to account for two or three of them before they get me," Bill promised.

"I may be a coward, but it seems to me that I can run a hell of a lot faster without a rifle and a couple of bandoleers of ammunition to weight me down. As for shooting it out with them, the way I shoot a rifle, they'd probably get me first anyway," I added.

Bill picked himself out a rifle which was to his liking from the hundreds in the pile, and we then set out in search of food. He also picked up two bandoleers of ammunition. Handing me one, he said, "Here, you can carry this. We may need it." There were hundreds of tin cans scattered about the area, and we examined every one of them, hoping to find one that had not been emptied. In desperation we searched the area from one end to another in quest of anything we might find that would relieve our hunger. It was all in vain. There was nothing to be found.

"Quiet! I think I heard something in the bushes!" Bill whispered. We ducked down and waited, Bill with his rifle drawn and ready to use if necessary. As we held our breath, waiting for another sound, we saw the outline of a skinny old horse making his way through the bushes toward us. Not nearly so startled to see us as we were to see him, he continued coming toward us. The Americans, Filipinos, and Japs had come and gone, but that old nag had survived the battles. He appeared glad to see us. I turned from him and continued my search, but Bill called me back.

"Ed, I have an idea. I know we haven't any matches to start a fire, but I'm sure I can start one from the muzzle blast of the rifle. I suggest we kill this horse and have ourselves some steaks. If I try to build a fire first, I might stampede the horse. Better shoot him first," he reasoned.

"Fine, if you can start a fire. I've been watching for matches but haven't found a one so far." At that stage I was willing to try anything. We had eaten horse meat on Bataan before, and I remembered the saying that Bataan would hold out as long as the 26th Cavalry held out. That was when we had been eating a lot of their horses.

Bill raised his rifle about two feet from the old horse's head and pulled the trigger. The old animal fell over on its side as if its joints were too stiff to bend, and died without lifting a hoof. With the bolo the Filipino had given us, we cut off a front quarter. The horse was so skinny that there appeared to be more meat on the front than on the rear quarters. Our greed and desperate hunger took the place of common sense, and we rolled the animal over and cut off the other front quarter.

We then broke open three or four cartridges and poured the powder in a pile. On top of that Bill placed dry leaves and twigs. With his new invention for starting a fire all set to go, he backed away and held his Army rifle about six inches from the pile and fired. The result was ridiculous. Instead of starting a fire, the blast from the muzzle blew away the powder, the leaves, and the twigs. "Fine!" I laughed, and Bill looked chagrined. We were right back where we had started toward building a fire. Several attempts at this convinced both of us that we would have to find some other way to cook our horse meat.

"Bill, I found a can a while ago with what I thought

was kerosene. Maybe if we put some on a blanket and fire into it, it will ignite," I suggested.

"It's worth a try."

I doused an old blanket with the kerosene, hung it over a bush, and fired into it several times without even the slightest hint of success.

We were both discouraged, but not ready to give up. Then Bill came forth with another idea. "Some years ago I was able to start a fire Boy Scout fashion by cutting a notch in a piece of wood and rubbing another to it."

"I've never been able to make that work, but let's try it," I answered.

"Before we start it," Bill suggested, "I think we'd better take our meat and get away from the road. If any Japs come along, they would see us before we had a chance to get away."

"Not a bad idea. Let's head up that trail."

We each threw our quarters of horse meat over our shoulders and walked about a hundred yards along the trail which led away from the road and back toward the foothills. There, beside a stream, we went to work on our new project. Each of us made a bow by tying our shoestrings to a stick, then cut a notch in the board, placed some tinder beside it, and started to drill. The midday sun beat down upon us as we worked desperately, pushing our bows back and forth to get the necessary friction between the sticks. At last Bill announced, "I'm beginning to get some smoke."

That was the nearest we had come to getting a fire started, and we both felt that at last success was with us. It would be but a few moments until we had a fire and were enjoying some good juicy steaks.

At that very instant the jungles rang out with bang! bang! bang! bang! We were being fired on by the Japs!

Quick as a flash we dropped everything and ran as fast as we could go. To our right was a steep hill, and our only avenue of escape was to run up the stream which led away from the road. Big boulders made the going difficult. Part of the time the water was knee-deep, and part of the time it was waist-deep. The banks on either side of the stream ran straight up for twenty to thirty feet so that it was impossible to turn off. After running for a considerable distance, I turned to see that I had left Bill far behind. At last I found a place where it was possible to scale the side and waited there for him. Then we ran a good distance on up the side of the hill and fell into a clump of bushes to catch our breath and rest.

"There's two ways to go now," Bill appraised our situation. "We can follow this ridge back down to the road, or we can go in the other direction back up into the mountains where we were before."

"That decision's not too difficult for me. Let's make our way back toward the road and wait till dark before we start out again."

We picked our way cautiously along the ridge high above the camp area which we had just left. Although we were traveling as quietly as possible, I accidentally kicked a rock about half the size of a basketball and sent it crashing down the steep hill toward the camp. The farther the thing rolled the louder it seemed to be, and it was only seconds later that we heard footsteps in the dry leaves from several directions. It seemed that a patrol had been looking for us, and when I kicked the rock they came running toward the source of the noise. We darted for the nearest cover, which was a clump of bushes. Shortly after we stopped moving the rustling in the leaves in the distance stopped too.

We knew it was a habit of the Japs to stalk their prey and hide motionless in a tree for hours at a time so we were afraid to move. It was about two o'clock in the afternoon when we went into hiding. We strained our ears and eyes trying to hear or see something, but there was not a sound to be heard. We remained silent without moving all afternoon and all night. In the light of day we were again afraid to move, so we remained in the clump of bushes all that day too. Too many times I had observed the curious little split-toed shoes that the Japanese wore in jungle fighting for the purpose of climbing trees I had also seen the rope which each of them carried to bind himself into a tree so that he could remain for hours.

Just as it was growing dark on the second day, Bill leaned over and whispered to me, "Ed, I've got a confession to make. I've been eating ants. They're a little bitter, but once I read where an explorer in Africa had eaten them without ill effects when he was desperate for food. Why don't you try some?"

"No, sir. Hungry as I am, those ants aren't going to do me any good, and I don't want the little things crawling around in my insides."

"I think I feel a little stronger since I ate them," he said.

We remained silent for about an hour. Then Bill said, "It's dark enough now so that we should be able to move without too much difficulty."

"Yes, surely they've gone by now." Cautiously we made our way on down the ridge, to find ourselves back in the banana field again. Again we feasted on a couple of green bananas before we got back on the road and continued our hike along the dark road to the north.

We found we were so weak by then that we were able to walk only about one kilometer (about six-tenths of a mile) before it was necessary to lie down and rest. Thus we made our way on up the pike, a kilometer at a time, with hopes of finding a friendly Filipino or food of some kind. All along the way there were dozens of automobiles and trucks that had been shot up. It was a battle-scarred, spooky country; but after walking for several hours up one long hill after another, we came at last to the open country between the two big mountains that made up the

Bataan Peninsula. We were then in flat country for a time. There were more piles of rifles and ammunition. In the dark Bill picked out another rifle.

Our pace quickened when we saw a light off to the right side of the road and up ahead of us. It would be a Filipino house where we could get some relief from our hunger, and we could not wait. We ran. As we drew near, the house turned out to be a big trailer. "Probably some Filipino family taking up housekeeping in one of the wrecked vehicles," I observed.

When we were within thirty feet of the vehicle we came to the startling realization that the occupants were Japs, not Filipinos. There were many of them, and they were busy chattering while they were preparing food and eating. The language we heard was Japanese and not Tagalog. By that time we were so close in that if we had been observed, we would have been more conspicuous by turning back than by going ahead. Instead of turning, we swung in a wide circle to the left, stepped up our pace, and got away from the place without being noticed.

Farther on up the road it started to rain. We slushed along from kilometer post to kilometer post and lay down to revive ourselves at each one. It was raining hard when we came to a sign that told us we were just one kilometer from Bagac, and we were heartened by the thought that in a few minutes we would be in a town where we could get some food. Again our pace became almost a run as we came nearer to the town. It was only a short distance, and we could see the housetops ahead of us. But as we drew nearer we found that the housetops were but the remains of what had been houses. The whole village had been burned to the ground, and all that remained of several blocks were the twisted tin roofs and other debris. How much farther could we go, and how much more disappointment could we take? Had we foreseen all these difficulties, our decision to walk across Bataan might have been different.

We walked on toward the coast, and after a time saw another light. It was probably another Jap outfit, and we would be no better off than we had been before, but we forged on to investigate. There were houses, several of them. Some were wrecked, but others were standing. We were sure they were occupied because some of them had lights inside.

"Rather than take a chance on their being Japanese, I suggest that we wait until dawn and see whether they are Filipinos or Japs," Bill said.

"I'm with you all the way. Let's wait over here in this old shack until we can find out what kind of people they are," I agreed.

The small hut we selected had the front wall torn away. The floor was about two feet off the ground. We sat down to wait, finding a blanket for each of us to put over our shoulders. The next thing I knew it was broad daylight and I was waking from a sound sleep. There lay Bill beside me, sound asleep and with his arms wrapped around his rifle. I shook him. "Bill, we'd better be moving." We looked the village over very carefully and were still unable to determine whether or not we were among friends.

"Bill, you cover me with your rifle, and I'll see what's in that house over there."

With the old blanket draped over my shoulders to cover my uniform, I walked down the street to investigate. As I approached one of the houses, a couple of dogs started barking fiercely. I watched them to see whether or not they were going to try to bite me. Then I looked up just in time to see two Jap soldiers coming straight at me about half a block away. I looked to the left and saw a single Jap coming toward me at about the same distance. There was nothing about their manner to indicate that they recognized me to be an American. At that instant the two dogs began fighting each other. I pulled my blanket up over my head, did an about-face, and walked leisurely in the other direction for several feet. Then I quickened my pace. When I was about even with the house from which I had started, I broke into a run and ran as fast as I could go to where Bill was waiting for me.

Then the two of us took off together cross-country as fast as we could go for about a quarter of a mile. When we stopped to look back, we saw nothing to indicate that we were being followed. Our big thrill came when we discovered that we had stopped in the middle of another cashew grove. Again we had a delicious feast on the tropical fruit. It was then Thursday morning, and it was the first food we had had since Sunday morning except for the green bananas and the ants which Bill had eaten. The fresh fruit literally melted in our mouths.

We had a new lease on life as we left the cashew grove and headed on north to find the Bagac-Moron road.

"Don't think we'd better try walking on the road again in the daytime. Let's get a little rest and go into Moron tonight," I suggested.

"Looks like a good place over here." Bill pointed to a spot beside a small stream. There were remnants of soldiers' equipment and first aid supplies all about the place, indicating that it had been an aid station. I browsed around for a while after Bill lay down to sleep; then I finally stretched out on the ground a few feet from him. I couldn't believe my eyes when I saw a dried-up mummy corpse lying on a stretcher not fifteen feet from where Bill was lying. "Who's your roommate?" I asked. But Bill was sound asleep and did not hear me. I slept, and did not think about the corpse again until we were a long way down the road, on our way to Moron. It was not yet dark, but we could see the road was clear for a long distance, so we continued our walk toward the town.

As we approached Moron we could hear gunfire, as if there were fighting in the village. We decided to wait beside the road until it was dark and we could get into the town without being observed and find out what was going on. As we waited, a small boy came walking down the road.

"Hey you!" Bill shouted. The boy was much surprised to see us. "Say, boy! What's all that shooting going on over there?"

Without answering our questions, the boy pointed to us and said, "You 'Merican soldiers."

"Yes, we're Americans, but what is that shooting in the town?" Bill insisted.

"We got much guns and ammunition and everybody shoots," was the answer. " 'Mericans left much ripels and boys all have ripels."

"Any Japs in Moron?"

"No, no. No Japanese in barrio," came the reassuring answer. "I take you to my home," he invited.

The three of us walked together down the road and toward the town. When we arrived we were received with a great deal of hospitality. The boy's family gave us wild pork, honey, rice, and papaya.

"We would like to find a boat big enough to sail across the China Sea," I told our host.

"But there are no such boats. The Japanese have confiscated all boats which they could use. The ones which they could not use they have destroyed!"

"But surely we can find one boat big enough to make the trip," I insisted.

"You will find none. All the boats are gone. This is

138

not the time to sail the sea. You like to stay here with us?"

"No, we cannot stay. We will go on to Subic Bay. Maybe we can find a boat there," I answered.

"But if you will stay, we can find a place for you to live and give you plenty of food. The Japanese are everywhere, and they will catch you unless you hide."

"We have to go," Bill supported me.

Our wait in Moron was exceedingly pleasant. We stayed for a couple of days, eating and resting and visiting with the natives. Toward evening of the second day we again headed out to the north toward Subic Bay, where we still had hopes of finding a boat in which we could travel to China. Around twilight we met a Filipino at a spring where he was filling a bucket with water. He was very interested in us, told us he liked Americans and hoped that the Americans would soon come back to the Philippines. When we turned down his invitation to come and live with his family, he finally said, as if it were his last hope of doing something for us, "You like beer, Joe?"

"Beer!" we both shouted.

"Yes. I have a can of beer. I will get it for you." He left his water can at the spring and went running across the field and over the hill to his house, about half a mile away. In a while he came running back with a shiny tin can in his hand and presented it to Bill. We both read the printing on the end of the can. It said "Corned Beef." The poor fellow could not read very well and thought it was beer. We thanked him kindly, told him we would drink it later, and went our way.

We walked all night, and at dawn found ourselves on the shore of Subic Bay where we met a fine-looking, middle-aged Filipino by the name of Salvador Savaras. We told him about our experiences and our plan, and again received the bad news about the possibilities for going to China. There were no boats big enough to make the trip, and it was not the right season to try it.

"There are Japanese patrols which come past here all of the time. We must be very careful. After you have had a good meal at my house I will take you to a place to hide," he promised us.

Salvador's home was on the shore, and we could look across the bay to Grande Island, which was at that time a Japanese fort. Mrs. Savaras furnished us with many kinds of delicious foods, including rice cake, wild honey, papaya, fried chicken, and many other things. It was good to be alive and free again. The kindness and generosity of the people touched us deeply, and we felt a warm affection for them.

After we had feasted at their home, Salvador guided us along the trail which led to a hut back in the hills. We remained there for several days. It was then the rainy season, and for several days we lay in the hut and listened to the rain patter on the thatched roof. In the evenings Salvador would take us back to his house, where we would visit with him and with his neighbors.

During the last few days of our visit with Salvador one of his neighbors was having a funeral celebration. People came in from around the community and sang and enjoyed a feast until late into the night every night for about a week. We learned that funerals were fun in the Philippines, but we told our friends we did not want to stay around long enough for them to enjoy ours.

Every evening at the funeral celebration we would tell Salvador of our intention to leave, and every evening he would insist that we remain at Subic Bay until the return of the American Army. We told him that fighting was our business and that even then we were receiving money from our government. Our government was not paying us to hide in the mountains somewhere until the war was over. He did not understand.

140

"Since we cannot go to China, it would be possible for us to sail to the southern islands if we had a small boat," I told him.

"But you should not go," he insisted. We saw that it was going to be necessary for us to be rude to our hosts in order to make our departure.

"We have definitely decided to leave tonight," I announced rather abruptly. "I will give you thirty pesos for your little banco." Salvador did not like the idea, but when he saw that we were in earnest, he gave in. When we were ready to shove off, we found that we not only had the banco, but he also gave us two mosquito nets, a new pair of shoes which fit me perfectly, cigarettes, matches, bananas, and a lot of other things to make our journey easier.

At last we were outfitted with a boat of our own and enough supplies to enable us to sail for several days at a time without having to stop for provisions. Bill and I had no doubt that we could sail from island to island until we could get a larger boat and then make our way to Australia, where we could join the American forces again.

It was with some reluctance that we said good-by to Salvador Savaras, his wife, and his kind neighbors, but we had one goal in mind—to get back to the American forces.

Our first obstacle in sailing was to get our little craft out of Subic Bay, past Grande Island, which guards the mouth of Subic Bay much the same as Corregidor guards the mouth of Manila Bay. For the past few nights the Japs had been swinging a search-light about the surrounding waters, and we knew that if we were ever spotted with the light it would be the end of our journey. We agreed to paddle our boat along the south shore of the channel until we got out to sea before putting up our sail. Our plan worked well until we hit a long shallow stretch studded with coral shoals. Several times the bottom of the boat scraped on the coral with a loud sound that we were

141

certain was audible across the bay. To prevent this from happening again, we waded beside the boat, one on each side, to ease it over the rocks and coral.

When we were about halfway past the island a strong wind came up, bringing a hard rain and big waves. The little boat pitched and bobbed and, from time to time, came down on big rocks so hard that we were certain it would break. It became necessary for us to pull it in to shore and wait for the rain to subside. There we lay on the leeward side of the boat for a long time to protect ourselves from the cold rain.

Soon the weather became calm, and we were again on our way. Though we had planned to wait until we were out of sight of Grande Island before hoisting our sail, our patience wore out; and in our eagerness to try out the boat we put the sail to the wind. A good breeze caught the sail as we let it out, and the little craft started skimming over the water with ease and grace. Bill handled the tiller, and I sat up front watching the water race past us.

At last we were on our way. We felt healthy and strong, for during the past few days we had eaten well, and we were well rested. We knew that two thousand miles of water lay between us and our destination, but however rough it got, it couldn't be more difficult than the eight-hour swim from Corregidor to Bataan or the five days of walking through the mountains of Bataan without any food. Every new gust of wind that filled our sail and caused our boat to leap along a little faster gave us a new thrill, for we were on our way.

We sailed all night, and when dawn came we pulled our little boat into shore and slept until darkness, when we could start out again. After two nights we had reached Luzon Point on Bataan and were getting ready for the biggest and most dangerous hop that we would have to make—the eighteen miles across the mouth of Manila Bay past Corregidor. The little boat showed only six inches above the water line, but with the outriggers we had confidence that it could make the trip.

Just before dark on June 8, 1942, we pulled the little boat down from her hiding place and shoved off. There was a good breeze from the north that carried us along at a very pleasant rate for the first few hours. Then we were able to see the black outline of old Corregidor to our left. We knew that Corregidor, like Grande Island, had huge searchlights which could be flashed out across the water.

It was a beautiful night for sailing, with big black clouds sweeping in toward us from all directions. They seemed to come toward us and then turn away, but all the while the wind stayed in the north and northwest, and we enjoyed a fast ride across the channel.

One big black cloud swept in from the southwest, and we were certain that it was going to put an end to our voyage. While I had my eyes fixed on it to see what it was going to do, Bill whispered, "There's a boat!"

A boat! I looked, and out under the cloud I was watching, about a hundred yards away and coming in our direction, was a small patrol boat. We held our breath while the craft passed behind us and faded into the darkness of the night.

By the stars it was about two o'clock in the morning when we were even with the Cavite shore on the south side of the bay, but we were still a couple of miles from shore.

"Let's head in a little, Bill. I don't like the looks of these clouds, and we don't want to be too far from shore when morning comes."

"But we're clipping along at such a good pace. I think we ought to make as much distance as we can while we have this good wind," he argued.

"All right, then. You want to keep on this course, and I want to pull in toward shore. Let's compromise

143

and pull in about halfway. How about that?" I suggested.

With that Bill pulled the boat around a few degrees to the left, a course which would not take us to land but would prevent us from going any farther to sea.

The wind was so good that we were literally leaping along, but we were so far from shore that even after an hour of sailing we did not seem any closer than we had been before. The waves started lapping over the sides of the boat, and I started bailing as fast as I could bail. I ws fighting a losing battle, and pretty soon found myself sitting waistdeep in water. It happened so quickly that Bill did not realize what had occurred until I told him that the situation had gotten out of control. There was only one thing to do. That was to down the sail and to start swimming the thing in towards shore. We had no idea how far it was to the shore, but after swimming the boat for a while, we learned that the distance was much shorter than we had expected it to be.

When we got near land, we were unable to find a place to pull the boat in. The night was so dark that the shore appeared to be a solid rock wall. At one place I held the boat back so the big waves would not carry it in, while Bill swam in to see if it were possible to find a place to bail the water out. He was gone for a long time, and came back with word that it was impossible.

"What the hell do you mean, impossible?" I asked impatiently. "You hold the boat and let me go in and look."

The waves were very big, and when I got within fifty feet of the water's edge I could see that they were beating the shore fiercely. They sent up a spray high into the air, but I swam on in just to make sure. My feet touched bottom just as a big wave was about to carry me in. By anchoring my feet and swimming frantically, I managed to get out without being carried into the rocks. There were cliffs everywhere, and if we had tried to take our boat in it would surely have been bashed to pieces. When I found Bill I apologized for not taking his word, and we agreed to look for a better place to go ashore.

We swam the boat on down the coast to where we thought we saw a cove. While we were swimming along I kicked something big and thought that Bill had swum under the water over to my side. But I was mistaken; there was Bill on his own side. Again I hit the thing with my arm. This time I splashed and churned the water so that Bill thought I had finally lost my mind. I had hit a big fish which was surely as large as I was, but after my dance he left me.

At last, after a long night's ride and a long swim, we pulled the boat onto the beach into a clump of bushes. The only sign of life we saw, when it was light enough to look around, were the tracks that some barefooted Filipino had left in the sand some time before. Just as we were about to lie down to sleep we looked out to sea and saw a gray Japanese patrol boat making its way out of Manila Bay to the south.

The sea remained so rough for the next couple of days that we were unable to continue our journey. It was miserable waiting, for our matches, rice, cigarettes, and everything else were soaked with salt water. For two days we ate uncooked rice soaked in salt water.

On the third day we convinced ourselves that the water was calm enough to sail again. We pushed off and got about fifty yards out from the shore when the waves started doing tricks with our little boat. The thing got completely out of control, and presently a big wave picked us up and set us back down upon the shore. In the process the outrigger on one side was snapped off, thus putting our little boat completely out of commission. We dragged it back onto the shore and set out walking. From my recollection of the island, it was only ten or fifteen miles across a stretch of land to the south shore, where we intended to pick up a more seaworthy craft.

We walked all night, most of the time along a railroad track. At dawn we selected a house and asked for food and lodging throughout the day. The Filipinos spoke no English but understood our needs, and after a delicious breakfast of rice and fish we lay down on the floor to sleep. At about noon we were awakened by a noise in the adjoining room. When we jumped up and looked into the other room we saw a fat, well-dressed Filipino arguing with the others.

"Hello. You Americans?" he asked when he saw us.

"Yes," answered Bill.

"I am the landowner. The boy came in town this morning and told me that two Japanese were sleeping in his house. They were afraid, and I came out to see what could be done."

We laughed at the idea that our hosts had taken us for Japanese but had been just as hospitable to us as if we were Americans. We visited and ate some more, and toward evening again set out on our way to the south shore. We walked all night, and in the morning found a Filipino who fed us and led us to a place in the hills where we could sleep without being disturbed. It was a small grass shack in the middle of an open field on a high hill. We could see the shore to the west and a big sugar factory in the green valley below.

As we crossed the field toward the shack we passed a plain, unmarked cross in the field.

"What is that for?" I asked.

"Oh, sir, that is where a soldier was killed. He had no identification. Nobody knows who he was, but his body rests here on the hillside." Our guide left us at the little hut, and we stretched out on the bamboo floor. It was cool and comfortable, and we slept well. About the middle of the afternoon I was awakened by Bill shaking my shoulder. I looked up into his startled eyes. He announced, "Ed, my rifle's gone."

"But where is it?"

"Somebody must have stolen it while we were sleeping. They could as easily have killed us."

Again we set out hiking before it had grown completely dark, and soon found that we had reached the little town of Balayan on the southern coast of the island. The people were so friendly that we were suspicious. At the first house where we stopped, the owner invited us in to have a dinner of fried eggs and wild pork. He said that he was a friend of the mayor of the city, and while we were eating he sent a messenger to arrange for an interview with the mayor for that very night.

The mayor met us in a field at the edge of town, and it was arranged that we should live in a little hut about two kilometers from town while arrangements were being made for our boat to sail to Australia.

Our hiding place was supposed to have been secret, with only a couple of persons knowing where we were located. On the first day we had forty visitors and on the second day we had fifty. The owner of the house explained that it was all right because they were all his relatives. Everyone who came to see us brought something to eat. We found ourselves surrounded with piles of coconuts, bananas, mangos, cans of spiced pork, cake, and many other delicious foods. The next few days were miserable. We did nothing but eat and visit with the people. With each new visitor it seemed the polite thing to do was to sample the food which he had brought. Soon we both reached the point when we were sick. Our lives were running in extremes, with too much of everything at one time and too little at others.

One thoughtful man brought along a pair of scissors to cut our hair, and did a reasonably good job, but when he undertook to shave me with a pocket knife called a *baliso*, without any lather, it hurt like being skinned alive. The audience was so pleased at the project that my pride kept me from stopping him after he had got started, so I suffered in silence.

After a few days Bill and I both got to the point where we agreed that we could stand it no longer. We had to get away from the food and from the people. Bill said bravely, to our host, "Tomorrow we are going down to the shore and take a boat and sail to Mindoro." Mindoro Island was a large island just to the south of Luzon and a very short distance to sail.

"Oh, but you can't do that," our host exclaimed.

"Can't do it? Who says we can't do it?" Bill demanded.

"Oh, but Señor Lopez will not let you go," he answered very calmly, as if to say, "It is against the law."

"And who, may I ask, is this Señor Lopez of whom you speak?" I inquired sarcastically.

"Señor Don Sixto Lopez. He is my cousin. You see, he owns all of this land. He will not let you go, but tomorrow his secretary will come to see you."

The next day a smart-looking Filipino in a white suit arrived upon the scene for an interview with us, and we learned that the desires of Señor Lopez were not as mandatory as the cousin had led us to believe the day before.

"It is the Señor's desire to be of assistance to you. You are very much at liberty to travel on if you wish; but if you wish, you may remain as long as you desire on the coconut plantation a few miles north from here. There you will be made safe and comfortable. There are already two Americans there. Perhaps they are your comrades. One is Chamberlain and the other Armstrong, and they have come from Corregidor," the secretary informed us.

"Don't think I know anyone by that name; do you, Bill?" I looked at Bill.

"Can't remember offhand. Might recognize them, though, when I see them. I sure hate to think of delaying our trip any more. Why, we've been away from Corregidor almost a month, and we haven't covered more than fifty miles."

"But we've got to get a boat and a good one, and I can't think of any better way, can you?"

"Then if you will go with him," the secretary pointed to another Filipino nearby, "he will keep you at his house until tonight, when a guide will come to escort you to the hacienda."

It was a long afternoon and evening while we waited for our guide to appear, but at long last a barefoot little man was seen coming across the field leading two diminutive white burros. Bill pointed to the animals and laughed. "Are we going to ride them or carry them?"

"Oh, they are very strong," said our host. When the little man drew nearer I asked him, "Are you our guide?"

He did not answer my question, but looked first at Bill and then at me and grinned.

"He does not speak English," volunteered our host. "Yes, he will be the one to take you to the hacienda."

"Well, that's fine. We should get along okay," I said. "A good way to keep from arguing, but would you mind explaining to him that we have escaped from the Japs and that we do not want people to see us or to know about us?"

"Oh, there is nothing to worry about. Everybody knows about you now," he exclaimed.

"Fine. That's just what we need right now more than anything else, a lot of good publicity."

Our host, recognizing my concern, said, "You do not need to worry. It is safe for you. The people in Balayan are your friends, and they will help you."

We thanked our host and bade him good-by; then we mounted our steeds and indicated to our guide that we were ready to go. In a short time we were making our way over the fields to the north.

10. Splitup

It was a beautiful night, with a big moon hanging in the sky. For most of the trip we could see the bay to the south of us dotted with lights, which we knew were the torches carried by the fishing boats. Ahead of us a mountain was silhouetted against the northern sky, and to the right we could see the famous Mount Taal breaking high above the horizon. Up ahead of me, Bill made a picturesque sight with his six-foot four-inch frame draped over the little burro. Then the silence of the tropical night was broken by Bill, singing, "Oh, I'm an old cowhand from the Rio Grande." Then, as we jogged along, we joined in songs serenading the moon.

Time and again we saw a little light in the distance, and each time hoped it was our destination, but each time it was just another house along the way where our guide could stop and chat with the occupants about the secret mission he was performing. The conversation was all in Tagalog, but we could make out enough to know that he was telling everything he knew about us. Our efforts to explain to our guide that we didn't want him to talk about us were in vain, and we went through the ordeal over and over again. At long last we pulled up to a house bigger than the rest, and our guide motioned us to dismount.

A young Filipino, much excited that we had arrived, came out of the house. "You come to see Marines?"

"Yes, where are they?" Bill asked.

"They are hiding near the creek. I will be the one to take you there," he volunteered. We followed him along a footpath into the middle of the coconut plantation, until we came to a little hut on the side of a hill near a stream. "Carlos, your comrades are here," he shouted. By the time we arrived at the hut, both the Marines were waiting for us.

"I am Carlos and this is Armstrong," one of them said. Both appeared to be well over six feet tall and to weigh about two hundred pounds.

In the conversation that followed, we learned that they had escaped from Corregidor a few days before us with some other Marines in a small boat. They had been ambushed by the Japs, and the others had been killed.

"What is the deal here, anyway?" Bill inquired. "Yesterday we told them that we were going to leave, and they told us we couldn't go because Señor Lopez didn't want us to go."

"Oh, Señor Lopez is the one who's taking care of us here, and boy, what care they give us! Never had it so good in our lives. The Señor and his two sisters live in Balayan, where you just came from, and also in Manila, but you will never see them. They'll send you practically anything you want and do anything for you, but they never come here. It really isn't safe because they're watched all of the time, and it would be their necks if the Japs ever found out about us being here."

"Well, if it wasn't known before, it will be known now," I said. "That damned guide of ours tonight stopped at every house between here and Balayan and told them all about us."

"Oh, there's nothing to worry about. Lopez owns all of the land as far as you can see in any direction. The people you saw work for him, and they all know about us," Carlos explained.

"What's the idea of Lopez being so nice to us when he's never even seen us?" Bill asked.

"Well, it's a long story, but we have plenty of time, so I'll just tell you all about it now." Carlos sat down at the foot of a coconut tree, and we all made ourselves comfortable as he explained the situation to us. "It seems that old Lopez is something of a Gandhi to the people in the Philippines. He is an old patriot from way back, and he was fighting for the independence of the islands even before the U.S. took over after the Spanish-American War. Then, when the U.S. did take over, he refused to swear allegiance to the United States. He even went into voluntary exile for about twenty-five years rather than do it. All the while he was traveling to England, France, and all over, trying to get freedom for his own country."

"Sounds like something out of a history book," Bill suggested.

"Yeah, he's a fabulous character, all right. There was a book published about the family once. This sister, Doña Clemencia, also took a trip to see President Teddy Roosevelt to try to get him to do something for the islands' independence; but—well, here comes old Walla." He interrupted his story as the Filipino boy who had guided us to the shack approached through the moonlit coconut grove.

"What's cookin', Walla?" Carlos shouted.

"Chicken and rice," was the answer.

"Hot damn! You'll like this!" Carlos cried as he brought a couple of bowls and spoons from the porch.

While Bill and I dug into the delicious food, Carlos continued, "Yep. They're some family, all right. I just hope that some day after the war I get a chance to come back here and get acquainted with them. By the way, the Filipino boy's name is really Braccio Evangelista, but we call him 'Walla' because whenever we ask him for anything, he always answers 'walla', which means I don't have any, or I don't know, or something like that. And, by the way, my name is really Reid Carlos Chamberlain, but they like to call me Carlos."

"How long have you been here?" I inquired.

"About a month. We expected to stop in just long enough to eat and rest. We may join the guerrilla forces, or we may try to get on down to one of the other islands. We've been waiting for some word from the Señor on just what would be the best thing to do," Carlos answered.

We told them of our plans and talked until late into the night. Then we all lay down on the bamboo floor in the shack and slept.

During the following days we found life at the Lopez hacienda very pleasant. We learned that the Señor owned all of the land for miles and miles about us, and we felt secure in our hiding place. We were in the middle of a four-or five-thousand-acre plantation, with plenty of room to move about without any fear of being seen.

Each day we swam in the cool creek nearby, climbed the coconut trees to shake down young coconuts, and read articles from the pile of *Reader's Digests* that were furnished to us. After a few weeks we had read all of them from cover to cover.

Sometimes we strolled along the trails up toward the mountains and visited with the natives along the way. It was the right season for roasting corn, and frequently we would spend an entire afternoon sitting around an open fire, roasting corn and visiting with the people.

On rainy days we remained in our hut, swapping yarns and making plans for our voyage to Australia whenever our boat was ready. Then sometimes we would make plans for the wonderful things we would do when we got back to the United States. First, we would all meet at the Coconut Grove in Los Angeles, and there, over a few bottles of champagne, we would all look back at these days and have a good laugh. Then sometimes Chamberlain would burst into song, "There's a coconut grove where I'll be confessing that I love you, etc."

Life through this period was not without its mixture of happiness and heart-rending sadness. We all knew that Gertrude, who made her home up at the big house where Walla lived, was pregnant. We eagerly awaited the day of the blessed event. Chamberlain had been playing nursemaid, and one morning when we heard a wild scream from the house, Armstrong, Bill and I went running because we knew the time had come. Gertrude, our mama cat, had given birth to two baby kittens. Our responsibilities had increased—two more mouths to feed. Armstrong, the big, blond Marine from Bruton, Alabama, was the silent one in our party, but after the kittens arrived he took a new interest in life. He took great pride in caring for them and making them comfortable.

It was but a few days later when a cloud of tragedy fell over our homestead. A small Filipino horse, which we had been nursing through a bad spell of sickness, grew steadily worse until life passed from his bloated body. But as one man's loss is another man's gain, our dismay was outweighed by the happiness of the large number of Filipinos who came throughout the day from miles around to slice fresh cuts of meat from the dead beast. For us the days when fresh horse meat looked good had long since passed, and we were all growing fat from the generous portions of food sent to us by Señor Lopez.

One rainy day while we were sitting in our hut marking time, as we had done for the past five weeks, Bill broke the silence with, "Do you suppose they really intend to get a boat for us, or are they just stalling?"

"Oh, I think they're working on it," Chamberlain answered. "You know how these people are. There's no hurrying them up. If you have the patience and can wait long enough, you'll make out okay."

"Yeah, but I'm rapidly running out of patience," I

objected. "Why, hell, we could have been halfway to Australia by now."

Then Armstrong, who rarely made any contribution to the conversation, said, "I like this place okay, but I'll be damned if I'm not about ready to pull stakes. I'd sure like to get back to civilization and see what's happening. We ought to just tell them that we are leaving in three days whether they have a boat for us or not."

We all agreed that when Walla came with the food that night, we would tell him of our plan.

When we told him, his answer was, "But by and by the boat will be ready."

"Sure it will. That's what you've been telling us for six weeks," Armstrong replied.

A couple of days after that Walla advised us that if we could wait for three more days the boat would be ready.

It was the latter part of July when our boat was ready for us, and we were escorted to the bay that very night. We were in high spirits as we slopped along the dark trail through the driving rain on our way back to Balayan Bay, about five miles away. It seemed fitting that it should be raining, for darkness and rain seemed to be a part of every important thing we had done since the beginning of the war.

Upon arriving at the bay we found that there was a fine boat waiting for us with all kinds of provisions, and it made us a little ashamed of doubting Señor Lopez. The boat was a twenty-four foot outrigger sailing craft with a stove, firewood, a fifty-gallon drum of water, a five-gallon can of sugar, a five-gallon can of spiced pork, two cans of cigarettes, a can of matches, a can of rice, a bushel sack of evaporated milk, quinine, a flashlight, and a sailing suit for each of us. The sailing suits were like those many of the local fishermen wore, and they would be helpful to disguise us. To us they looked more like pajamas than clothing a person would wear in the daytime.

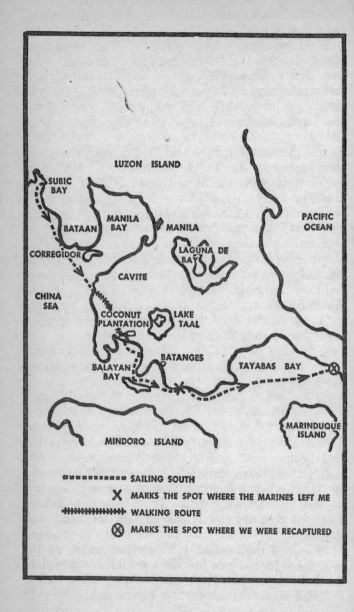

SAILING SOUTH

✕ MARKS THE SPOT WHERE THE MARINES LEFT ME

WALKING ROUTE

⊗ MARKS THE SPOT WHERE WE WERE RECAPTURED

Just before we left, one of the men, a member of the Lopez family, presented me with a valuable compass. "This," he stated, "belonged to my uncle who was a mariner. We value it rather highly, and if you ever have an opportunity, we would appreciate it if you would return it to us." I assured him that I would take good care of it, and we shoved off into the blackness of Balayan Bay.

With our usual bad fortune, we ran into a storm a couple of hours after we had shoved off, and when dawn came we found that we had been blown far off course. We were in the northeast part of Balayan Bay, just a few miles from where we had started, and to the east we could see Mount Taal. As a result of the adverse winds, it took us two nights to get out of Balayan Bay and on our way.

After five miserable nights of sailing we found that we had traveled little more than twenty-five miles. "At this rate it will take us twenty-five years to get to Australia," Bill calculated.

"Yeah, but at least we're moving," I said. "The winds won't stay like this forever."

"The trouble," Chamberlain added, "is that the winds blow fine in the daytime, but at night, when we are sailing, they die down. I think we ought to sail in the daytime, at least until we get away from Luzon; then we are not likely to be seen."

"Yes, but that's just when we're most likely to be seen, if we try sailing in the daytime," I argued. We had been sailing all night and we were tired, impatient, and argumentative. It was getting light, and we were heading in toward shore to spend the day.

"You know, I think we ought to have some breakfast and then shove off and sail all day," Bill suggested.

"I second the motion. If that wind comes up the way it has for the past few days, we'll leave this place far behind us in a few hours," Chamberlain said.

"Well, I'm sure not for it," I declared. "Not with

157

these patrol planes coming over every day and the Jap patrol boats working up and down the coast all of the time. I think we ought to try it this way for a couple more nights; then we will be out of the danger zone."

"Well, let's take a vote on it," Chamberlain suggested, looking from one to another of us.

"Good idea. I'm in favor of it," said Bill.

"You can count me out before you vote, because I'm not willing to sail in the daytime under any conditions, and that is all I have to say. That's just one risk we don't have to take," I said.

Armstrong spoke up again. "I think we ought to sail on today, so it looks like we got you outnumbered, Whitcomb."

"Okay. You can outvote me, but you can't force me to go. I don't think you've got the nerve to sail off and leave me, and if you do, I don't think you'll get very far."

That was stronger language than they were used to from me, and I left them little choice but to call my bluff. After we had pulled the boat ashore, a Filipino invited us all to come to his house for breakfast. There we ate and discussed the matter of sailing in the daytime at length. After we had eaten, the other three made their way back to the boat, and I was taken to the home of a Filipino where I would sleep for the day. The little Filipino house was high in the hills, and before I lay down on the floor to sleep I took one last look down at the shore where the boys were preparing to shove off.

Before I got to sleep I heard someone calling my name. It was Bill. "Ed, you've got the quinine bottle with you. Don't you think we'd better divide it up?" My feeling that Bill had not really come for the quinine was confirmed when he went on with, "Please think it over, Ed. We've come a long way together. Let's not split up now."

I said, "If you sail away today, we are splitting up,

158

because I am not willing to take a risk that isn't necessary."

"Well, we are going," he said, and stuck out his hand. We shook hands and parted friends, and he turned and was gone.

It was with great sorrow that I parted from Bill. Although I had known him only a few weeks, I had learned to have a great deal of respect for him. From the moment I first met him after the fall of Corregidor, I felt that he was the type of fellow who could make a successful escape. In our travels I learned that he was a bit determined, but so was I. For that reason we had sometimes quarreled when it came to making a decision. I was always the more conservative, perhaps too much so, but we had got through some tough spots together.

I was dead tired and dropped off to sleep shortly after Bill had left. After some time I was suddenly awakened by the familiar rat-a-tat-tat of machine gun fire. I jumped to the window just in time to see a Jap patrol boat firing on a sailboat out across the water. My first thought was that it was the boys, and my heart sank. But as I peered down the shoreline to my left I could see the outline of our little sailboat as she disappeared around the point in the distance. Then I knew they had gone, and I was alone. I slept deeply until late in the afternoon.

When I awoke, I found myself alone for the first time in many months. There was no one to say, "Let's get started walking," or "Let's go this way," or "Let's go that way." I was my own boss. I could go where I wanted to go and do what I wanted to do, but my situation was not clear. When I had argued with Bill and the others, I had been so dazed and so tired that I did not know what I was saying. All I knew was that I wanted to get some sleep and that I did not want to be caught at sea by a Japanese patrol boat. I walked to the window again and looked down toward the point where the boat had disappeared, hoping that I might see them coming back to pick me up. There were no boats to be seen in any direction. I walked down the hill to the shore and sat on the beach until long after the sun had gone down.

So ended my association with the United States Marines. Somehow, I felt I would never see them again. I knew they were impatient to get back into the war. What could be said about men like them—men who wouldn't quit or admit defeat—men who survived one battle after another and came back for more until they found their peace in a bloody grave? They were the true heroes of the wars. They would know no victory parades or rows of ribbons on their chests. They would know only the final peace that comes to every man, be he king or knave. There must be some special place in heaven for men like Reid Carlos Chamberlain, Army Armstrong and William Harris, who would give their lives so that we on earth might live in peace.

11. New companions

For the next few days I stayed around the village, resting and visiting with the people. I showed them the old trick of how to make an egg stand on end, and they all thought it was very funny. Whenever I was introduced to anyone new I always had to do the trick over again, and everybody laughed as if it were the first time they had even seen it.

The people decided that I was to stay with them for the duration, just as the people had done at every place we had been before. I was tired of arguing the point over and over, so this time I just picked up my knapsack one night, told my host I was leaving, and started walking. I had heard rumors that there were two American miners at a town fifteen kilometers down the coast, and I decided to see if I could locate them.

It was about three o'clock in the morning when I came upon a man loading his boat and getting ready to sail back to Balayan. He was alone, and I walked out to talk to him.

"Como esta usted?" I shouted.

"Como esta?" he answered.

"Do you speak English?" I asked.

"Oh, yes," he answered in good English. "I knew you were American when I first saw you far down the shore." I was surprised and disappointed, because I felt that my Filipino disguise was effective.

"How could you tell?" I asked.

161

"Oh, it is easy to tell by your size and by the way you walk," came the answer.

"I have heard that there are two American miners along the coast here. Do you have any idea where you could find them?"

He told me where I could find the Americans and directed me so I could find my way, but when I reached the house he had pointed out, I found that the Americans had moved on down the coast. The occupant of the house invited me to eat and get some rest before continuing on my way. Before I had slept very long, I was awakened and told that the miners had returned. I was introduced to a tall, blond-haired fellow about twenty-eight years of age who said he was Ralph Conrad from Oakland, California, and to Frank Bacon, about thirty-five years old, from El Paso, Texas.

My first question was, "Are you military?"

"No, we are mining engineers from Baguio. We are civilians," Conrad answered.

Then Bacon added, "We were working in the mines at Baguio when the war started, and for the past eight months we've been dodging the Japs. We have just finished getting a boat ready to sail to Australia."

"That's funny, because that's just where I'm heading," I said. Then I told them how I had been traveling with the Marines and how they had left me.

"Our boat is plenty big, and you're certainly welcome to come along with us if you want to," Conrad said. "We've got everything ready but our sail, and it may be a couple of days before it is ready. We'll shove off then."

It seemed too good to be true that I should find another ride to Australia in so short a time. I found Ralph Conrad and Frank Bacon to be very resourceful persons. With the engineering background, they showed a great deal of ingenuity. Before we started on our trip, it was agreed by all that we should sail only at night and stay reasonably close to the shore whenever possible. They had both spent eight months dodging the Japs while walking the two hundred kilometers from Baguio to the south shore of Luzon, and they were very cautious.

The Filipinos in the vicinity were friendly and very helpful to us and made our preparations much easier.

It was just about dark when we shoved off from the shore at a point about fifteen miles east of Batangas and headed eastward into the night. It was a great thrill to see the sail fill with wind and to watch the outriggers cut through the waves as we sped along. A good northwest wind carried us along at a rapid gait, and after sailing for a few miles we came to an open bay. With the wind blowing as it was, there was little question in our minds but that we could sail across the bay and reach the opposite shore long before daybreak. We decided to sail directly across Tayabas Bay.

After sailing until dawn, we found that we were still a long distance from the shore. The wind was still good, and there seemed little chance of being caught by the Japs. Frank managed the tiller, Ralph sang and told stories, and I sat and watched in different directions for patrol boats.

It was about eleven o'clock in the morning when we finally pulled up on shore and started looking around for something to eat. A few Filipinos gathered to talk to us, but they did not show the same friendliness as the people had shown at the other stops along the way. When no one invited us to his house to eat, we took our bag of rice into a hut and asked if we could cook it there. They agreed reluctantly, but after the rice started to cook they offered bananas and other foods. The atmosphere was strange, and the people stood around silently. We sensed that there was something wrong.

"I'll stay with the boat and our provisions while you and Frank go in and eat," I suggested.

"We won't be long, because I think the rice is ready now," Ralph said.

It seemed no time until they were back to the boat, and it was my turn to eat. As I sat on the floor of the Filipino house eating my rice and bananas, I looked out of the door and saw a sight that made my hair stand on end. There were Ralph and Frank beside the boat with their hands high above their heads and surrounded by at least a dozen Filipinos with drawn pistols. I jumped up and ran to them as quickly as I could. "Wait a minute here. You're making a mistake!" I told the Filipinos. Then one of them pushed his gun into my chest and pushed me into the middle of the ring.

I repeated, "You're making a mistake. We are friends of the Filipinos." But my words fell on deaf ears. One of the group took a rope from our boat and tied our hands together. I talked to the leader as persuasively as I knew how. I told him to name his price—we would pay him anything he asked. We were certain that it meant death to us if we were turned over to the Japanese, for a proclamation had been issued several months before, ordering all civilians to report to internment camps. I knew that applied only to Ralph and Frank, but I also knew that I would be killed if they learned I was an escaped prisoner of war. I was not in uniform because mine had worn out weeks before. For a shirt I wore the Filipino sailing uniform, which looked like the top to pajamas, and for trousers I had a pair of ragged blue denims.

They paid no attention to my pleas, and after our hands were securely tied they directed us to march. Then they formed a circle around us and walked us about two kilometers to a little town. Women and children looked from the doorways and windows as our procession moved up the street. From their expressions I knew that they felt sorry for us, for they knew we were being turned over to the Japanese.

From the first day of the war I had experienced

every form of degradation. I had been bombed, strafed, shelled, shot at, and starved; but nothing had ever been so completely humiliating as being led through the streets with my hands tied.

At last we reached the Municipal Building, where we met the mayor of the town of Agdagnan. We were thrown in jail. There we learned that the mayor and his chief of police were pro-Japanese. They would probably be looked upon with great favor by the Japs for turning us in. Inside the jail, the mayor explained to us that it would be for our own good if he turned us over to the Japanese so that they could put us under their protection in the civilian internment camp in Manila.

"I am going to turn you over to the Japanese, whether you like it or not," he advised. "It will be to your benefit if you sign this paper stating that you have turned yourselves in voluntarily. The Japanese are very nice people, and they will take good care of you."

I stood silent while Ralph and Frank explained to the mayor that we were civilian miners traveling from Baguio to Australia. When the sheet of paper was handed to me, I signed the name Robert Johnson because I had heard Ralph and Frank both mention the name Johnson many times in the past few days.

When we were alone in the cell, I told Ralph and Frank what I had done. "Who was this Johnson you've been talking about?"

"Fred Johnson was the superintendent of Le Panto Mines," Frank said.

"Where is he now?" I asked.

"He left the Philippine Islands on the last Pan-American Clipper to get out of here. He's no doubt back in the States."

"What was his first name?"

"Fred. Fred Johnson was his name, but he is much older than you," Frank told me.

"Then I'll tell 'em I'm Robert Johnson, son of Fred Johnson."

We were all very nervous while we waited for the arrival of the Jap patrol. After dark, while sitting in the cell, I suddenly realized that I had my silver wings and dog tags in my pocket. If they were found on me it would be a dead give-away that I was military personnel. I took out the dog tags and bent them until I was able to break each one in four pieces. Then came the problem of what to do with the pieces. There was an old pillow in the cell, and I pushed the pieces of dog tags into the center of the pillow through a tiny torn place in the tick. The silver wings were too bulky to put in the pillow, as I was only able to break them once. Later that night I threw the pieces as far as I could through the iron bars of the window into the weeds outside. Then I tore a seam along the front of my sailing suit and stuffed a couple dozen quinine tablets inside.

We felt certain that we would be shot when the Japanese arrived.

Early in the morning I asked for permission to go to the toilet, thinking I might possibly find a way to make my escape. The toilet was about fifty feet from the jail, and it was apparent to me that I was being watched by an armed guard each step of the way. On the return trip to the jail a young Filipino girl walked near me and said, "God be with you, and God protect you." I knew she understood our predicament, and I felt very much comforted by her blessing.

It was only a short time until a Japanese patrol of ten soldiers with automatic weapons on their shoulders and hand grenades tied to their belts ushered us out of the jail. The officer in charge was a good-natured fellow who seemed quite amused that we had been able to move freely in the Japanese-occupied territory without having been captured before.

We were put on a train and taken to area headquarters near Legaspi, where we met the commanding officer. When he heard our story he leaned back in his chair and had a good laugh. He, too, thought it was funny that we had been able to stay out of the way of the Japanese military so long.

"It will not be long before you will be returned to the United States," he told us. "The Japanese are victorious everywhere. Your navy is being destroyed, and your planes are being shot down in large numbers every day." He then showed us printed charts indicating the large number of American warships which had been sunk and the large number of American planes which had been downed. By comparison, he showed us the very small number of Japanese warships and planes which had been destroyed. "You see, we are winning the war, and it will not be long before the United States will be forced to surrender." We had no reason to believe that he was telling the truth; on the other hand, we had no reason to believe he was lying. If the Americans were having any kind of success at all, they should have recaptured the Philippines long ago. The war was then in its ninth month, and we had never yet seen an American plane or ship except those we had when the war started—all of which, we knew, had since been destroyed.

"The place for you is in the internment camp in Manila at Santo Tomas. The people live very well there and you will be protected for your own safety."

If there was one place in the world I did not want to go, it was to Santo Tomas Civilian Internment Camp. It was no place for a fighting man. Wouldn't Bill, Armstrong, and Chamberlain laugh if they could see me sitting inside an internment camp with the women and children? I was an Air Corps navigator on a B-17. I had told my father back in Indiana that we would probably defeat the Japanese in about six months. The war had been on more than nine months, and here I was on my way to a civilian internment camp to wait until the war was over, regardless of who won.

12. Santiago prison

It was August 14, 1942, when we were loaded into a staff car with two neatly dressed Japanese Military Police as escorts and started on our way toward Manila. The staff car was a new 1941 Plymouth and more comfortable than anything we had ridden in for a long time.

"How long will it take us to get to Manila?" Frank asked our driver. The Jap turned around and shook his head, making signs that he could not understand our language.

Ralph leaned over and whispered to Frank and me, "Don't let them kid you. I'll bet they speak English better than any of us. Better be careful what we say."

There was very little to be said at that stage. As we rode along I remembered how we had talked earlier of turning ourselves in to an American Army post in Australia. There would be no trip to Australia; we were headed for Santo Tomas Internment Camp to spend the duration of the war.

We needed time to think. The occurrences of the past forty-eight hours had us completely baffled. It was unbelievable that the Filipinos had turned us in —that they had betrayed us. I had served and fought side by side with Filipinos at Clark Field, Bataan, and on Corregidor, and they had really proved themselves to be loyal friends when Bill and I were at their mercy in the jungles. I would never have believed that there was a Filipino on Luzon who would betray us, and yet it had happened.

Ralph, Frank, and I had a lot of talking to do, but that could wait until we were in Santo Tomas, where we could be alone. I had to learn more about their friend Johnson and more about the mining business.

We clipped along over the green Philippine countryside. That part of the island had been virtually untouched by the war, except that every bridge along the way had been destroyed by the rear guard of the American-Filipino Army. Our demolition boys had done an excellent job, but now the Americans were paying for it the hard way. At every bridge we saw skinny, half-naked American soldiers working like slaves in the torrid sun, rebuilding the bridges, and it was necessary for us to cross the streams on improvised wooden bridges.

We stopped at noon at a small town to have lunch in a Filipino restaurant where we were allowed to order as we pleased. The three of us sat at a separate table from the Japs, and got in some fast talking as we feasted on a meal of scrambled eggs and rice. The many Filipinos about us were obviously curious, but they had been well disciplined by the Japanese —there was no demonstration of any feeling toward us. The meals were not paid for when we left.

By the middle of the afternoon we approached the outskirts of Manila, and I felt a strange unreality as we rode down Dewey Boulevard toward the Manila Hotel. I remembered a peaceful November evening when I had looked out across Manila Bay to see a big red sun sink into the distant China Sea. Again I saw the little humps of land rise out of the western horizon and knew they were Bataan and Corregidor. In November they had been part of a beautiful picture as I looked out across the bay from my hotel window, but now they looked more like the black edges of hell, pushed up out of the water from deep below.

We passed the Manila Hotel, passed Jap soldiers drilling on what used to be the green golf links beside the Walled City; then a Japanese sentry saluted our escorts as we drove through a big stone archway in the high stone wall and on into famous Fort Santiago, built by the Spanish many years before. It was there that José Rizal, the Filipino patriot who was known as "the George Washington of the Philippines," had been imprisoned in a dungeon. Our car pulled to a halt in front of a headquarters building, and we were ordered to get out. Our escorts directed us up the steps and instructed us to wash our hands in Lysol solution before entering the building. Then we were turned over to another Jap, and our escorts left.

"Bring all things and put them here," our new jailer directed. We placed our two Army knapsacks, a blanket roll, our money, and a straw basket of rice on the counter. They were put in square bins behind the counter. We were then led back out of the building and across the lawn to wait until arrangements were completed for our transfer to the internment camp. But as we were escorted through a door to an inner court, we suddenly realized for the first time that we were being herded into a prison. Behind the iron fence in front of us we could see a long row of wooden cages. I walked over and looked between the wooden slats into a room packed full of people.

"Any Americans in here?" I asked.

No one answered. They only stared at me. Then the Jap guard took me in tow, and with a push and a couple of ape-like grunts started me on the way down the line of cages. When we stopped I asked an old, gray-bearded man behind the bars, "Any Americans in here?"

"I am the only one," he whispered. "Shh-h-h! You are not allowed to talk." By that time the guard had the wooden door unlocked and opened. I started to step in, but he jerked me back and made a sign that

I was to take off my shoes before entering the cell. I removed them and placed them at the end of a long line just outside the cell. With that, the Jap gave me a little shove that sent me into a world unlike anything I had ever seen. What I saw looked like something out of an old movie; it did not seem real. I felt like a giant standing there with a room full of haggard, expressionless faces staring up at me. The big wooden door slammed shut behind me. I said, "Hello."

There was no answer. They just kept on staring. Finally someone pointed to a sign on the wall. It was a notice in three languages—English, Japanese, and Tagalog—for the benefit of the cosmopolitan clientele, to the effect that we were being detained by the Japanese, that we should not communicate with our cellmates, that from 7:00 a.m. until 7:00 p.m. we should sit upon the floor, and that from 7:00 p.m. until 7:00 a.m. we should lie upon the floor. There were twelve prisoners in the room beside myself.

After reading the house rules, I settled on the floor beside the old gray-bearded American. "You are not allowed to talk," he warned me again. As I looked at the man, I saw that his white hair and whiskers hung down to his shoulders, and his skin was almost as white as his hair. He was very thin, and his left hand was paralyzed and withered. He wore only a pair of B.V.D.'s. He leaned over to me. "It is all right to whisper, but don't let them catch you. Don't tell anyone in here anything; you don't know who you can trust." Then he asked eagerly, "What do you know about the war?"

"I've been in the jungles ever since the war broke out. But I heard that Corregidor and Bataan have been taken over by the Japanese," I lied.

"We get news from time to time when a new prisoner comes in, but most of us have been in here for a long time."

"These others. Are they Americans?" I asked, nodding toward three men across the room.

"No. The old bald-headed man over there is McCullough Dick. He is a Scotsman, and he was editor of a weekly newspaper here in Manila. I am also a newspaperman. My name is Roy C. Bennett, and I was the editor of the Manila *Daily Bulletin* until after the war started. The other two over there," he nodded toward the others, "are Frenchmen, and the rest are Filipinos, Chinese, and Japanese."

I could tell from his manner that Mr. Bennett was glad to have someone to visit with, but while we were whispering I heard a loud shout ring out down the hall, "Ro Col" Everyone in our cell jumped up from the floor and formed in a line facing the front of the cell. "This is roll call. Stand beside me and after I say "ichi," you say "ne," he instructed. Down the corridor I could hear the sounds at one cell after another, coming closer to us. Soon a Jap guard stopped in front of our cell; Bennett called "ichi," I called "ne" and it went on down the line, san, shi, go, roku, hichi, hachi, ku, ju, ju-ichi, ju-ne, and ju-san. We had counted off in Japanese. It was the first of a large number of roll calls we were to have at odd hours of the day and night. I stuck to the number two position for several days until I found I could fill in any spot down the line.

Again we sat down in our positions around the wall, and Bennett and I continued visiting until suddenly everybody jumped up again. This time they lined up in front of a tiny window about four by ten inches in size, in the middle of the front of the cell. Someone outside passed in little saucers of rice with a few green leaves on top. Each in turn grabbed his saucer, ran back to his place along the wall, and started gobbling it up. There were no eating utensils; they ate with their hands. When it was my turn, I took my saucer of rice and sat down on the floor beside Bennett. A weary-looking creature sitting on the other side of me leaned over and whispered, "That's right! Eat it all. You've got a fat belly." I did not have a fat belly. I did not have an appetite either, so I handed it over to him.

Shortly after that everyone lay down on the floor. I assumed that it was 7:00 p.m., but had no way of knowing for sure. I wondered how they knew. Anyway, I lay down too. There was no bedding of any kind, and the hard wooden floor was uncomfortably crowded with thirteen people lying in an area of about twelve by thirteen feet.

I lay awake a long time, thinking of the chain of events that had led up to my being there and of the things Mr. Bennett had told me. I was waiting for the light to go out, but after a while I realized that it was not going to go out. A twenty-five-watt bulb hung in the middle of the cell and seemed to grow brighter as the night grew later. If darkness brings horrors, having a light all of the time is twice as bad. If it were dark, you could imagine that you were somewhere else—that you were back home lying on the living room floor—but with the light on you cannot get away from reality. You are in a cell with a group of weird-looking people, and it looks as if you are going to be there for a long, long time. The Japs had tricked us into thinking that we were going to the civilian internment camp, but instead had thrown us into prison. Ralph and Frank were in other cells, and it was impossible for me to see them or to talk to them. How would I ever find out about Johnson if I could not talk to them? I turned and rolled and tried every position to be comfortable, but comfort was not to be had on the hard wood floor.

At long last dawn came to Fort Santiago prison. When the prisoners again sat themselves around the wall of our little room, I observed that there were small holes about one foot square cut in the floor in each corner at the back of the cell. In the hole to the right was a water pipe with a faucet slightly below the level of the floor. The pressure was so low that it was almost necessary to put your lips to the pipe in order to get a drink. In the other corner, to the left, was a can under the floor which was used as a toilet. It was emptied once a day by someone who reached under from the outside and took it away, but the nauseating stink was always present in the cell. Other than these two luxury items, there was no furniture of any kind in the room—no blankets, no mosquito nets, no mattresses.

Several of the men were deathly sick with dysentery and made many trips to the can throughout the course of the day. When they begged for a doctor, the Jap guard laughed and said, "You eat too much."

The side walls and the ceiling were of plywood, but along the front there were wooden bars three by three inches square, placed about an inch apart, extending from the floor to the ceiling. All of our food was passed in through the tiny portal in the middle of the bars, and the door was opened only when new prisoners were brought in or when someone was taken out.

From talking to Bennett I learned that the military police followed a definite pattern in making their arrests and bringing people to Fort Santiago. "Two or three Japanese police will call at a house and ask for the person they want. These calls are most frequently made about four in the morning when everyone is asleep. If the person they are looking for answers the door, he will be brought in without even having a chance to get dressed, to tell his family where he has gone, or to bid them good-by," Bennett explained.

"But why are these people brought here?" I asked.

"Various reasons, crimes against the Japanese which the people themselves sometimes don't even understand. Some of the people in here have no idea why they are here. Sometimes they remain in prison for months before they are questioned."

"Have you ever been questioned?"

"Oh, yes. Several times, but that was months ago. They used to take me out and question me for long periods at a time. I kept telling them that they were wasting their time because everything I had said against the Japanese was in black and white in my newspapers, and there was plenty of that," he chuckled. "It was all very foolish for them to keep asking me questions. Finally they got the idea, and they haven't questioned me for months."

"Will they question me?" I asked eagerly.

"You may be called out today, or tomorrow, or the next day, or you may not be called for several months. Maybe never at all. There is no way of predicting what they might do," he answered gravely.

I watched and waited and dreaded the prospect of being called out for questioning. There was little I could tell them, for it would be impossible for me to account for my whereabouts since the beginning of the war nine months before.

Life in the crowded cell became routine, broken only by the appearance of the little man at the front of the cell three times a day with a saucer of rice for each of us. Sometimes there would be a few green leaves on top of the rice. At other times there would be small, bony pieces of fish. On Sunday morning and on Thursday morning, in place of the bowl of rice we received a saucer of milk with some sugar and a small piece of bread. After the first couple of days I found myself eating as the others did. When my bowl of rice was handed in through the window I grabbed it, ran to the corner, and devoured it like a hungry dog.

In the afternoon of the second day a handsome Filipino dressed in a white gabardine suit was thrown into the cell. He was black and blue from head to foot, and his suit was badly soiled. I learned that he had been a candidate in a recent election in one of the provinces and had defeated the Japanese candidate. The election had been declared unfair, but he won a second election by an even greater majority than before. In order to get him out of circulation the Japanese had brought him into the prison.

Among our other cellmates was a sixteen-year-old Chinese boy who had been charged with stealing a fountain pen in Manila. Whenever a new guard stopped to read the names on the little wooden tags hanging on the front of our cell, he always called out the Chinese boy's name. When the Jap asked questions that the boy could not answer in Japanese, he would make signs with his fingers. It turned out that the Japanese characters for the boy's name meant "the heart of a horse." That amused the Japanese, and they teased him about it.

One of our cellmates was a Japanese. He had dried blood on his shirt, and his clothing was torn from a fight on the docks of Manila. He only remained with us for two days.

One of the cells at the other end of the line was filled with Filipino women. To the best of my knowledge they were furnished with the same facilities we enjoyed.

Each day three or four persons were taken from our cell for questioning. Some were returned to the cell beaten until they were black and blue. Sometimes they were dumped into the cell so badly beaten that they could not stand, and fell in a heap on the floor until they were revived. Others were never brought back at all. I learned that Fort Santiago was a place dreaded by all Filipinos, and it was easy to understand why. Throughout the night and day we could hear the screams of persons who were being tortured, and it was terrifying to realize that I myself might be called out for questioning. I hoped that they would never call me, because I knew I could never explain my past activities to their satisfaction. I kept wondering what had happened to Ralph and Frank and whether the screaming I heard might be one of them.

The only comfort I found in life was from my long visits with Mr. Bennett. Whatever the man lacked in physical fitness was made up for by his guts and grim determination. His wife and two young daughters were in Santo Tomas Internment Camp, and he had little knowledge of their condition.

"When I first came here, my wife was on the outside and was able to send me medicine and vitamin tablets," he told me, "but I have received nothing from her for a long time." Then he laughed. "A funny thing happened. Once she tried to send in some salt, but the Japs turned it down. Later she put it in a bottle and labelled it NaCl, and it came through without any difficulty."

In our conversations I learned that Mr. Bennett was from Kentucky, that he had been educated in journalism at the University of Missouri, and that he was considered an authority on Far Eastern affairs. Before the war he had made a number of speeches which were broadcast on a nationwide hook-up in the United States. I also learned that he had been married by Doctor Parker at Hanover College in Indiana, but I could not tell him that was only twenty-five miles from my home because to Bennett I was Robert Johnson from Miami, Arizona. Perhaps he sensed that there was something wrong with me, because he never tried to pry into my past experiences. We both felt that the less we knew about each other, the better it would be in case the Japs tried to pit us one against the other.

Time and time again Bennett asked me how I thought the war was coming along, and each time a new prisoner was brought into the cell he got all the news he could. It was August in 1942, and the best information we had was that the American forces were still far to the south of us in the Pacific. I remembered what the Jap colonel had told us about Japanese successes, and I heard very little news to convince me that his story was untrue.

Bennett once told me of a conversation he had had with General MacArthur in Manila before the war. "I had considerable knowledge of the Japanese build-up and of the strength they had. I told General MacArthur that I hated to see a reputation as great as his end with a venture as doomed to failure as an attempt to defend the Philippine Islands against the Japanese."

"What did he have to say about that?" I asked.

"He said that he could never keep the Japanese from invading the Philippines, but he was sure that by the spring of 1942 he could have an army so strong that it would make an invasion so expensive the Japanese could not afford it."

"Well, they did it whether they could afford it or not, and here we are," I said.

Then, after thinking a while, Mr. Bennett added, "To tell you the truth, I have always been a lot more concerned about the Chinese than I have about the Japanese. The Japanese are a small nation with limited resources, whereas the Chinese have unlimited resources and unlimited manpower. If that country ever develops its resources and establishes a modern army, it may become a real threat to us."

"I'm not so sure that the Japanese aren't a real threat to us as things stand now," I observed.

While we were talking, I heard the Jap guard outside shouting something. The faces in our cell turned toward me. I listened, but could not understand what the guard was saying. Someone pointed to me, and then, like a flash, I realized. He was calling Roberto Johnson.

13. Lead-pipe questioning

I jumped up and ran to the front of the cell. Each time the guard called I shouted, "Aye," until he finally stopped in front of our cell.

I looked out through the portal to see a little Jap with thick glasses holding some papers in front of him and peering up at me. Again he said, "Roberto Johnson?"

"Aye."

Again he looked up. "You Roberto Johnson?"

"Aye."

He thumbed through the handful of papers, stopped, and came forth with the question, "Namo?"

"Roberto Johnson," I answered.

By that time my heart was pounding so hard that I could hardly speak. Did it mean that I was finally on my way to Santo Tomas to join the other American civilians, or was I on my way to be questioned and tortured like the others?

The big iron bolt of the door screeched up and down until the door swung open, and I stepped out into the world. He closed the door and pointed down to the line of shoes, indicating that I was to find my own. Then the two of us walked down the long line of cells to the gate, across the soft green lawn, up a flight of stairs, and into a room. There he left me with two Japanese, an officer and an enlisted man, who had been waiting for me. The room was furnished with a table and three chairs, one at each side of the table and one at the end. There was no other furniture, but over against the wall I noticed a piece of pipe about three feet long and three-quarters of an inch thick, and a pick handle. I was directed to sit at one side of the table. The officer sat across from me, and the enlisted man, who turned out to be an interpreter, sat at the other end of the table.

"What you name?" The question was asked first by the Japanese in his own language and then relayed to me by the interpreter.

"Robert Fred Johnson."

"What you father's name?"

That question and all that followed were first in Japanese and then interpreted.

"Fred Johnson," was my answer.

"You mother's name?"

"Betty Johnson."

"Where you home?"

"Miami, Arizona."

"When you come to Philippine Islands?"

"I came to the Philippine Islands in July, 1941."

"How you come to Philippine Islands?"

"I came on a Swedish freighter."

"Why you come to Philippine Islands?"

"I came to the islands to work with my father in the mines here."

Little did I know as I made up the answers to the Jap's questions that I was projecting myself into a world of make-believe in which I would live for the next year and a half of my life. I told them that my father, Fred Johnson, was the superintendent of the Le Panto Mines of the Nielson Corporation, that I had been named Robert Fred Johnson in honor of my dear old father, that I had studied pre-med three years in Miami, Florida, that I had worked for a Doctor Miller in Tucson, Arizona, for two years, and then had come to the Philippines to work in the mines.

The officer wrote each of my answers down in Japanese as the interpreter relayed it to him. With each question he peered at me out of eyes like those of a vicious snake, and inhaled air through the corners of his mouth with a hissing sound, which added to the snake-like effect.

The questioning went on and on for a couple of hours. I told them that I was in Baguio on December 8, 1941, when the war broke out, that I had met Ralph Conrad and Frank Bacon there and had gone to a place called Lusud, thirty miles east of Baguio, where we remained for three months. I also told them that we started our long hike from there to Batangas, south of Manila, that we had made our way through Balete Pass where we argued and split company, that I had hiked alone for six weeks until I reached Batangas, where I fell ill with malaria, and remained until Bacon and Conrad found me there about July 15, 1942.

Strange as the story sounded, it was much more believable to the Japs than the truth would have been. Had I told them that I was a lieutenant in the United States Army Air Corps, that I had navigated a Flying Fortress from the United States to Clark Field, been bombed out of Clark Field, escaped from Bataan, escaped from Corregidor, and tried to sail to Australia in a tiny sailboat with outriggers, they would never have believed me.

According to International Law I was then in the category of a common spy, since I was wearing civilian clothes in enemy territory and denying my connection with the military. However, I knew that the Japanese were not playing according to the rules. I remembered a little Jap on Corregidor who had scoffed and said, "Ha! Japanese law is International Law."

After what seemed like a very long time, and when I had answered every conceivable question about myself, the session ended, and I was taken back to my cell. All eyes were on me as I stepped back into the miserable enclosure and looked around at my cell-

181

mates. I sat down beside Mr. Bennett along the wall.

"How did it go?" he whispered after the Jap had left the front of the cell.

"Not bad. They just asked me a lot of questions about myself and how I happened to come to the Islands." Bennett looked at me, and I knew he was wondering just what I had told the Japanese. I was never able to tell whether or not he suspected I was in the military service. Whether he did or not, he seemed to take everything I said at face value, and did not pry into my background.

"Do you think they will call me again for questioning?" I whispered.

"There's no way of knowing. They may call you back again tonight, or tomorrow, or the next day, or they may never call you again. You just can't tell."

I wondered how I would remember all of the things I had told them—that my birthday was July 17, the name of my girl friend, the route I had taken from Lusud to Batangas. I had made it a point to give a fictitious answer to every question in case they tried to compare my answers with any military records which might have come into their possession. I was afraid I had gone too far—that I had built a web in which I myself might become entangled.

That night I could not sleep. I kept running the story I had given the Japanese over and over in my mind so that it would be familiar to me.

The next day I prayed that I would not be called again. I had told them everything I could possibly tell about myself except the truth. Late in the afternoon, when I had finally convinced myself that they would not call me, I heard a sound down the corridor which made me flinch. "Roberto Johnson." I stood up at the front of the cell and called "Aye" again until the Jap arrived. Again I was led out across the lawn and back to the interrogation room.

The snake-eyed Jap looked at me and rattled off a long phrase, and the interpreter relayed it to me.

"You must tell the truth. If you tell the truth, it is very good for you. You will be sent to Santo Tomas with your friends. If you do not tell the truth, you will be killed." Again it was the same series of questions. "You name, you father's name, you mother's name, where you live, how you come to islands?" Somewhere down the long line of questions the Jap deviated into some new subject matter about what happened on the first day of the war in Baguio. Again the questioning lasted for a couple of hours, and I was returned to my cell.

The questioning periods continued day after day, with sessions lasting from two to six hours. Each day we reviewed the questions of the previous day until the whole story of my own background became very familiar to me. But each day I received the same admonition. "You must tell the truth. If you tell the truth, it is very good for you, and you will go to Santo Tomas with you friends. If you do not tell the truth, you will be killed."

Back in the cell at night I would lie and wonder how it would feel to be shot. Would it happen at night or at dawn? Would they do it at Fort Santiago, or would I be taken to some place in the country?

One night in the cell I looked up to see a Jap standing a short distance away with a rifle pointed directly into my face. He pulled the trigger, I saw the flash, and everything was still. It was only a nightmare, but it was so realistic that from that instant on I was sure I knew how it would feel to be killed.

About the sixth time I was taken for questioning, the Jap officer was particularly courteous and polite to me. Instead of glaring tensely at me, he pulled out a package of American Lucky Strike cigarettes and offered me one. It was like graduation day back at school, when the teachers treated you like a human being. The Jap spoke softly and pleasantly instead of harshly. I thought at last I had convinced him that

I was telling the truth, and I would soon be on my way to Santo Tomas.

After the usual preliminary questions about my name and my father's and mother's names, etc., he asked, "You say Filipinos took care of you when you had malaria. Who were Filipinos who helped you?"

"I don't remember their names. Most of the time I called them Joe and they called me Joe," was my answer.

"But you remember some names?" he insisted.

"I am sorry that I cannot remember any of them."

"But one name? You can remember the name of one Filipino?" he pressed me.

"I was very ill, and I just don't remember."

He was nice about it and seemed to understand my difficulty in remembering. I decided that he was really not a bad fellow after all, and that this was just about the end of the questions he had to ask me. My cigarette burned short as I inhaled the smoke into my lungs and then exhaled, watching the gray cloud roll out across the room. It was not a long session, or at least it did not seem long until I was on my way back to my cell, fully satisfied with the way I had outsmarted the Japs.

The next day when I was called for questioning I was no longer frightened as I had been in the past. I walked into the little room and took my usual chair. I had no sooner got comfortable than the Jap officer jumped to his feet with a wild oath in Japanese. The interpreter relayed the message to me that I was not to sit upon the chair, "You not good enough to sit on chair on same level with Japanese. You sit on floor."

I slid off the chair onto the floor and looked up at the Jap, who was still in a rage. "You tell the name of Filipinos who helped you."

"But I don't know their names. I called them Joe. They called me Joe. Their names are not easy to pronounce or remember." My statements were not translated back to the officer by the interpreter.

"You tell the names of Filipinos," demanded the interpreter.

"I don't know. I don't know."

While the Jap raged on, the interpreter picked up as much of his statement as he could. "Americans think they better than Japanese; think they better than Filipinos; think they better than black people." As the Jap's fury increased, the interpreter seemed to be frightened. Finally he stopped trying to enlighten me on the verbal bombardment I was receiving. The officer's eyes flashed as he sputtered and hissed at me in Japanese. Finally he drew back and delivered a slap across the face, followed by more and more slaps in rapid succession, first with the palm, then with the back of the hand.

We carried on an endless session by ourselves, without the interpreter. The Jap would scream out at me in Japanese, and I would answer in English that I could not remember. Then there were more slaps, followed by several kicks in the side with his foot. I did not know exactly what he was saying, but I was certain that he was taking out on me all the hate he had for the American people.

Just when I thought he was about to stop, he stepped back and blurted something to me. I could not believe my eyes when I saw the interpreter hand him the iron pipe that leaned against the wall. Surely he would not hit me with it! Perhaps it was just a threat to frighten me.

"You think of names," he demanded. I thought and thought. I thought of Salvador Savaras at Subic Bay and his sweet young wife who had cooked such wonderful meals for us when we were starving after our walk across Bataan. I thought of the Lopez family at Batangas who had risked their lives to shelter and protect us. I wondered if I might give some fictitious name, but I knew it would result in an investigation, and any Filipinos suspected would be shot. I had heard too many stories of how Filipinos had been

185

killed in cold blood without a trial on suspicion of helping Americans. The Jap waited.

When my answer finally came it was, "I don't know." The Jap seemed to understand what I had said, for he drew back the pipe and struck me a blow across the back that seemed to paralyze my whole system. There were many more blows, but they were merely dull shocks as they struck my spine and shoulders.

He stopped and looked down at me, saying something that sounded sympathetic. Then the interpreter asked, "What is the matter? You cry. You a woman?"

"No, I'm not a woman," I shouted. "If you're going to kill me, shoot me. Please don't beat me to death!" I raised my hand to him and went on, "I have told you everything I can tell you. There is nothing more I can say. If I have told you a single lie, go ahead and shoot me."

The officer waited while the message was translated back to him by the interpreter. It seemed to satisfy him. He put the iron pipe back in the corner. When I tried to stand up, I felt that the bones of my back and shoulders were surely broken.

I started toward the door, thinking the questioning was over and they were ready to take me back to my cell. The Jap stopped me. He said something in a different tone than he had used before. I looked at the interpreter, anxious to know what he had said. "This is Japanese justice. You like this or your kind best?" was the question. I shook my head to indicate I did not like it. The Jap smiled and led the way back to my cell.

By the time we got to the cell big welts had swollen up on my back where the sharp end of the pipe had hit me, and my left arm was swollen above the elbow to almost twice its normal size. When I entered the cell I wanted to fall upon the floor as I had seen others do, but instead I made my way over to the wall and dropped down beside Mr. Bennett. No one in the cell seemed to suspect what I had gone through, and after a while I leaned over to Bennett. "They gave me an awful beating today."

"I had hoped it would never happen." He looked down at me sympathetically. "It might be better if you wouldn't make that known to the others." Still he did not ask me why I had been beaten or what questions they had asked me. As we talked, the Jap appeared at our cell again and unlocked the big door, motioning for everyone to come out. "What's this for?" I asked eagerly.

"We get to take a bath," was the answer. I stood up and joined in the line as we filed out through the corridor into the open court. There was a water spigot where each person was allowed a few seconds to wash his hands and face and body. Some took off their shirts to rinse them out, while others washed only their hands and face and feet. I did not take off my shirt because I did not want to expose my bruises to the others.

I was not called for questioning for the next few days, but about the time I was getting rid of my soreness, I began having headaches and a fever. I knew the feeling well and was certain that it was malaria. For four days I was allowed to lie on the floor instead of sitting against the wall. Instead of the regular diet of rice, I was given rice porridge. Every day I asked for quinine, and every day I got the same answer, "By and by the doctor come." The doctor never came, but I got some relief from the quinine that I had smuggled in the seam of my Philippine sailing uniform.

Bennett advised me of the hopelessness of my plea for a doctor. "Some time ago there was an American in the next cell who cried for quinine for days. One day we didn't hear him anymore, but we saw him carried out of the cell unconscious."

On the fifth day I felt a little better, and when the

187

guard learned of this, I was again summoned for questioning.

I was still very weak, and on the way to the interrogation room I wondered if the Jap would beat me again. Somewhere there was a limit to the amount of torture I could take. Somewhere there was a limit to the amount of fiction I could remember.

In the interrogation room with the same officer and interpreter, I noticed that the pipe and pick handle were still leaning against the wall. I also noticed that the manuscript of questions and answers had grown to be almost an inch thick, all written in Japanese characters which I could not read or understand. The session started the same as all the others, "If you tell the truth, it is very good for you. If you lie, you will be killed. You have not told the truth, and unless you tell the truth you will be killed." We carried on from there with the usual list of questions, starting first with my father's name, my mother's name, etc. Some of the routine was hard to remember because I had thought of it very little during my sickness.

When we came to the part about spending three months at Lusud, east of Baguio, with Ralph and Frank, the answers became difficult. I could tell by his attitude that the officer was not satisfied with my replies to his questions.

"Your two friends have described this place very well," he insisted.

"Yes, but that is the way I remember it," I answered.

The Jap pushed a piece of paper in front of me on the table and handed me a pencil. "Now you draw *mapo* Lusud," he demanded. If only I could have spoken to Ralph or Frank for a second, it would have been easy. In all the days we had been in Santiago I had only seen each of them a couple of times, and those were only fleeting glances as I passed their cells. The job before me was to draw a map of Lusud, a place where I had never been. I drew what I thought was a typical Filipino barrio with a school, a few shops, a stream, and the usual number of trails leading from the village The Jap was not impressed with my work of art, but rather expressed the attitude that he had finally caught me on something which I could not explain.

"Your companions draw a map and it is not like the one you draw," he exclaimed. Then I realized I was in a trap. All of the personal background material I had given them had been easy to fabricate, but when it came to comparing my knowledge of Lusud with that of the two miners who had lived there for some time, I was faced with a difficult proposition. I racked my brain for an answer. Perhaps Mr. Bennett would know. He had traveled all through the islands, and there was a possibility that he might have been in Lusud. He was my only hope, since there was no possibility of questioning either Ralph or Frank about the matter.

Instead of the usual two-hour questioning period, the Jap continued on into the night. Each time I drew a map he looked at it, asked me some questions about where the Filipinos lived who helped me or where the other Americans were hiding, then tore up the paper and threw it on the floor with a wild oath. He was playing cat and mouse with me. Each time I tried to draw the map I felt I had the combination he wanted; but again my drawing would be torn up and thrown upon the floor.

Finally, about ten at night, after about six hours of questioning, he gave me a pencil and paper and said, "Take this to you cell and draw mapo Lusud. Put in the houses and buildings, the roads and trails, the fields and forests, where Filipinos live who helped you, and where other Americans hide. You work tonight until you finish mapo. You do not finish mapo tonight, you bring paper tomorrow and finish mapo here."

The longest and most difficult questioning period had come to an end. I was taken back across the inner court to my cell.

I trudged wearily across the soft wet grass of the court beside the little Jap who had been questioning me all evening. His steps were quick, and he seemed to be feeling very superior. He knew that he had me trapped, that I would spend the night fretting in my cell, that I would be even more worn out the next day. It was as if I were already doomed—as if I had an incurable disease, and it was only a matter of time until it would be all over. I was at my wit's end and too tired to think about it.

I had thought a lot about the possibility of attempting an escape from Fort Santiago. After the Japs had beaten me with the iron pipe, I was certain that I could have overcome both of them and dived off the high wall into the Pasig River. It would have been almost certain death, but still there was a slim chance that I might have made it.

As we walked across the court I could see that the stars were shining brightly in the sky. The sight of them only made me feel sick, as I had felt sick a few days before when I saw a map of the United States crumpled in a pile of debris. There were Los Angeles, Tucson, Miami, New York, and all of the places that held so many wonderful memories. I was sure beyond any doubt that I would never see them again.

We reached the line of cells, and the officer turned me over to the guard and disappeared across the court. Everything was quiet as we walked down the long corridor. All the prisoners inside the cells were lying on the floor and trying to sleep. Outside my cell I laid my pencil and paper on the floor and took off my shoes before entering the cell, but as I looked up I saw the guard was unlocking the wrong door.

"Wrong cell!" I started to say. Oh, my God! He was opening the wrong door. It was Ralph's cell. If only I could get through that door and have a few minutes to talk with Ralph, it would solve all my problems. I stepped in quickly, the big door slammed shut behind me, the iron bolt screeched into place, the lock clicked, and the guard was gone back to the other end of the line.

I stood in a daze for a moment, looking over the bodies crowded together on the floor at my feet. One of them looked at me and began to mumble. "You're in the wrong cell. Get out or you'll get us all in trouble."

I held up my hand with the palm toward him, "Shhh! It is all right. It is all right." I climbed over the bodies to Ralph and shook him.

"Make room so I can lie down quickly," I whispered.

"How'd you get in here?" he asked, much surprised. He looked five years older than when I had last seen him. His whiskers had grown out, his face was thinner, and his eyes were sunken.

"Think the guard made a mistake. Here, draw me a map quick before he comes back. Draw me a map of Lusud. That guard might find out his mistake and be back any minute."

Ralph took the pencil and sketched out the town very quickly. "I want the streets, trails, streams, fields, woods, and where other American and Filipinos live." As Ralph sketched, I fired one question after another at him until I gained a fair idea of the story he had told the interrogator. There were some big differences in the story I had told and the story he had told, but I knew I would have a chance to straighten things out a little with the Jap.

"What kind of a mine is this that I'm connected with?" I asked. "They've never asked me that question, but I'm sure they'll get around to it sooner or later."

"Copper," he answered, "they haul the ore down to Lingayen Gulf, where it's shipped away."

"And where is this Fred Johnson who is supposed to be my father?" I asked.

"Why, I thought I told you. He went back to the States on the last Pan-American Clipper to leave the islands. That's a real break for you, because if they check the records they'll find that there really was a Fred Johnson. As a matter of fact, they've probably already checked the records," Ralph surmised.

"Yeah, probably they have. Do you suppose they really have any intention of ever taking us to Santo Tomas? My man promises me every day that if I tell the truth, we will go soon."

"It's hard to tell what they'll do next. Have you had a chance to talk to Frank?"

"Not a word. I've seen him only a few times. Looks okay. If they would just give us a few minutes to talk things over, we could clear this whole thing up in a short time. I sure have had a hard time explaining my activities that first day of the war. They wanted to know every breath I took. I told them that I was out at our mine, and when I heard about the war starting, I drove into Baguio. Said I stayed there most of the day until I went out east to your mine, where I found you," I said.

"That's not what I told them, but they probably won't go back to that now. They haven't asked about it for some time. By the way, do you know why they've been grilling you so much about your activities around Baguio?" Ralph asked.

"Haven't the slightest idea, but I sure wish they would keep away from that place. The closest I've ever been to it was five thousand feet up when we flew over it in a bomber."

"Well," Ralph said with a smile, "the fact is that the Le Panto Mine was blown up several months ago, and they thought we had something to do with it."

"Where did you get that news?" I asked.

"This character who is questioning me finally told me that. Wouldn't it be a hell of a thing if they punished us for that when you didn't even know the mine existed until you made up that story?"

"Yeah, but a lot of the damnedest things have been happening, you know." I added, "Say, have they got rough with you yet?"

"Yeah, he clouted me with a strap a few times. Did they get you?"

"Did they get me! Christ, he almost killed me with an iron pipe. Then he slapped me and kicked me until I was almost unconscious. Really, I thought my time had come," I said. "I can't think of anything else, can you? Maybe I better get back to my cell before morning. If that bird ever finds out I was in here, it might cause more trouble."

"I can't think of anything else. Probably be a good idea for you to get out of here. Good luck to you," Ralph stuck out his hand.

"Thanks, and the same to you. I don't know how I can ever thank you," I said.

With my paper and pencil in hand, I walked back to the front of the cell and called to the guard. There was no response. Then I waved the paper out of the little hole in the front of the cell and shouted, "Hey!" My voice rang out as in a tomb; still there was no answer. Then in a moment the lights went out for a few seconds. After that a guard came creeping cautiously toward my cell as if he were expecting some trick. I tried to explain to him that I was in the wrong cell. He did not seem to understand what I was saying; he walked back toward the other end of the corridor. I could see that it would be harder to get out of the cell than it had been to get in. Presently an officer approached, and I explained my difficulty to him. "I am in the wrong cell."

"Your name," he demanded.

"Robert Johnson. I belong in the next cell," I pointed to the left. "I was put in here by mistake."

He read the little wooden tags on the front of the cell and then walked over to my cell and read our tags. Then he called the guard and gave him an order in Japanese. The guard unlocked the door, and I stepped out. The officer pointed at the paper I held in my hand and motioned me to give it to him.

"No, it's mine," I insisted.

He looked at the map. I held my breath to see if he would return it. What a break that would have been, after all I had gone through to get it. I stuck out my hand, and much to my surprise he handed the paper back. The door to my cell was opened, and I stepped in with my map clenched in my fist as if someone were going to take it away from me.

In my own cell everyone was oblivious to what had happened. It was well after midnight when I made my way across the row of bodies to settle down in my own place on the hard floor for the night. Before I went to sleep I picked up the paper and had one long, last look at it. So that was Lusud, where I was supposed to have spent the first three months of the war with Ralph and Frank. It was no wonder that the Jap was not satisfied with the maps I had drawn of the place. They did not resemble it in any respect. I could have drawn a map of Luzon in detail, or Bataan, or Corregidor, and shown where the Japanese forces had made their landings and where the Americans had made their retreats and withdrawals. But Lusud—that was a different story.

There was no doubt that Ralph's story would coincide with the story Frank had told, since they had been together ever since the beginning of the war. The only part that would be different would be the part that concerned their relations with Robert Johnson. Without him they both could have told the truth and been in Santo Tomas long ago, but Ralph Conrad and Frank Bacon were loyal Americans and loyal friends who were willing to risk their lives to save another American. If I were not successful in straightening out the story I had told the Japanese, they would face almost certain death along with me.

I was almost asleep when there was a loud noise from the other end of the corridor. "Roll call! Roll call!" A roll call was almost certain to follow anything as unusual as a person being put in the wrong cell. The drowsy prisoners jumped into line, and the roll call went off like clockwork from one end of the corridor to the other. Soon it was all over and quiet again.

The next morning the routine in our cell was just as it had been on all the other mornings that I had been there. The little Jap came down the row with his bucket of rice, dipped a heaping saucer for each of us, and handed it through the window. We devoured our food quickly and had nothing more to do until he came again. Bennett and I visited and watched while a couple of other prisoners were taken from the cell for questioning. At one time, when I hear some planes in the distance, I ran and pressed my face against the wooden bars in the front of the cell and looked high into the sky to see a couple of Japanese trainer-type planes doing acrobatics. Then I sat and looked up through the bars at the green grass of the court and the well-kept trees. It was then I came to realize for the first time that the confinement itself was the most terrible part of our ordeal. I felt then that if I had freedom to go where I wanted to go and do what I wanted to do, I could tolerate any other type of punishment which might be coming to me.

It was mid-afternoon when I finally heard my name being called down the corridor. I was on my way again for another period of interrogation, but this time I had my map of Lusud well in mind and a much better idea of the story I would tell the Japs.

The questioning went well, and I felt that if ever they were going to send us to Santo Tomas it should be soon. All of my answers semed to please the snake-eyed interrogator, and it was not long until I was back in my cell waiting for another night and another day to pass.

Some time just before dark, while I was sitting along the wall with Bennett, I heard someone whispering my name outside the cell in back. Who could it be? Surely Ralph or Frank had not succeeded in getting out. I crawled over toward the back of the cell as inconspicuously as possible and saw a man I recognized as Norman Reyes. He was holding a roll of paper and motioned that he was about to deliver it to me by pushing it back under the floor in the can we used for a toilet. Norman had been a radio announcer for General MacArthur's *Voice of Freedom* on Corregidor, and I always believed that he was the one who broadcast the story about the boys playing "Slap the Jap off the Map" by throwing bread at each other.

I grabbed the roll of paper out of the can, stuck it in my pocket, and went back to my regular position along the wall. After dark, when everyone had laid down to sleep and I felt sure no one was watching me, I pulled out the roll of paper and read it. It was a very long message which had been written on toilet paper by Frank Bacon, giving me the entire story he had told the Japs. The paper was flimsy, and a portion of it had got wet, making it very difficult to read.

Each line I read dampened my spirits. By the end of the letter it seemed to me I had very little hope of working out a story which would tally with the one Ralph had previously told me and the one I read on the paper. It had been necessary for each of my friends to tell many lies in order to tie me in with their experiences since the beginning of the war. But their stories had not been the same.

I lay there all night trying to figure out a way to patch up my story into a happy medium between the one Ralph had told and the one Frank had told. It seemed impossible. Then, in the course of the night, one possibility presented itself to me. Up until the time I had been accidentally put in Ralph's cell, I had been thinking only of myself and had shown very little concern for the two friends who were trying to save me. The only way I could possibly clear the two of them was to make a complete confession to the Japanese and to explain that my two friends had lied only to help me. We were facing almost certain doom unless something happened very soon.

The next morning, after breakfast, the guard again lined us up outside the cell for our bath. During the short time I was in front of Ralph's cell I thought I heard him whisper, "Have you told them yet?" I didn't have a chance to answer, for we were moved away immediately. "Have I told them what?" I asked myself. Did he mean had I told them the story that he told me; or did he mean had I told them that I was an Army officer and that they were innocent civilians trying to protect me? I made up my mind then that the next time the Jap called me for interrogation, I would tell the truth. What Ralph and Frank had done for me was much more than could be expected of any person. I would not see them go through another day of torture for me.

That afternoon when the guard called my name I was glad to hear it for the first time since I had been in Fort Santiago. For the first time I was glad to see him as he appeared in front of the cell calling "Roberto Johnson." But when he opened the big door and I stepped out, I saw a sight that made me gasp. Down the corridor ahead of me were Ralph and Frank, both putting on their shoes. I had missed my chance, for we were being taken out to be executed.

The Jap led the three of us down the corridor and out across the court. My friends were both hollow-eyed, be-whiskered, and ragged, and their faces were solemn. Without a word we looked from one to another, all with the same question in our eyes. "What are they going to do with us?"

This time we were led to a different building where we were ordered to stand in the hall and wait until the jailer conferred with another Japanese. There was no conversation as we waited, for there was nothing to be said. Presently the Jap took Ralph into a little room where they remained for approximately five minutes. When they returned, Frank was taken into the room for a shorter time. At last it was my turn. Inside the room was a large-scale map of the lower part of Luzon Island. The Jap pointed at it and said, "You will tell me where you got your boat when you started sailing."

I studied the map carefully as if I were completely unfamiliar with the area. There was Balayan where the Lopez family had been so wonderful to us. There was Mount Taal, Batangas, Tayabas, and all the other places so familiar to me spread before my eyes. I selected a spot remote from anything or anybody I knew anything about and put my finger on it. "It must have been right along here," I told him.

Back in the hall the Jap announced, "Ralpho Conrado, Franco Bacon and Roberto Johnson will be taken this day from Fort Santiago to Santo Tomas University."

14. Santo Tomas

None of us really believed that we were being transferred to Santo Tomas Internment Camp. Since our arrival in Fort Santiago we had been told daily that if we told the truth we would be sent to Santo Tomas, but we knew we had not told the truth. We knew that the Japanese had thick manuscripts of all the false information we had given them in answer to their hundreds of confusing questions. We had been tricked before, and there was little reason to believe that we would not be tricked again. We were sure of only one thing—that wherever we were being taken and whatever they were going to do to us, it could be no worse than what had already happened to us in Fort Santiago.

We were led out across the court and back to the building we had first entered when coming into the Fort. Again we were ordered to wash our hands in the Lysol bath at the top of the steps before entering. There we waited while a clerk at the desk just inside the door was given our names and ordered to bring the possessions which we had placed in the wire bins when we checked in, almost three weeks before. There was our basket of rice. There was my khaki knapsack which I had carried all the way from Bataan. On the inside of the flap I had drawn a calendar for the last few days in May and the month of June, 1942, so that Bill Harris and I would not lose track of time during our hike across Bataan and our sailing trip to Australia. There was also the money which Ralph and Frank turned in, and my thin cotton blanket which Lopez had given to me. My heart skipped a beat when the clerk threw down on the desk a Mobil gas map which belonged to Ralph and Frank, upon which they had traced their two-hundred-mile hike from Baguio to the southern part of the island and which contained the names of Filipinos who had helped along the way. The information on the map was what the Japanese had been seeking to get from us through questioning and beating. Frank hastily slipped it into his pocket as we were ushered out of the building and back down the steps to the waiting Japanese staff car. This time it was a tiny black automobile of Japanese make, and our escorts wore the uniform of the Japanese gendarme.

We were on our way again, but we had no idea where we were going. We passed through the main gate and through the high stone wall of the Walled City into Manila. Again we saw all of the modern buildings and the beautiful Manila Hotel, but they meant little to us. Our spirits were deadened by the deception, torture, and misery of the past few weeks, until we were afraid to believe that we were actually being taken to the civilian internment camp. We sat silently, waiting and wondering, as we passed over the Pasig River at Jones's Bridge and on through the city. At last we pulled up in front of a big black gate where a sentry saluted our driver and opened the gate for us.

Spread out before our eyes were the magnificent buildings of Santo Tomas University. Hundreds of men, women, and children were walking about the well-kept grounds. It was the first time I had seen American civilians in more than nine months, and it was a good feeling to see clean-shaven men in well-kept clothing and women and children in neat, clean dresses. It was almost like Sunday afternoon in the park back home.

All eyes turned to us as the little Japanese car

drew nearer to the main building. I felt conspicuous and self-conscious, for we all had several weeks' growth of beard, our hair was shaggy and our clothing ragged. My clothes were the ones I had been wearing on that unhappy day when our sailing trip to Australia was brought to an abrupt end by our capture: a faded Filipino sailing suit for a shirt, a pair of blue jeans with holes in the seat, and shoes with a loose sole. The crowd gathered nearer as we unloaded with all our worldly possessions draped over our arms and made our way into the office. There we registered with the American-British committee which had internal control of the camp.

"What is your name?" asked the secretary, looking up at me.

"Robert Fred Johnson," I answered without hesitation.

"And what is your business affiliation?"

"Le Panto Mines."

"Le Panto," he repeated. "Let's see, how do you spell that?" With that question I suddenly felt as if all eyes were on me. "L-a-" I paused, because I did not know how to spell it.

"L-e P-a-n-t-o," someone volunteered, and the secretary looked at me suspiciously.

As soon as Ralph and Frank were registered, we were directed to a big gymnasium to the left of the main building, where we were to be quartered for the duration of our stay in Santo Tomas. There we found row upon row of Army cots with sheets and blankets, each with a mosquito net hanging above it ready to let down when night came. Ralph and Frank were quartered in another part of the gymnasium, and I did not see them as I went about getting used to the new surroundings.

"There's a fellow just outside the door where you can probably get a haircut after while," a fellow in a neighboring bunk suggested.

"What time does he get here?"

"Should be there in a few minutes."

I found the place to take a shower and shave, and by the time I got out-of-doors the barber was waiting. I sat on a box while he cut away handfuls of hair from my head. It was the early part of September, 1942, and I hadn't had a haircut since Bill and I arrived at Balayan back in the middle of June.

"I just got in camp today. A couple of other fellows and I from Baguio thought we could keep from coming in to camp, but they finally caught us and brought us in," I volunteered.

"I saw you when you came in this afternoon and figured you probably would be around to see me," the barber answered.

"They've sure got things fixed up nice in here. Looks like everybody lives pretty comfortably.

"I don't mind it so much, but a lot of the people in here were pretty wealthy on the outside—had large houses, servants, and all that. But they're beginning to get used to this kind of life now. The worst part of it is being locked up and not being able to go anyplace," the barber said.

"But the grounds seem very large, and you can walk around and visit with your friends." I paused, then continued, "There sure are a lot of people in here. I never imagined there were this many Americans in the Philippines."

"Oh, they are not all Americans. There are quite a few British people in this camp and a few Dutch. You know, anyone who marries a British subject automatically becomes a British citizen, and they are all subject to being interned even though they might be full-blooded Filipinos."

"About how many are there in all?" I asked.

"There's about thirty-five hundred at the present time, but that number will be reduced when those who are going to Shanghai leave here," he answered matter-of-factly.

"Shanghai? Who's going to Shanghai?"

"A few weeks ago the Japanese commandant put out word that there would be a Japanese ship sailing to Shanghai and that he would take applications for transfer. But I think only about a hundred have signed up."

"What's their idea for wanting to go to Shanghai when they have things so nice here?" I inquired.

"In the first place, there are a lot of people in this camp who are from Shanghai. When the war broke out every ship at sea for miles around made for Manila Bay, thinking that it was the safest place to be in time of war. As a result, we have a lot of people in camp who were either on their way to Shanghai from the United States or Australia or on their way to other places from Shanghai. They tell us there is no internment in Shanghai and that people who sign up to go there will be free to live in the city as they please."

As the barber whacked away at my hair, I wondered if there was any possibility at all of my getting on the ship to Shanghai. I remembered Bill Harris telling me what a fabulous place it had been when he was stationed there. He had explained to me that the Japanese held only a narrow strip along the coast of China. If a person could get through to the interior he would have no trouble making his way on back to Chungking. Bill and I had been headed for China when we made our swim from Corregidor. What a stroke of fortune it would be, I thought, if I could get on that ship for Shanghai and finally accomplish the mission on which Harris and I had set out, back in May.

As these thoughts ran through my mind, the barber flipped off the apron and shook the hair onto the ground. "Well, you look like a different fellow now," he observed.

"I feel like a different fellow. Say, by the way, I haven't got a cent of money to pay you."

"That's perfectly all right. Glad to do it for you.

Now if you go over into that building," he pointed to a building to the west of where I stood, "there's an American Red Cross office where you can probably get some better clothes than those you have on. They also have toothbrushes and some other items that may be useful to you."

I thanked him and hurried over to the Red Cross office, where I was able to get a pair of walking shorts, a polo shirt, and a pair of low-cut canvas shoes. After that I found a huge dining area to the rear of the main university building where there were eating utensils and generous portions of food.

That night, when I lay down to sleep, it all seemed too good to be true. There would be no roll calls to interrupt our sleep, we would not be awakened by the screaming and moaning of prisoners being tortured in the middle of the night, and the next day there would be no long periods of interrogation. Again I could think of home, for at last there was a possibility that the American forces might return to Manila before the Japs called us out again for questioning. It might take them months to investigate the stories we had told; they might never learn the truth about us.

As I lay there on my cot I tried to remember every word the barber had told me about the ship that was going to Shanghai. I had not pressed the subject too far because I did not want him to know I was interested in the trip. In one way or another, I felt I must get out of Santo Tomas as soon as possible, for sooner or later, it was certain to become known that I was a soldier. The more I thought of it, the more I wished that the night were over so I could find out more about the Shanghai trip.

The next morning I learned that Ralph and Frank had gone to the hospital for treatment. I also learned that almost everyone in camp thought that all three of us were United States soldiers. Whenever anyone questioned me about it, I would tell them that Ralph and Frank were actually mining engineers. That would generally satisfy their inquisitive minds. But I found one fellow who was not so easily satisfied. Walking between the buildings on the second day in camp, I was stopped by a tall, thin man. "Boy, don't you think you're skating on pretty thin ice?"

"What do you mean?" I inquired.

"Why, passing yourself off as a miner. Don't you know all of the mining people in here know each other by now, and it won't be long before they have you pegged?"

I thought for a couple of seconds and answered, "But as long as they are all Americans and British, I can't see that it makes any difference."

"That's where you're wrong," he fired back. "Now, don't get me wrong. I'm all for you, and I happen to be a miner myself. I know both Ralph and Frank; but there are just a lot of people in here you can't trust. Don't talk. Don't tell anybody anything."

I thanked him for his advice, but felt no better for having talked to him. I could not believe that people together behind barbed wire, as we were, could not be trusted; however, it was not long before I came to have some respect for his viewpoint.

As soon as possible in the morning I made my way over to the office of the Japanese commandant. I was able to talk with him after a very short wait. He was an old gentleman with a kindly manner and spoke very fine English compared with what I had been used to hearing from the Japs in Santiago. I got to the point at once.

"I am Robert Johnson, and I just got into camp yesterday."

"Yes, what can I do for you?"

"Well, I understand that there is a boat sailing for Shanghai in the near future, and I would like to go if it could possibly be arranged."

"Oh, I am very sorry for you," he replied, "but the list for sailing has already been prepared. There will be no names added to the list, and no names will be removed."

It had all been too good to be true. That was the end of the line as far as going to Shanghai was concerned. I tried not to show my disappointment, but said as calmly as possible, "I would like to ask you one favor."

"Yes, what is it?"

"I would like for you to take down my name, and if there is any possibility at all, I would appreciate it very much if my name could be added to the list."

"I will be glad to do that," he answered.

He then gave me a form to fill out, upon which I wrote my name and a couple of fictitious names of people for references in Shanghai.

Once outside the office I suddenly felt that I had made a big mistake in being so insistent. The Japanese commander could only conclude I was eager to get out of Santo Tomas at the first opportunity. If he were to check my record, that in itself could lead to more questioning.

The next few days in the camp were very pleasant. I got acquainted with the people and the physical aspects of the place. There was much to be seen and learned, but my chief interest was in determining the possibilities for escape in case it became necessary. I walked from one end of the grounds to the other, examining the fence and the surrounding territory. My conclusion was that getting out of the grounds would be the easiest part of escaping; however, getting away from the big city presented a much more serious problem. Then my enthusiasm for escape was dampened when I heard that four men had been shot to death when they tried to run away from the camp.

The thirty-five hundred people in the camp lived in luxury compared with anything I had seen since the beginning of the war. Chow was served two or three times a day—generous portions of beef stew, rice, and vegetables. Many of the people had been able to build small houses of their own from bamboo and other materials which the Filipinos brought to the main gate. Families sometimes prepared their own meals and enjoyed all the comforts of home in these houses, where they were allowed to remain throughout the daylight hours in comparative seclusion. However, there were many hundreds of other people who could not afford such luxury and had to make the best of dormitory life. There was always some activity going on: discussion groups, classes, work groups, shows, and many other things.

At a given time each day hundreds of faithful Filipinos would appear at the main gate with all manner of supplies and provisions for the internees. They provided a constant source of news from the outside world by way of messages smuggled inside the packages.

And so life went on inside Santo Tomas Internment Camp in September, 1942, with all thirty-five hundred prisoners faring well, but with each one counting the days and the hours that passed and waiting patiently for the good news which might indicate that the American forces were on their way to the Philippines. No such news was forthcoming. The war had long since left the Philippines, and the only news was that the American forces were waging a bitter struggle with the forces of the Japanese far below the equator in the steaming jungles of New Guinea.

In the hospital at the other end of the compound I was able to find my friend, Frank Bacon. Civilization was not agreeing with him, he looked worse than he had looked at any time since I had known him.

"How are things with you?" I asked when he looked up.

"Oh, hell, they tell me they think I've got a bug and may be here for a long time. This is a swell place though, and I don't mind. Oh, by the way, meet my bunkmate," he said, nodding to the patient in the adjoining bed.

We exchanged greetings. Frank continued, "I told him all about you, so it's all right to talk. What have you been doing?"

"Oh, I've been getting acquainted with the place. Think I may go to work in the kitchen tomorrow scrubbing pots and pans. I like this place, except that I get a funny reaction from some of the people. One of your old friends jumped me and told me I would get in trouble with the story I'm telling."

"Well, don't worry about it. If he's a miner, he's okay," Frank assured me. "By the way, have you seen any of these Army nurses? There must be fifty or sixty of them in here."

"Yes, I saw a couple who looked familiar, but didn't know them well enough to speak to them. Hope I don't bump into anyone I know in here." I added, "Yesterday I went over to the commandant's office and applied for passage on that ship to Shanghai."

Frank had not heard about the ship, so I explained the details to him. "You'd better get over and see if you can't get on it too. If we ever got up there, it would be no problem at all to escape back to Free China.

"Well, I don't think I would be up to anything like that after what we've been through in Santiago. Does Ralph know anything about this?"

"Don't know. Haven't had a chance to talk to him."

"He may want to go. He thinks they've just put us in here while they're checking on the stories we told them, and that we'll be back in Santiago as soon as the investigation is over."

"Well, it doesn't seem like there's much chance of my getting to make the trip. The commandant told me that there would be no names added to the passenger list, but one way or another I'm going to have to get out of this place. People keep asking me questions. When I went back to see about that job in the kitchen, those guys kept asking me questions, and I don't think they'll be satisfied until they get the truth about me."

We talked a little longer before I took my leave and walked back toward the main building. Sitting at a table under the dining shelter were a couple of American Army nurses who looked slightly familiar to me. There was no one else near, and it seemed like a good time to find out who might be in camp that I would know. I approached them and introduced myself. "I'm Bob Johnson from the mines up at Baguio. Used to know some of the Army nurses and was wondering if they'd happen to be in this camp."

The girls looked at me skeptically. One asked, "What were their names?"

"Seems like there was one girl by the name of Ann Williams and another by the name of Alice Hahn," I ventured.

"Oh, sure. They're here. We live together. Ann should be along here any minute. I'm waiting for her now."

"Where is she now?" I had to find her immediately, to warn her to go along with my story.

"I think she's in the fourth cottage in that line over there," a nurse pointed, "but she'll be along here any time."

"Think I'll see if I can find her. Thanks a lot." I nodded and hurried off in the direction of the cottage she had pointed out to me.

I started to knock on the wall of the cottage just as a familiar face turned toward me. "You're eh . . . you're . . . Oh, I can't think of your name," she stammered, looking me over from head to foot.

"I'm Bob Johnson, and I would like to speak to you a moment, if you please." There were other girls present, and I nodded for her to come out onto the pathway. She looked at me, puzzled.

"I'm Ed Whitcomb from Corregidor. Don't you remember when I visited Drachenberg in the tunnel and told you that we were going to escape by swimming back to Bataan?"

"Oh, sure. I remember, but what are you doing in here?" She was still puzzled.

"Well, it's too long a story to tell you now, but I was captured by some Filipinos who turned me over to the Japs. I told them I was a civilian and that my name was Robert Johnson, and here I am. The important thing is that you do not act as if you knew me. Also, I would appreciate it if you would tell any of the other girls who might recognize me to keep mum about it until I get out of here."

"Oh, you can count on us." She smiled reassuringly.

"Whatever happened to poor old Drachenberg? I've thought about him a lot of times," I inquired.

"Drachenberg was moved from Corregidor to Bili Bid Prison right here in Manila. He is much improved, but still in bad shape."

"Did you ever hear anything about Jim Dey and the others?"

"I think they were all taken to Cabanatuan POW camp north of here," she replied.

"Sure hope Drack makes it through all right," I said.

"I hope you do too." She smiled again and stuck out her hand to bid me good-by.

"Thanks again. I appreciate your help. They tell me you can't trust everybody in this place." I left Ann and headed back toward the gymnasium, feeling confident that she and the other girls would keep my secret.

15. Transfer

From that day on things went pretty smoothly in
Santo Tomas. We had good food to eat and a dry,
comfortable place to sleep. It was a pleasant existence, but always in the back of my mind was the
thought that one day an armed Jap would come into
camp looking for Robert Johnson. I knew that when
that happened there would be no more long periods
of questioning, for by that time they would have
learned all the facts—that I was an escaped prisoner
of war, passing myself off as a civilian. Each night I
went through the different possibilities of escape, and
some nights I even walked outside and stood for long
periods to see if there were any activity I should
know about before trying my getaway. But always
it was peaceful and quiet, and always I came back
and climbed into my bunk, reassured that it would
be an easy matter to get away when the right time
came.

Each afternoon I worked in the main kitchen,
washing dishes, scrubbing pots and pans, and clean-
ing up the kitchen. There were only three or four
of us, and it was generally quiet around the building
because most of the people in camp took their siestas
at that time. For comfort and convenience we wore
only a pair of wooden clogs, a pair of tight-fitting
shorts, and an apron of some kind. Periodically, the
fellows I worked with set upon a system of interrogation to find out more about me. They seemed certain
that I was connected with the military forces, but

gained little support for their theory in the answers I gave to their many questions. Finally, one day, the young fellow working next to me admitted to me privately that he had been in the Army Air Corps at Nichols Field when the war broke out.

"Well, why didn't you go with the Army instead of coming in here?" I inquired.

"I wasn't with my outfit at the time they evacuated the field, and I didn't get a chance to join 'em." He looked about him and then went on, "There are quite a few soldiers in here. A lot of people think you're one." He stared me straight in the eyes.

"Naw," I sighed. "But sometimes I wish I were. Were you a pilot?"

"Hell, no," he said briskly. "Do you think if I was an officer I would be doing this kind of work?"

We heard an unusual amount of chattering out in the hallway, but we paid little attention to the noise. Then one of the other fellows spoke up, "They say they're bringing some prisoners in here who just got in from the southern islands."

Someone else answered, "Sounds like that might be them now."

We went on with our work, scrubbing away on the big baking pans, but when we heard the new prisoners coming in we turned to see a group of United States Army nurses in uniform file into the room. Some looked familiar as I glanced up at them; then, all of a sudden, one looked straight at me, threw out her arms and came running toward me crying, "Whit! Whit! What are you doing in here?"

Everyone stopped and looked. "Look, you must be mistaken," I pleaded, looking into her face and shaking my head. "You must have me mixed up . . ."

"No. You're Whit. Don't you remember me? I'm Evelyn Whitlow." By that time I had walked her a few steps away from the others so that I could explain the situation.

"Not so loud. Not so loud! Now listen to me. I can't tell you now, but I'll explain to you later."

"But what are you doing in here, and what are you doing dressed like that?" She looked at me and laughed.

"I'll tell you later; it's a long story. For now, just call me Bob Johnson and warn any of the other girls who might recognize me not to say anything."

Evelyn had never been in a civilian internment camp and had no idea how different it was from a prisoner-of-war camp. She had been one of the group of nurses who were flown from Corregidor in a seaplane in the attempt to escape to Australia, a few nights before the fall of Corregidor. Their seaplane had struck a snag while taking off from one of the southern islands, and they had been taken prisoner on the island of Mindanão. How well I remembered her, and how I wanted to reminisce about the days of Bataan and Corregidor! I remembered her asking the chaplain to autograph her Bible, and how she had stumbled across the wheel chair occupied by Emanuel Quezon, president of the Philippine Islands, when she closed her Bible and stepped back to thank him. But there was no time to talk about such things.

"Look," I whispered, trying to rush her along with the rest of the nurses, "you please keep quiet about seeing me, and I will see you later and explain the whole thing to you." She agreed and left me.

Back at the sink the ex-soldier observed, "She knew you pretty well, didn't she?"

"Yes, didn't think I knew her at first. Had a date or two with her back before the war in Manila," I lied casually and went on scrubbing the pans.

I felt more and more insecure in Santo Tomas as the days went by, despite the fact that life was pleasant for one not accustomed to such luxury. It seemed to be common knowledge that there were a number of soldiers and sailors in camp, and I sometimes wondered if it would not be better if I simply made a clean breast of it with the internees, told them the truth and let them know that my safety depended upon their helping to keep my secret. That would at least have taken me out of the "suspicious character" class and placed me with all the other known military personnel. As it later turned out, however, the course I followed proved to be the wisest.

An enterprising soldier, who was also pretending to be a civilian, arranged a space in the third floor hallway of the main building with a bed and a certain amount of privacy. He then rented this space out to various couples who wanted to be alone. His business operation was soon called to the attention of the American-British committee in charge of the affairs of the camp, who ordered the entrepreneur to cease and desist. The soldier defended his position with, "Look, there are other people in this camp who have their own rackets. This is mine. If you report me to the Japs, I'll go to them and tell them a few things I know." The committee took a dim view of such insubordination and took corrective measures, and the soldier made good his threat. He went to the Japanese commandant and told him, among other things, that there were a large number of people from the Armed Forces hiding in the camp.

The Japanese issued a statement that they knew the names of all the people in camp who were connected with the military, and that these would be severely punished unless they turned themselves in voluntarily. A few days later a truck rolled into camp and hauled away twenty-five ex-soldiers and -Marines —including the entrepreneur himself. To my knowledge they were never heard from again.

But that was not my fate, for I kept my secret locked deep inside and watched and waited. A whole week had gone by since we had come into camp, and the excitement of our arrival had died down. Even the Army nurses were much less interested in me than I could have wished.

I lay on my cot one afternoon, relaxing after my chores in the kitchen were finished. I was feeling very much at peace with the world when, above the usual mumble of men's voices across the room, I distinctly heard someone speak the name of Robert Johnson. I was completely jarred out of the peaceful state of mind which had been mine for so short a time. I raised up in time to see an American approaching my bunk. "Johnson, they want you over at the commandant's office right away." I do not remember ever seeing the fellow before, but he knew who I was.

"What's it about?" I asked as calmly as I could.

"They got you on the list, and they got to get more information . . ."

"What list?" I interrupted as we rushed out of the gymnasium on our way to the commandant.

"The sailing list for Shanghai."

"You don't mean it," I replied, beside myself with surprise and joy. "Well, you know, I had no more idea of getting on that boat than I had of flying to the moon."

After the brisk walk to the commandant's office, I was advised that before sailing I must have a physical examination.

"Where do I get it?"

"You will go with me to the city tomorrow at ten in the morning," the commandant replied.

That came as a shock which dampened my enthusiasm for the whole affair. Why go to the city for an examination? There were plenty of doctors in Santo Tomas. I had heard nothing about any of the others going into the city for their examinations.

As I walked back toward the gymnasium, it all became clear to me. That was the way the Japanese would do it. They would say that I was being taken into the city for some purpose, and I would wind up again in Fort Santiago. That was the way they had got us into Fort Santiago in the first place. They had told us how wonderful Santo Tomas was and how fine it would be for us to associate with all of the other Americans. Then they had driven us directly to the prison instead.

I spent a miserable evening and night, with the memories of the horrors of Fort Santiago still fresh in my mind. I knew I could not stand another siege of such treatment without cracking under the strain.

Late in the night I looked about me to see everyone asleep. How I resented it! Hundreds of civilians who had done nothing since the beginning of the war except sleep and eat—there they were, all sleeping peacefully as I debated over and over in my mind whether or not the time had come to try to make my escape.

At last I slipped out from under my mosquito net and sneaked outside. No one saw me. There was not a sound except for the heavy breathing and snoring from the various parts of the room. Outside, the sky was clouded, and there were no stars or moon to be seen. It was dark over by the wall. Again I did as I had done almost every night since I had been in camp; I stood watching, waiting, and thinking. Then I turned and went back to bed, where I fell asleep in a very short time.

Some time during the night I was awakened by a weird voice crying out into the stillness. At first I thought I was dreaming; then it became real. The voice was screaming:

> "I'm a wild Scotsman,
> Ha! Ha! Ha!
> But I want to be a wild duck,
> Quack, quack, quack."

It went on over and over again amid the mumbling of a group which had gathered on the balcony of the gymnasium. I did not go up to the balcony to investigate it, but word came back to our area that some fellow had smuggled some whisky into the camp and had taken too much.

When he became too noisy and the others attempted to quiet him, he took up his wild duck routine and held off everyone by swinging a baseball bat wildly in front of him. Each time someone tried to close in, he swung the bat back and forth and cried out again:

> "I'm a wild Scotsman,
> Ha! Ha! Ha!
> But I want to be a wild duck,
> Quack, quack, quack."

It was some time before the confusion came to a halt, and then all was quiet again.

The next morning at the appointed time I waited at the commandant's office. He stepped out of his office to the waiting car, looked at me and said, "You Robert Johnson?"

"Yes, I'm ready to go." I climbed into the little black car with the feeling that it was my last ride. The little car rolled out of the main gate and followed the same course which had brought us from Fort Santiago to Santo Tomas Internment Camp. I felt weaker and more helpless each block we traveled. But when we came to the street that would have taken us to Fort Santiago, the little auto continued straight toward the pier and pulled up in front of a large building. What will it be this time? I asked myself.

The commandant and I unloaded, and I tagged along as he hurried up the steps to the third floor of the building. There he had a hurried chat with a Japanese naval officer, and I wondered what means of torture they were planning when the officer turned and looked at me. There were more words between them. Finally the commandant saluted, received a salute in return, did an about-face, and we were on our way back down the stairs. I asked no questions and received no explanation of what had gone on as the little car made its way back to the gates of Santo Tomas. There was no rhyme nor reason to what had happened; but by that time I should not have expected reason from the Japanese.

Two days later, September 12, 1942, just ten days after I had been ushered into Santo Tomas, about ninety Americans and British who were to make the trip to Shanghai assembled in front of the main building to wait for the busses which would take them to the pier. Many of the people were heavily laden with suitcases and bundles. But I, clad in a pair of walking shorts and polo shirt, carried only a paper bag with a toothbrush, shaving equipment, towel, washrag, and a bar of soap. We were about to embark upon an eight-day sea voyage which would take us to a foreign land full of adventure and mystery. But adventure and mystery were the last things I wanted, and up to the very moment I stepped upon the bus I watched and waited for the Jap who would come and call me aside.

It seemed that everyone in camp turned out to see us off. Both Ralph and Frank were there, slightly bewildered at the speed with which I had managed to get away from the camp.

"I sure wish you fellows were going with me," I said.

"Maybe it's better this way," Ralph suggested.

As I shook hands with both of them I said, "I don't know how I can ever thank you for all you have done for me. There should be some sort of a medal for the kind of bravery you have shown. Anyhow, your chances of getting through this thing will probably be a hell of a lot better without me."

"That's right," answered Frank. "Our stories jibe, and there are enough people in camp who know us—we shouldn't have any more trouble."

"Best of luck to both of you. If things go right, I'll escape from Shanghai to the interior where I can join the friendly Chinese," I said.

"It might be better if we don't stay around you too much now. Can't tell who might be watching," Ralph warned. So they withdrew into the waiting crowd, and I stood alone waiting to climb on the bus. It seemed only seconds until we were whisked out of the main gate again, through the streets of Manila and down to the pier to the waiting ship.

16. Shanghai

It was mid-afternoon when our group of Americans and British loaded onto a twenty-five-hundred-ton Japanese freighter by the name of *Maya Maru*. There were no markings upon the ship to indicate to American planes or submarines that there were American civilians aboard the ship, and it did not take us long to learn that the trip was not being made to Shanghai just for our personal benefit and convenience. The space allotted to us was below the main deck and barely large enough so that everyone could lie down. Adjacent to our space were quartered some two hundred Japanese combat soldiers. Also aboard the ship were twenty Formosan prostitutes who were being returned from the southern islands to their native land on rotation. Down in the hold below us were some two hundred horses which had been captured from the American forces somewhere in the islands, and in the forepart of the ship were two American-made automobiles. Also sharing our space were sixty Hindus with their long flowing robes draped about their bodies and their caste marks conspicuously painted on their foreheads. All in all, it was an interesting cargo of animals and humanity, and the thirteen-hundred-mile trip from Manila north to Shanghai promised to be a memorable voyage.

Although we were all loaded and ready to go by late afternoon, it was completely dark before the motors started turning over. I felt a thrill when I realized that at last I was on my way to China. Months had passed since Bill Harris and I had started to China, and it seemed ironical, after all that had happened to us, that the Japanese were furnishing the transportation I needed to get to China and to escape back to the friendly forces.

I counted the seconds and minutes until I could feel the ship moving, for I was still very much aware that Fort Santiago was only a few hundred feet down the shore from where we were located. There was still the fear in my mind that a Jap soldier would drag me off the ship and back to Santiago prison. Then, just as if my thoughts had been a premonition, again I heard a Japanese calling the name of Johnson. It was like a dream, but there he was, right before my eyes, calling "Johnson! Johnson!"

Quickly I stepped back so that he could not see me as he passed by with his flashlight. But in a couple of seconds he was back with a well-meaning American who was pointing me out to him.

"You Johnson?" The Japanese pointed his finger into my face.

"Yes," I answered meekly.

"You doktor?" he asked.

"No!" I answered. "I'm no doctor." Perhaps, I thought, he was looking for another Johnson who was a doctor.

He flashed his light on the roll of papers in his hand and then came back at me again, "You no doktor?" Again I answered, "No. No doctor."

"Come home! Come home!" he commanded with a couple of backhand waves which meant I was to go back to my quarters.

I watched and listened intently until I saw him locate a Doctor Jensen who was a fellow-passenger aboard the ship.

Such minor misunderstandings could happen a hundred times under normal circumstances, and a person would never give them a second thought. To me they were horrible moments which frightened me now that I was on the threshold of a successful escape.

It was only a matter of minutes later when we could feel the motion of the ship, and we knew we were at last under way. There being nothing else to do, each of us found his place in the area which had been allotted to us and made his bed on the hard wood floor of the middle deck with no blankets and no bed clothes.

At dawn the next morning we were allowed to go on the top deck. I was much surprised to see that we were still in Manila Bay, approaching the channel to the north side of Corregidor, which leads from Manila Bay into the China Sea to the west.

The North Channel seemed to be the crossroads of the world for me. Ten months before we had winged our way across it in giant bombers fresh from the United States, armed to the teeth with machine guns and bombs and ready to conquer the world. Then, five months later, we had escaped across the channel in a tiny boat with a hole in its side and with the enemy hot on our tails. After our drubbing on Corregidor, Harris and I had swum those very waters in our effort to get started to China. After we found out we would be unable to sail to China, Bill and I had again sailed across the channel on our way southward toward Australia. Now, after going the long way around, I was again on my way through the channel toward China.

The Americans and British strained their eyes looking at Bataan and Corregidor, but all that they could see were the dense jungles of Bataan and the rocks of Corregidor. Although I was surrounded by Americans I felt very lonely, for the sights which meant nothing to them reminded me of Lieutenant Croxton, of Dey, Renka, Drachenberg, and the thousands of others I had known. I felt a sudden desire to speak out and tell my fellow Americans all about it. I wanted to point to that scar over on the side of the hill and tell them that was where Bataan Airfield had been located; over to the left was Cabcaben Field, then farther west was Mariveles where our American forces had surrendered. On the other side of the ship to the south was Corregidor, with Kindley Field, which we had patched up for the Japs. Just below that and to the left was where the Japs had made their landing on Corregidor, and over the hill from that was Monkey Point, where we had an old relic of a seventy-five millimeter cannon. That hump on the island was Malinta Hill, and just over on the other side was where we left eleven thousand miserable Americans and Filipinos starving and dying. Thoughts flooded my mind as I remembered the events of the dimmed, distant past.

I felt a hand on my shoulder and we slightly startled when I turned and looked straight into the eyes of a Jap.

"Go," he ordered.

Everyone else had gone below while I was carried away with my thoughts. I must go too, for the Japs did not want me to see their "impregnable fortress of Corregidor."

In the area below deck the passengers were preparing for their morning meal. Most of the Americans and British had brought along some provisions and were gathering in little groups to spread out their meal. For those who had brought no food it was possible to get ten little bowls and a bucket of rice and fish adequate for ten people from the ship's galley.

The ship's provisions were not satisfactory to the Hindus, and they had their own supplies. They also had bowls and utensils for mixing up the concoctions they ate. Each one of them seemed to be as busy as the proverbial cat on the tin roof, grinding, mixing, and flavoring their various dishes. It seemed each one prepared his own food, and no one would eat food that had been touched by another person.

In our area I got acquainted with some of my fellow passengers who offered to share their canned food with me. There was a young lady named Jean, a tall, skinny fellow named James Montague who seemed very quiet and reserved, and an elderly lady whose name I never learned. Since I was the only one who had nothing to contribute to the feast spread out on the deck, I felt the least I could do would be to entertain them with a story. They all laughed when I told the story about a character in the gymnasium back in Santo Tomas a few nights before screaming:

> "I'm a wild Scotsman,
> Ha! Ha! Ha!
> But I want to be a wild duck,
> Quack, quack, quack."

Everyone was much amused, but it was a source of no little embarrassment to me a short time later when I learned that the "wild Scotsman" was the tall, skinny James Montague who stood by, listened, and laughed heartily as I told the story. I also learned that James Montague had spent eight months in Santo Tomas because he had been inebriated and missed his ship for the United States a few days before the war started.

Later in the day I engaged one of the Japanese soldiers in conversation. "You go back home to Japan?"

"No. Go to China," he replied in broken English.

"But when you get this close to home, can't you get a furlough for a few days at home?" I persisted.

"Japanese soldier not going home," he insisted. I was later told that a Jap soldier would be a disgrace to his family if he were to return to his native land before victory had been won.

These Jap soldiers were packed in much the same as we were, each man having about twelve square feet in space. They slept on the deck with no bunk or cot of any kind. At lunch time one member out of each group of ten would go to the galley and return with a bucket of rice and fish for the whole outfit, and then they would sit around in the same space and enjoy their meal.

To keep in shape, one group after another was taken out onto the deck where they engaged in calisthenics and formed in lines, each one chopping at the one in front of him with judo chops.

For discipline it was not uncommon to see an officer slapping a subordinate across the face, first forehand and then backhand. The subordinate might step backwards as he was slapped, but no one ever resisted.

While watching the Japanese and their curious antics I was startled to see a familiar face. Mingling with the officers and men on the other end of the ship was Norman Reyes, the trusty from Fort Santiago who had smuggled the note from Frank Bacon to me. I never talked to him during the voyage and never knew for certain whether he recognized me.

We plowed northward through the China Sea for several days in a convoy of four small transport ships, escorted by a lone destroyer zigzagging back and forth ahead of us. It offered no more protection from American submarines than did the dummy wooden gun mounted on the superstructure of the *Maya Maru*. Not one of us aboard the ship knew of the hundreds of thousands of tons of Japanese shipping which the United States submarines had sent to the bottom in the sea lanes we were traveling. Nor did I imagine that thousands of my friends from Bataan and Corregidor, including Jim Dey, would be sent to their watery graves by American planes while being transported north in the same manner that we were being moved.

Life at sea was more than my malaria-racked body could stand, and after a couple of days I was flat on my back with a high fever. Through the generosity of the people about me I was furnished with a cot from somewhere, a quilt for a cover, and more food than I was able to enjoy.

A few days later everyone was ordered to remain below deck for a long period of time. The ship had stopped, and there seemed to be a considerable amount of activity on the deck. When at last permission was given to go on deck, I climbed off my cot and went up with the rest of the passengers. We were tied up in a harbor which was a beehive of activity. Some of our cargo, including the prostitutes, was unloaded, and other cargo was loaded onto our ship. Across the harbor from us we saw a huge American transport loaded with supplies. It was the S. S. *President Harrison*, which had been captured by the Japanese earlier in the war. Across to the east we could see the green hills of Formosa, and I was surprised at the vast expanse of the island.

Formosa was the island we had wanted so badly to bomb, but we had been blasted and our planes destroyed before we ever got the chance. Walt Seamon and I had traced it off on one map after another that night after the Japs had bombed Clark Field. It was a strong link approximately halfway between the Japanese mainland and the Philippine Islands. If it had been bombed as Clark Field was bombed, the Japanese effort in the Pacific would have been greatly slowed down. But it had not been bombed, and it was making a great contribution to the Japanese military successes. I felt sick, sicker than I had been before, and made my way down the ladder and back to my bunk. I was more determined than ever that if it were humanly possible to do so, I would get back to the friendly forces and get into the war again.

Sometime in the afternoon or night the *Maya Maru* pulled out of Takao Harbor and continued on north toward Shanghai. After a couple of days I began to recover from my illness, and I realized that within a matter of hours we would be reaching Shanghai. What would it be like? I knew nothing about Shanghai except that it was a big city on the China coast, now under the control of the Japanese. Where would I go, and what would I do? I had no idea. There was no one on board the ship I could talk to. Everyone else seemed to know where he was going and what he was going to do when he got there. Perhaps I could find a place to hide and stay until I had sufficient information and provisions to start my trip back to Chungking. But that was hundreds of miles, and there were many problems which could only be worked out as they arose. I had to talk to someone—I needed help.

In conversation with my fellow passengers I learned that there was a young married couple in our group who worked for *Time* and *Life* magazines, and I felt that if there were anyone aboard I might confide in, it would be they. Their names were Carl and Shelly Mydans. I watched them to see whom they associated with, and waited for an opportunity to talk to them alone. There were other newspaper people aboard, I learned, including Russell Brines and Royal Arch Gunnison and his wife. I had to make a decision, but could not bring myself to do it. Everyone seemed completely wrapped up in his own problems, and I was so bewildered at the prospect of making my identity known to anyone while we were still aboard the ship that I did little more than enter into casual conversation with any of my prospects.

About eight days after we had left Manila we sighted the Chinese mainland. After hours and hours of sailing, we headed westward into the Yangtze Estuary. It was completely dark when we finally rounded a bend in the river and saw the magnificent city of Shanghai spread out before us. In Manila, the Japs had told us there would be no internment and that we would be free to live as we pleased. What they had not told us was that Shanghai was the "Paris of the Orient," that we could live like kings, and that all the wonderful things of the world were ours for the asking, simply because we were Americans and British.

As we neared the dock, different groups of people gathered together and pointed out various familiar landmarks, for most of the passengers had been in the city before. Many of them had lived there for years. I could hear different passengers telling their friends where they could be located. It was then I first became seriously concerned about where I would spend the night. Perhaps I might walk about the streets all night or find some place to rest until morning. I stepped off the ship with no idea of where I would go or what I would do. In the crowd I picked out Mydans and called him aside. "Where are you going to be? I have a serious problem that I want to discuss with you. My name is Bob Johnson and I don't know just where I'll be," I said.

"We don't know ourselves. We may be in the Palace Hotel," he answered, looking at me curiously.

"I'll probably be looking you up," I said, feeling sure now that he was the man I wanted to talk to. I followed the crowd walking out of the customs building and into the street.

"Truck for the American School. Truck for the American School," someone was shouting.

"What does that mean?" I asked the person next to me.

"Anyone who doesn't have a place to go can go to the American School, I suppose," was the answer.

Without any further invitation I climbed onto the truck and waited until it was loaded. We were hauled for two miles through the city, and at last we pulled up in an area which resembled the campus of a small college. It was the American School, and we were immediately directed to the dining room where a delicious meal of ham and eggs was waiting for us. After that we were assigned to our quarters and told that we could stay there as long as we desired.

That night I slept peacefully on a comfortable cot in a dormitory, little realizing the wonders of the city of Shanghai which lay about me.

Dawn of September 20, 1942, ushered in a new day and a new life for those of us who had made the trip from the civilian internment camp in Manila to the city of Shanghai. The atmosphere was pleasant and cheerful as I dressed and walked out onto the campus of the American School. A glance down the long cinder driveway told me that the gates were open and there were no Jap guards. We were free to go where we wanted to go and do what we wanted to do, as they had promised us. I walked up into the dining room in the main building and found friendly Americans waiting to serve whatever I ordered for breakfast.

There were few people in the dining room; I sat across the table from my newly acquired friend, James Montague. "The food's fine," he stated as he pushed his fork into the steaming scrambled eggs on his plate. "Just tell them what you want."

"Looks good to me."

It was just as if we were back in the United States, and I began to feel like a civilian again.

"How do you spell your name again?" Montague asked me casually.

"W-h-i-t . . . oh, I mean Johnson. J-o-h-n-s-o-n. Robert Johnson!" I looked at Montague, but he smiled unconcernedly and went on eating as if he had not heard me. There was no further conversation about the name or the blunder. It was the only time in the year and a half that I used the name of Robert Johnson that I ever made the slightest bobble. The stateside atmosphere had thrown me completely off guard.

"Ever been in Shanghai before?" I asked.

"This is my first trip," he answered rather formally and in an accent that sounded somewhat British. "Are you acquainted here yourself?"

Before I could answer, a tall blond man of about forty approached our table. "You fellows who came in last night will have to go to the French police headquarters to get your identification cards."

"Identification cards for what?" Montague fired back.

"The Japanese require that all persons living in this part of town carry identification cards with them."

"But I have my passport," Montague argued.

"Yes, but you'll have to get a French identification card too," our informant said.

Life was not to be as simple in Shanghai as I had imagined. I knew that I must decide quickly whether to obtain an identification card with the French police or whether to escape. I knew that I must find Carl Mydans, the *Life* photographer, and talk it over with him before I did anything else.

"Excuse me, but I have a lot of things to do," I told Montague, and left the table without finishing my meal.

Clad in my walking shorts, polo shirt, and low tennis shoes, I walked out of the American School campus and down the long street which led back to the docks. Although there were many rickshaws and streetcars, the two-mile walk was necessary because I did not have the few cents to pay my fare.

It was about the middle of the morning when I knocked on the door of the Mydans' room in the Palace Hotel. Carl Mydans opened the door. Shelly, a pretty dark-haired girl, greeted me with a friendly smile, and I felt at ease immediately.

"Well, Mr. Mydans, I am in trouble. They say I've got to get an identification card with the French police, but I want to talk to you first. I want to get out of Shanghai and back to Chungking. I don't know whether to go now or to wait a few days.

If I wait I must register with the French police."

"What is it? What's your trouble?" he asked, looking at me sharply.

"Well, you see," I hesitated, "you see, I was with the Army in the Philippines."

"In the Army!" Mydans repeated in a hushed voice. His eyes brightened. He thought a moment, and then directed me to sit down in the middle of the floor. He checked the hall door and listened at the door to the adjoining room. Then his wife and he sat down in the middle of the floor with me. "You can't tell when you might be overheard," he warned. "Tell us all about it."

They both listened patiently as I told my story from the beginning, stopping me from time to time for more details. When I finally finished I felt tired and weak from nervous exhaustion. I had never told anyone the complete story before, but I felt certain beyond any doubt that I had done the right thing.

Mydans looked at the floor for a few seconds and then said thoughtfully, "It has cost our government thousands of dollars to train men like you. It's a long way back to Chungking. Shelly and I were there before we came to the Philippines. The best thing would be to find someone we can trust who will give you advice and help on getting back to Chungking."

"That's been my plan all the time; but, frankly, I have no idea who that might be."

"Well, give me a little time, and I will see what I can find out for you."

"But I've got to get over to the French police for my identification card," I said.

"You just wait until you hear from me before you go to them. In the meantime, here's fifty bucks for you. You will be needing money."

I was overwhelmed at the idea of receiving so much money at one time, but the important thing was that Mydans had believed my story. I thanked him and his wife and left the hotel feeling much richer for the money I had in my pocket and much happier with the thought that I had friends upon whom I could rely. I walked from the hotel down along the Bund, the wide street between the river and the tall buildings of the city of Shanghai. The waterfront was teeming with sampans, the streets were swarming with Chinese humanity, and all in all, Shanghai looked as if it would be a very interesting place to live. I took the crowded streetcar all the way from the waterfront back to the American School.

In a couple of days Carl and Shelly Mydans turned up at the American School. They had walked out, partly for the interesting hike and partly for the purpose of loading up on reading material from the American School library. We visited for a few moments in the library, and then walked out onto the lawn where we could talk.

"There's a Mr. Henningsen who is president of the American Association here in Shanghai. From what I can learn of him, he should know more about the possibility of your getting back to Chungking than any other person I would know of," Carl advised me.

"I've heard of him. But where do I find him?"

"He has an office downtown in one of the business buildings. I expect someone here at the school could tell you the address."

"Well, I'll see him just as soon as I can possibly get there. I still haven't got my French police identification card," I said.

"Let us hear from you as soon as you have talked to him," Carl said warmly.

"I sure will, and thanks." As they started to leave, I called them back and asked, "How much do you think I ought to tell him about the story?"

"There shouldn't be any question about him. You'll probably have to tell the whole thing in order for him to help you," Carl suggested.

They left me, and I went into the office to inquire where I could find Henningsen.

By mid-afternoon I was back downtown and in an office waiting to see Mr. Henningsen. At the reception desk sat a man I took to be Japanese. I was shocked, for I knew I could not trust my story to anyone who was friendly with the Japanese. He looked up at me and in clear, perfect English asked, "Did you want to see Mr. Henningsen?" It was unbelievable. I had never seen an oriental person who sounded so much like an American.

"Yes, I want to see Mr. Henningsen," I answered abruptly. My first thought was that the man was a ventriloquist, for it did not seem possible that the voice I heard was coming from an oriental.

"Mr. Henningsen will see you in a few moments. He is busy now. Won't you sit down?"

I sat down, to wait anxiously until I was finally admitted to the inner office.

Mr. Henningsen was a fine-looking gentleman a little over six feet tall. He greeted me warmly, and I immediately had confidence in him. Still worried about the front office, I asked, "Who is that fellow out there?"

"Oh, that's Peter Kim. Don't worry about him," Henningsen said, as if he sensed my concern.

"Jap?"

"No, he's a Korean, and he feels about the Japs just like we do," Henningsen laughed. From then on I had no hesitation in telling my story to Henningsen. He listened patiently as I went over the details much as I had done with the Mydans, but I was still uncomfortable. The story did not seem real even to me. I had lied to so many people for so long that the truth sounded strange to me.

All the time I was wondering just how this man would react to the yarn I was telling. I had never been certain that I was doing the right thing by passing myself off as a civilian. As the fellow in Santo Tomas had told me, it was thin ice; and way down.

inside I was not sure just what people would think when they learned the truth.

When the story was finished I watched his face to see what his reaction would be, for his expression had not changed throughout the entire story. When I ended he stood up and put his hand on my shoulder, and I suddenly had a feeling of self-assurance.

"You've come a long way," he said, "but the trip to Chungking is next to impossible. I don't feel that this would be a very good time for you to start the trip."

"But I would like to get started as soon as I can. The longer I stay here the more difficult it will be," I protested.

"Do you speak any Chinese?"

"Not a word."

"It would take a lot of preparation, and it just isn't something you can do immediately. Give me some time, and I will talk to you later about this."

I thanked him and started to leave. He asked, "Are those all the clothes you have?"

"These are my best," I said.

"Then you'd better come with me. I have some things over at my apartment you may use." We walked from his office to his downtown apartment, where we learned that his shirts, socks, underclothing, shoes, and suits fit me perfectly. In a short time I was converted from Robert Johnson, the refugee, to Robert Johnson, the sheik of Shanghai, with the help of a suit which fit as if it had been made for me, a pair of Florsheim shoes, and an Arrow shirt with a respectable-looking tie. It was Bob Johnson Day in Shanghai, and I was winning all the prizes. In addition to the clothes, Mr. Henningsen gave me another fifty dollars in cash, so I was not only well dressed, but also more prosperous than I had been for a long time.

I never knew of all the kind deeds Mr. Henningsen did as president of the American Association, but I felt that I had found a man among men. When I thanked him and stepped out onto the streets of Shanghai again, I was an entirely different person. I was sure it would be easier to pass myself off as a civilian miner when I was dressed respectably than it had been when I was a shabby fugitive.

Upon Henningsen's advice, I went directly to the French police and obtained an identification card without any difficulty. It consisted of a picture, finger-prints, and a lot of French writing that I could not understand. Later, upon instructions, I went to the Swiss Consulate and obtained another identification card with equal ease. The important thing was that I had an identification card with my picture and with Robert Fred Johnson written under the picture. It made it easier for me to convince myself that I was really Robert Fred Johnson. There was nothing in all Shanghai to remind me of the days gone by.

In Manila the Japanese had promised us that there would be no internment in Shanghai and that we would be free to travel about the city as we pleased. But what they had not told us was that we would have all the good things of life at our beck and call— that there were fine modern theaters with good movies—that there was a fabulous race track in the heart of the city—that there were restaurants which served delicious exotic dishes—or that the city was loaded with beautiful women, including American, British, Dutch, French, White Russian, Chinese, Japanese, and Eurasian. Nor did they tell us that the rate of exchange was very favorable. When we arrived, one American dollar was worth twenty Chinese dollars. Within a year the inflationary spiral carried the value of one American dollar to ninety-six Chinese dollars. We found ourselves paying twenty-seven Chinese dollars for a five-course dinner in the finest clubs and restaurants, but it was only about twenty-seven cents in American money.

During the first few weeks in Shanghai I was able

to learn very little about the prospects for my proposed trip to Chungking. I developed a frame of mind much like that of a fugitive from justice. I realized that my days of freedom were limited, and felt that I must get the most out of life while I could. In that frame of mind I drank deeply of all the worldly pleasures which abounded in the "Paris of the Orient." Through it all I felt guilty and insecure, knowing that this luxurious existence might be brought to an abrupt end at any instant.

17. Malaria—and hope

One morning, just after I had got up and prepared to start out on another day of adventure in the city, there was a loud knock on my door. Thinking it was one of the fellows from down the hall, I shouted, "Come in." When there was no answer I threw open the door and found myself standing face-to-face with three Japanese in civilian clothes.

"We are from the Japanese gendarmes. We have come to ask you some questions."

My first thought was how to get away from them. I stepped back and said, "Won't you come in and sit down?" Much to my surprise, they filed past me into the narrow room so that I was between them and the door. I felt weak and pale as I waited for the first question. The spokesman sucked in a mouthful of air through his closed teeth with a hissing sound, just like the Jap who had interrogated me at Fort Santiago. "You have a Japanese wife?" he asked.

Then it struck me. The fellow in the next room, Henry Francis Parks, had told me he was married to a Japanese girl who lived over in the Hongkew section of town across the creek.

"You are looking for the fellow in the next room," I answered. "I'll go get him for you." With that I went running out of the door and down the hall. Apparently they had not understood me, because they all came running along behind me. I stopped and looked into Parks's room. He was not there, but I found him down the hall and was much relieved when I was certain he was the one they were seeking. Parks was a musician, and among his other activities he had been president of the Amateur Radio Operators Association before the war. The Japs were interested in radios and came by to question him every few weeks.

Back in my room, I was nervous and weak. I lay on my cot most of the day with a headache and fever. Finally, I was feeling so bad that someone called a missionary doctor who ran an infirmary at the American School. She was Dr. Hyla S. Watters, a rugged little lady about five feet, three inches tall, with her hair chopped short like the high school girls used to wear back home. After looking me over and taking my pulse and temperature, she said, "Boy, it looks like you've got malaria."

"I've had it before, and I wouldn't be surprised," I answered.

"Best thing we can do with you is get you down to the infirmary while you still feel like making the trip," she advised. I gathered together a few belongings and walked with her over to another building where she had a number of cots and some hospital equipment.

The siege of malaria brought to an abrupt end my meandering about in that paradise of the Far East. I lay on the hospital bed with headaches and a high fever, and night after night in my dreams relived the tragic and horrible incidents of the war back on Bataan and Corregidor. Long sequences of activities went through my mind as clearly and as vividly as if I were seeing and living them for the first time.

Then one morning Dr. Watters appeared in her usual cheerful frame of mind and announced, "Bob, I have an idea. There is a kind of treatment which may work on the type of malaria you appear to have, if you want to try it."

At that stage I was willing to try anything, and told her so.

She turned and went into the other room. In a few minutes she returned with the largest syringe I had ever seen in my life. Though there was no one else in the room, she leaned over and whispered to me, "Now this is salvarsan. It is a treatment that is used for syphilis, and it may just cure your malaria." She looked at me. "Don't tell anybody that you are taking this. They may get the wrong idea."

"I hope it works," I said, just before she jabbed me and drained what looked to be about half a pint of the green liquid into my system.

"I'll probably have to give you another one of these later," she said, covering the syringe and disappearing into the other room.

In another couple of days the fever was gone, and thanks to old Doc Watters, I never had malaria again.

Dr. Watters became one of my dearest friends from that time on. She was a graduate of Smith College and Cornell Medical School and had interned at Bellevue Hospital in New York. Most of her sixteen years in China had been spent at Wuhu, far up the Yangtze River, where she had worked in a Methodist missionary hospital. When the Japs took over she came to Shanghai. She was spending her time there pedaling her bicycle from one school to another, giving medical attention to little Chinese, Russian, British, and American children. Her one hope in life was that the war would soon end so that she could return to her hospital at Wuhu.

After my recovery I worked some with her. We rode bicycles across town to a convent school where, along with the Catholic sisters, I worked at grinding up dried eggshells in an old-fashioned stone mill. This produced calcium, which Dr. Watters administered to her hundreds of child patients who were suffering from a lack of milk in their diets.

Days passed into weeks and weeks into months, and I became so completely wrapped up in the activities about the city that I gave less and less thought to the trip back to Chungking. The magnificent autumn weather faded into winter. Early in November we awoke to find the ground covered with snow. On the morning of that first snow, all of the residents of the American School were shocked by the news that the Japanese had suddenly rounded up the most influential citizens of the American and British community and thrown them into what was known as a "political prisoners camp." I was particularly shocked to learn that my friend Henningsen was among those who had been taken away. I had lost the one person who could have helped me prepare for the trip to Chungking.

The Mydans suggested that I move from the American School and take a room at the Palace Hotel where I could be nearer to them. The move was a pleasant one, for there I was able to have a pleasant room with a private bath, a fireplace, radio, innerspring mattress on my bed, and a wonderful view of the river. We ate our noon meal in the luxurious dining room of the hotel, where a White Russian orchestra played soft music and the menu was loaded with indescribable foods. Evenings, we would sometimes sit on the mat in front of the fireplace in our rooms, eating Chinese chow with chopsticks and drinking hot buttered rum, or go to parties in the French quarter with our many friends. Life had never been so good. It was a long way from the Philippines. It was also a long way from Chungking and from any prospect of ever getting back to fight with the American forces again.

The Christmas season of 1942 came and went, and we were all so busy with the activities of the season that I gave little thought to the way I had spent Christmas in the jungles of Bataan just one year before. There was little thought or talk of Christmas back in the United States. It was too remote in distance and time to occupy our thoughts.

The Japs added to our prestige when they required

that every enemy alien wear an armband when he was on the streets or in public. The armbands were made of bright red material with a large A for American and a large B for British and a number to identify each person. The chief effect of the arm bands was that they distinguished us from the thousands of White Russians in the city who could claim citizenship to no country.

All good things must end. The fabulous life we were all enjoying in the enchanting city came to an abrupt end when we were notified that all Americans, British, and Dutch were to be interned in a concentration camp for the duration of the war. When it became known that I was to be interned at the camp called Poo Tung across the river from Shanghai, along with all the other single male adults, the Mydans and Dr. Watters intervened for me with the Japanese and requested that I be put in the same camp with them because of my malarial condition. Though I had not suffered the slightest indication of malaria since the treatment the doctor had given me, I offered no resistance to the idea. I felt certain that life in the camp with the American and British families would be more pleasant than life in an all-male camp.

Things happened rapidly from the time we received our first notification until we assembled at the Columbia Club with all of our worldly possessions, waiting to be transported by the Japanese to our internment camp.

It was about the middle of the afternoon, February 1, 1943, when we unloaded in a compound on the western edge of Shanghai formerly occupied by Chapei University. There were only two large buildings, although the barbed wire fence about the place contained approximately four acres of ground. It was not nearly as large or as pleasant a place as Santo Tomas. In all there were only about one thousand American, British, and Dutch internees. As in

Santo Tomas, we were allowed to set up our own organization for the internal affairs of the camp.

Gone were the private rooms with the radio, fireplace, and hot buttered rum. Instead, I had fourteen roommates, a cot, and a box at the foot of the bed to hold my knife, fork, spoon, and chopsticks. Among my roommates were businessmen of Shanghai, a couple of ex-Army officers from World War I, William Hines, secretary to the Shanghai YWCA, Bishop Roberts of the Methodist Church, a couple of engineers, and an ex-millionaire.

In a short time camp life became organized and routine. There were schools, religious services, plays, dances, and baseball games. Everyone who was able to do so assumed certain duties. Jimmy James, who had owned and operated several well-known restaurants and night clubs in Shanghai, became one of our chief cooks and bottle washers. Carl Mydans, from *Time* and *Life* magazines, was one of the chief editors of the camp newspaper. Dr. Watters worked in the camp infirmary with several of the other doctors. I worked in the infirmary clinic as an assistant to Mrs. Jean Arnhold, who had previously taught pathology in one of the Shanghai universities.

Our work kept us busy from early morning until night, taking blood counts, malaria smears, urinalyses, and blood sedimentation tests, and examining what seemed to be millions of stool specimens of persons suspected of having dysentery. During an epidemic of whooping cough we took blood counts on practically all of the children in the camp. I became personally unpopular with the young children—they would run to their mothers when they saw me coming.

Dr. Watters never asked me any questions about my background; however, I felt certain that she suspected me of being connected with the armed forces. She seemed to take particular delight in an assignment she gave me one day of painting a Jap soldier from head to foot with a sulphur solution as a treatment for his scabies.

During the month of our internment in Chapei there were relatively few incidents to cause uneasiness, such as there had been in Santo Tomas. I was content with the peaceful life until one morning in the laboratory, Jean Arnhold broke the silence with, "Bob, did you know people are talking about you?" I was completely surprised, because I knew that Carl and Shelly Mydans were the only ones in camp who actually knew anything about me. I was certain they had said nothing.

"Talking about me? Everybody in camp gets talked about, don't they? What are you hearing?"

"Oh, that you're a deserter, or that you jumped ship, or something like that," she stated as casually as if she were accusing me of not going to church on Sunday. From her tone it was apparent that she was not the slightest bit concerned about the truth or falsity of anything she had heard, but I became completely choked up and could not talk. I worked with my microscope for a time before I finally asked her to come out into the hall.

There, with my voice filled with emotion, I said, "Jean, I do not know what you have heard about me or what anyone is saying, but I want to tell you this—I have never jumped ship or deserted from anything." As I talked, inexplicable tears rolled down my cheeks.

Jean laughed and waved her arms. "Oh, Bob. Don't think anything about it. I don't care what you have done. Forget that I ever said it." She tried to comfort me, but I felt that she had not understood. We went back to work, and nothing was ever said about the subject again.

It was only a couple of days later that I was injured while trying to steal home in a baseball game. I slid on the ground and scraped the skin off a large area of my hip. Immediately, I ran from the ball diamond to the infirmary on the other side of the compound to have it treated. The doctor on duty was Dr. Worden, a former Shanghai physician who had lived for some time in Japan. Although I was well acquainted with him and his family, I had made it a point to stay away from him in camp after I learned of his close friendship with Buddy Uno, a Japanese war correspondent. Uno had written *Corregidor, Isle of Delusion,* a book about the Japanese invasion of the island of Corregidor, in which he had participated. The book had been in the bookstores in Shanghai, and I had read it.

In the infirmary Dr. Worden sat me on the edge of his examining table. He turned on his powerful light, which shone down directly in my face as I looked up at him. Before he looked at my wound, he looked me straight in the eyes and said, "Bob, I hear you are a deserter from the Army."

I looked straight back at him, and without flickering an eyelash answered, "That is ridiculous. Where did you hear that?"

"Just heard it," he answered. "Now, let's see—say, you've really lost some skin there." With a professional touch he dressed my wound and put a big bandage over it, and I felt much better.

There was no more conversation with Dr. Worden about the subject. Although I saw him every day, he never mentioned it again.

From the day we reached camp there was talk that there would be a repatriation of American civilians. There had been one such exchange of civilian prisoners several months before I arrived in Shanghai, and as the months passed in Chapei the rumors increased steadily. One thing seemed more certain than anything else—even if there was a repatriation, there was little or no chance that I would be included.

In the evening after the dinner hour, various groups and individuals would promenade about the big rectangular driveway in front of the main building. As we walked and talked each evening, I would look out across the open Chinese countryside to the west where the sun set and think about the possibility of the long, long hike to Chungking. By that time I had grown soft in the easy life of peace and quiet, and had decided that I would attempt escape only in an emergency. My enthusiasm for the trip was not strengthened by the statement from our commandant which had been read to us and then posted on the bulletin board in the main building. It read:

I, the Japanese Consul and the Commandant of this Civil Assembly Centre, give instructions to all to assemble here today. Unfortunately, the prevailing international circumstances have deprived you of your right to free life and necessitated to you to enter this place. However, this is your safest refuge where your rights are best guaranteed and the only abode you are now permitted to live in. You must therefore cope with the rules and regulations and make the best possible efforts in the carrying out of this place with a spirit of mutual harmony and with the thought that this is your home, loving it and enjoying your life and duties given to you. Thus to live in peace and happiness is the wisest and best way for you. On this I emphasize. If, contrary to the above, you should violate the regulations, you shall be punished according to penal regulations. Should any of you attempt to run away from this place you might be shot to death by our guards. This you must remember. You must read carefully the regulations which are handed to you.

One night Carl, Shelly, and I were sitting on the front steps of the main building after the curfew. Everyone else had gone to bed. We were whispering and laughing about the various amusing events that had taken place in camp over the past few weeks.

Suddenly we heard a disturbance down by the main gate, about a block away. We listened silently, as we recognized a Jap patrol with rifles and bayonets marching in the gate and down the road toward us. I knew that Carl and Shelly were thinking the same thing that I was thinking as we sat watching the patrol come nearer and nearer. They halted in front of us, and the officer asked a question in Japanese which none of us could understand. Receiving no satisfaction from us, he marched his patrol into the building and up the steps to the office of the commandant. We waited for several minutes before the patrol came stamping back down the steps, turning down the hall, and halted exactly in front of the door to the room where I was supposed to be sleeping. I peeked around the corner and watched them as they stood at parade rest for a minute. Then they picked up their rifles and marched off into the night. No one seemed to know why they came, what they did while they were there, or where they went.

We speculated for a while about the purpose of their visit to our camp, and then retired to our respective rooms for the night.

A few days later the camp was buzzing with excitement. Definite word had been received that there would be a repatriation of American citizens in the near future. We were notified of the priority which would be given to certain categories. Aged and sick persons were put in category A. In category B were women with children, and on down the alphabet through C, D, E, and F—married couples, husbands whose wives had been previously repatriated, etc. At the very bottom of the list, in category G, were healthy young males. We knew that only a limited number would go and that there was no possibility of category G being included. The important thing was that the process of repatriation was getting into operation, and there was a possibility that we might all get to go home sometime before the end of the war.

In the late summer of 1943, word was received that the repatriation would begin in August or September. We had been in the internment camp more than six months, and the life had become humdrum and routine. During the months we had been there we had heard little news of the outside world or the progress of the war in the Pacific. From notes which were smuggled into camp we gained the impression that the American forces far in the south Pacific were beginning to roll toward the north. General MacArthur's forces had captured some small islands in the vicinity of New Guinea, but they were islands which we had never heard of before and seemed very far away. As far as we were concerned, it was possible that the war would last for many years, and our best prospect for getting home was by way of another repatriation if it ever came about. We were helpless, and the prospects for such future repatriations seemed remote. Nevertheless, we all rejoiced in the good fortune of those who were about to make the trip back to the United States.

We were waiting for the list of names of those who would go when I met Mydans in the long hall of the main building. He ran toward me and shouted, "You're going, Bob! You're going! You're on the list!" I was too astonished to speak. "They're taking all of us who came up from Manila on this ship, and our passage will be applied against the Manila quota," he explained, and shook my hand.

It was too much to comprehend. We found Shelly, and the three of us talked excitedly about the unbelievable stroke of good fortune which had come our way. They were as much pleased as I, and I was certain that their intelligent guidance and counsel had led to the success of my Shanghai venture. With them in my confidence I felt a sense of security I never enjoyed with any of the hundreds of other people I knew in Shanghai except Mr. Henningsen. Without their companionship the months of waiting would have been much more difficult. Without the hundreds of dollars they had given me for my support and comfort, Shanghai would have been a different place.

From that day until September 20, 1943, there was so much excitement in Chapei that the place took on an entirely new look. All of the little animosities and problems that had developed during our internment melted away, and everyone was happy. Only one thing was important—unless something totally unexpected happened, we were on our way back to the United States.

Finally, the wonderful, wonderful day arrived when several hundred of us assembled in front of the main building with our worldly possesssions. It was a beautiful day, with the sun shining and the skies clear and blue. Everyone was happier than he had ever been during his stay in Chapei until we started loading on the busses that would haul us across town and back to the Bund. Then there were few dry eyes in the crowd as the little camp band struck up the tune to:

> My country 'tis of thee,
> Sweet land of liberty,
> Of thee I sing.

There were tears of happiness and tears of sorrow all mixed up together as lifelong friends and relatives bade one another good-by, realizing that they might never see each other again. The sounds of the cheering and the strains of the music faded as we pulled out of the main gate, which we had entered seven months before.

The busy city of Shanghai took no notice of us as our little caravan of busses wound its way through the streets and down to the docks to our waiting ship.

It was just exactly one year since our little band

of refugees had arrived in Shanghai from Manila; and I was certain that if I lived to be a million, I would never live another year as memorable as that one.

There was little delay at the docks, and soon we were loaded onto the *Tia Maru,* a French passenger ship which had been commandeered by the Japanese early in the war. We sailed to Hong Kong, the Philippines, Saigon, Singapore, then through the straits between Java and Sumatra and across the Indian Ocean to the colony of Portuguese Goa on the western side of India. We took on passengers at all of the stops, and the ship became quite crowded.

At Goa we met the Swedish ship *Gripsholm,* which had brought Japanese civilians from the United States. There at the port of Goa, without ceremony, but with much exaltation, the passengers from the *Tia Maru* exchanged ships with the passengers from the *Gripsholm.*

Stepping onto the *Gripsholm* was like stepping into heaven. It represented freedom and everything we had been dreaming of for so long. It was a neutral ship, and for all intents and purposes we were free from the domination of the Japanese.

There were all kinds of delicious foods spread out on white-covered tables with rich-looking silverware, American cigars, cigarettes, and everything good. What was more important, however, was that there were magazines and newspapers from which we could learn what had happened in the United States and in the world while we were out of circulation. There were phonograph records and movies that we had never heard of. We were nearer to America than we had been for many months.

It was mid-October, 1943, when the *Gripsholm* sailed from Goa to Port Elizabeth, South Africa. The citizens of the town greeted us with open arms and gave us a royal welcome on the day we spent ashore there. Then our giant luxury liner sailed on across the South Atlantic to Rio de Janeiro, one of the most beautiful cities in the world. Again we were given the plush-carpet treatment during the twenty-four hours we spent ashore.

Then came the leg of our voyage we had all been looking forward to. After Rio our next stop was to be New York City. Until we reached that stage of the voyage we never fully realized that we were really going home. For the first time it seemed almost a certainty that I would get to the United States alive, and I began thinking more and more about home. I had not received a letter or written one for almost two years, and strange ideas about home began to run through my mind. A lot of things could happen in that time, and regardless of their importance, there was no way that the family could have let me know about them. Were they all well and alive? Would there be great changes, or would everything be the same? In a very few days I would know the answers.

From Rio the trip went fast. It seemed no time at all until we found ourselves, one gray December morning, looking out across the water at the Statue of Liberty and New York Harbor. As I looked up at the monument, I realized for the first time that I had just completed a trip around the world, for it was from that same spot on the surface of the earth that Walt Seamon and I had waved good-by to the old statue when we sailed off for navigation school in Miami, three years before. As I looked at the statue, I thought of Seamon and of the night we sat in the headquarters of the 19th Bombardment Group at Clark Field and traced off maps of Formosa.

Who had ever made such a trip around the world? As cocky second lieutenants we had flown our shiny new Flying Fortresses to the Philippines to conquer the Japanese. We had seen our beautiful planes destroyed on the ground by the Japanese right before our eyes. Then there had been Bataan, Corregidor, Fort Santiago, Santo Tomas, Shanghai, Chapei. I should have been happy—happy to be alive and happy to be free. But that was not my feeling. I was as sad as I had ever been in my life. I could not forget that we had been defeated. We, with the autos that traveled faster, the planes that flew the highest and the fastest, and the athletes who excelled in more sports than those of any other country in the world, had been defeated.

18. "Hello, Mom"

We milled around on the deck of the *Gripsholm* in the early morning of December 9, 1943, waiting for the gangplank to be opened so that thousands of repatriated citizens could step once again on American soil. Already there were hundreds of people waiting behind the barricade down on the dock to greet their friends on the ship. There would be happy reunions between relatives and friends when the people from the *Gripsholm* were able to stand once again on American soil.

For me there would be no such reunion. No one knew I was coming home. Nevertheless, I was anxious as the next person to get off the boat, for until I was on land I could never be certain of my freedom. Since the *Gripsholm* was a neutral exchange ship, it might create a very embarrassing situation for her officers if anyone discovered that I was military personnel. The possibility of discovery at that late date was so remote that I gave it very little thought until a friend approached. "Bob, they're looking for you."

"Looking for me? Who's looking for me?"

"I don't know who it is, but they're asking everybody for you."

At that time I was standing very near the gangplank, hoping to be one of the first to get off the ship. "Well, they'll just have to keep on looking, because I'm getting off this ship as soon as I can," I answered.

The words had scarcely left my lips when a well-dressed young man I had never seen before approached me. "Are you Robert Johnson?" he asked, looking me straight in the eye.

"Yes, sir."

Then he leaned forward and whispered, "Are you also Edgar D. Whitcomb?"

I nodded, much bewildered.

"Where are your things? I'll take you off the ship immediately," he said.

I pointed to a bag near the gangplank. "This is all I have."

"I'll help you with it," he volunteered. Then he whispered something to the Swedish officer who was guarding the gangplank, and the two of us, carrying my big suitcase, started down the gangplank before I had an opportunity to say good-by to any of my fellow passengers.

I turned back to get a better look at a husky Navy commander who had just boarded our ship. He had several rows of decorations under the submarine insignia on his chest, and when he grabbed Ellie Watkins in his arms, I was sure he was Bud Watkins, from Manila. I knew Ellie had been aboard ship since Manila, but she had not recognized me. We passed them by and made our way down to the dock.

Later, word spread across the *Gripsholm* that Robert Johnson was a deserter or a spy and that he had been taken off the ship by the FBI.

At the gate where the hundreds of people were waiting to greet their friends, a port official stopped us and asked, "Your name, please?"

"Robert Fred Johnson," I replied, looking back at my escort.

"One moment. I'll see if there is any mail for you."

"I'm sure there is none," I told him. The FBI man flashed his badge and directed me to continue on down the line past the eager, waiting crowd. As we passed in front of them they all looked at us, and I looked into the face of each one of them, hoping that by some miracle I might see a face I had seen before.

In a taxi on the way to Grand Central Station, the FBI agent informed me that I was to proceed directly to Washington, D.C., and report to a certain address which he gave me. "But you are not to make any attempt to contact any of your friends or anyone you have ever known before, and under no circumstances are you to talk to anyone about your experiences," he warned. He gave me a ticket and directed me to my train. Then he wished me good luck, shook my hand, and departed. Whether I was under surveillance for the remainder of my trip to the capital was of no consequence to me. Under normal circumstances a citizen might well become shaken up by being taken off a ship and whisked to a train by the FBI. As far as I was concerned, I welcomed their assistance as well as any investigation they might wish to make.

In Washington, I found the hotel room I had been directed to, and my knock on the door was answered by an Army major. He was the spitting image of General "Vinegar Joe" Stilwell and seemed to have a great sense of humor. He laughed at everything I said, and I laughed at everything he said. I have never determined whether he was an unusually funny man, or whether I had suddenly developed an unusual wit, or whether I was high as a kite from the homecoming reception I gave myself in the club car of the train between New York City and Washington. In any event, our visit was brief. Again I was warned not to make any attempt to contact any of my friends or talk to anyone about my experiences. The warning sounded much funnier coming from "Vinegar Joe" than it had sounded coming from the FBI agent in New York.

Following the major's instructions, I checked in at the Hotel Lafayette under the name of Edgar D. Whitcomb and went straight to bed. The following morning a lieutenant colonel picked me up at the hotel and drove me straight to the Pentagon Building;

that is, he attempted to drive me straight to the Pentagon Building. He was much embarrassed when, after winding around from one cloverleaf to another, we found ourselves headed back toward Washington. I wondered if there were any significance in the fact that the colonel got lost. Did it have anything to do with the reason it was taking the Allied Forces in the Pacific so long to start rolling?

In the Pentagon Building, the headquarters for the armed forces of the United States, I felt very much like old Rip Van Winkle. There were generals, admirals, colonels, majors, and captains in droves, and women dressed in Army, Navy, and Marine uniforms. There were more American officers and men working under one roof in that building than there had been on Bataan and Corregidor combined. I could not associate the conditions of scarcity and want which we had suffered in the Pacific with the seeming abundance of everything in Washington. One thing was certain—I had the answer to a question which I had asked myself many times on Bataan. Are the people back home working really hard to try to save us? If they had ever known there was a Bataan, they had forgotten it long ago.

A fat colonel in the intelligence service interrogated me on my escapes and the circumstances surrounding my taking the name of Robert Fred Johnson. When he thought he had my story well in mind, he came forth with what was probably his first original idea since the beginning of the war. "It seems that about the only thing left for you is for you to be interned for the duration of the war."

"Interned for the duration of the war," I repeated. Surely the man realized that I was an American and on his side.

"Yes, if it ever became known to the Japanese that an American Air Corps officer had been repatriated on a civilian exchange ship, it might be impossible to negotiate any more exchanges of civilians," he explained.

"Where would that be?" It was completely incredible to me that anyone should entertain such an idea. I could not believe that the colonel was speaking seriously.

"I have talked with some of the other intelligence officers about your case, and it has been suggested that you be put up in some hotel where you would continue to live under the name of Robert Fred Johnson. You would, of course, not be able to contact your family or any of your friends until the end of the war."

The idea was too fantastic for me to comprehend. It would have been better if Bill and I had accepted the offer of the Filipinos to take care of us until the Americans returned to the Philippine Islands. For that matter, we would have been no worse off back in the internment camp in Chapei for the duration of the war. It was beginning to look to me as if getting back in the hands of the American forces was about the worst thing that could have happened. I would be like the man without a country.

We continued our interviews for several days. At quitting time in the evening, I would take a bus back to the Lafayette Hotel and spend my evenings walking the streets of my nation's capital. For the first two weeks after my return to the United States, I never saw or talked to anyone I had ever seen before. Though I was assigned on orders to duty with the military intelligence service, I still wore civilian clothes each day to the Pentagon building and each night as I roamed about the city alone. How long would it take them to decide my case? It seemed impossible to me that there should be any question about my status.

After the first couple of days at the Pentagon Building, I spent all my time at a typewriter in an empty room, writing the complete details of my experiences from Clark Field until the time I arrived in Washington. Then, after a couple of weeks, the colonel suggested, "There is some chance that you might go back into the Army under your present name." I could not believe it. It had surely taken a high-level staff discussion to reach that decision.

"Why not?" My patience was almost gone. "The enemy has no record of my real name in any camps I was in. They never got my name on Bataan or on Corregidor. On Corregidor I had a number, 0-200, but they never had my name. Then in Fort Santiago, Santo Tomas, Shanghai, and Chapei I went under the name of Robert Fred Johnson with a number assigned to me—C-143. There is no way under the sun that the Japs would ever know that Edgar D. Whitcomb and Robert Fred Johnson were the same person."

"Well, now that might just work. We'll have to take that up and let you know," he replied.

At last we were coming around to it, the only sensible decision to be made.

After that discussion I began to feel at last that I was nearer to the time when I would be going home. Then thoughts of home and of the little village of Hayden in southern Indiana came into my mind. There, many months ago, I had left my mother, father, brother, and sisters and four grandparents. I had not heard from them in more than two years. As the time when I would hear from them and see them again drew closer, it became a little frightening; for I feared things might not be as they were before. Although I was at last back, free and healthy, I was more lonely on the streets of Washington than I had ever been during my stay in Shanghai. There I had many friends and many happy times, but the first two weeks back in the United States were desolate, lonely, and dreary. Waiting was easy, for the weeks, months, and years in the Philippines and China had taught me a great lesson in patience, and the danger and suspense had faded away the moment we stepped

257

from the gangplank of the *Gripsholm* onto American soil. But I was afraid of the future.

Each day when I went to the Pentagon Building I hoped that some decision would be reached and that I could be on my way. At last, during the second week of my excommunication from society, my colonel friend announced, "It has been decided that you should be returned to active duty in the Air Corps under your real name. You will be given a couple of weeks' leave to visit your family, then you will report to the Army Air Corps Redistribution Center in Miami, Florida, for reassignment."

"Say, that's great! Does that mean that I can call my family now?"

"Sure. Any time," he replied. "But there's one thing I can't impress upon you too strongly. You are not under any circumstances ever to leave the continental limits of the United States or to enter the Asiatic Theater of operations again for the duration of the war. If you try it, you will find yourself facing a court-martial."

"Yes, sir," I replied, but down inside I felt a shock. The one thought I had in the back of my mind was to return to the Pacific and help finish the job we had started. It did not seem fair to me that some colonel in the Pentagon Building, who had never been out of his swivel chair so far as I knew, could tell me that I must spend the remainder of the war in the United States.

"Another thing: before you leave the Pentagon Building, Colonel Wray of the Air Corps wants to see you. After you see him I want to go downtown with you to get you measured up for a new uniform which the Army is going to give you."

"Fine, sir. I'll be back as soon as I see Colonel Wray."

At Colonel Wray's office I told him that I was Ed Whitcomb or Robert Johnson, and that I understood he wanted to see me.

"Say, boy, I understand you've had quite a time of it."

"Yes, sir. But it's all over now, and I'll be going back home to Indiana tomorrow."

"Is that right? I'm from Muncie, Indiana. I'll be flying out day after tomorrow, and you can go with me if you want to."

"Thanks just the same, but I hope to be there before then."

I left Colonel Wray and went back to the Intelligence Colonel, who took me to get my new uniform. Then I was once again Edgar D. Whitcomb, dressed in a full uniform with second lieutenant's bars on my shoulders and a pair of silver wings on my chest. Robert Fred Johnson, who had occupied my body for a year and a half in a world of fantasy, disappeared from the face of the earth.

At long last the time had come when I could call the folks at home, tell them that I was back safe, and ask about each of them. Instead of rushing to the first phone I could find, I waited until late in the evening when I was back in my hotel room. It was not something that could be done from a pay station or from someone else's office. After the weeks and months and years, what was the difference whether I called that day, the next day, or the next week?

What a moment it was! It was cold and dark out-of-doors when I picked up the phone in my warm room at the Lafayette Hotel. I was about to call a little town in Indiana and ask to speak to Mrs. John Whitcomb, who had been waiting anxiously for two years for some word from her son. How long those years must have been. She had kept a little radio playing all night beside her bed and cried herself to sleep night after night in the early days of the war while the news had told of one crushing American defeat after another. Only a mother could understand the feelings she must have had.

What a mother she had been! I remembered her

telling us that she had never lived in a house until she was seven years old, because her father was in the railroad construction business, and the family lived in construction camps in all parts of the country. As I thought of Mother, memories came back to me of a time when she had stepped into the middle of a street fight among several big, tough men. She grabbed the arm of one of the toughs as he was about to clout his adversary with a tire tool, and stopped the fight while a crowd of bewildered town folks looked on. She had been a nurse, and I remembered how she had been called many times from the care of her family at all hours of the night and day to attend young mothers in childbirth, dying old folks, and patients with a hundred kinds of sickness. I remembered how she had once waited six nerve-racking weeks for me when I was fifteen; I had run away from home because I thought I would never get to see the world otherwise. I saw Chicago, Boston, New York, and Washington, but the journey came to a sudden halt when I was arrested in Hamlet, North Carolina, for riding a freight train, and sentenced to thirty days on the road gang. The officials wired home, mother telegraphed ten dollars to pay the fine, and I was released after spending the night in jail.

Then, after all the troubles I had caused her, I had gone off to war and got lost. One terrible day in August, 1942, she had received a telegram from the War Department, informing her that her son was missing in action somewhere in the Philippines. In August, 1943, she had received a second missing-in-action telegram.

As I picked up the phone, I prayed to God that everything would be all right at home.

"Hello, operator. Long distance, please. I want to call Mrs. John Whitcomb in Hayden, Indiana."

There was a short wait before I heard the call going through to Pittsburgh, Indianapolis, and Seymour.

Then, "Hello, North Vernon, this is Washington, D.C., calling Mrs. John Whitcomb of Hayden, Indiana."

"Hello." Mother was on the line.

"Hello. This is me. It's your boy, Ed, back home again," I shouted.

"Who?" she asked; and I could tell that she knew but could not believe it. From then on the conversation was hazy, even to me, but I learned that everyone was the same as when I had left, and told them I would be on my way home the next day.

19. Full circle

It was just five days before Christmas, 1943, when I arrived in Hayden; and needless to say, there had never been such a Christmas at the Whitcomb home before. Neighbors and friends flocked in for miles about the countryside to see the fellow who had escaped from the Japs, until I began to feel like a man from Mars. A big Christmas tree was decorated brightly, and stacks of multi-colored packages were placed around it. In the kitchen there was a turkey almost too big for the roasting pan, the biggest ham I had ever seen, and everything imaginable good to eat. Besides all that, I had on deposit in the bank more money than I had ever thought I would own in a lifetime. It seemed that I had just stepped through the pearly gates into heaven and everything was even more wonderful than I had ever imagined it would be.

The family and town were very much the same as when I had left more than two years before, except that I had suddenly become the most important topic of conversation among the two hundred inhabitants of our village. What had happened in the war seemed of little importance to them. The important thing was that I had returned home safely. Word had got about that the details of the escape were secret, and the people were considerate enough not to ask questions. The North Vernon *Plain Dealer* simply stated, "Lt. Edgar D. Whitcomb is spending the Christmas holidays with his family."

The greatest change in the home town was that most of the fellows of my own age were away in the military service, fighting and winning battles. The newspapers and radio told of advances and victories by the American forces, and the thought that we had been defeated in the Philippines kept coming back into my mind. While I was at home, enjoying myself and having all the good things in life, my old friends were dying in the Jap prison camps of the Pacific. I became restless before my two weeks were over, and before the end of my leave I was glad to be off to Miami to the Army Air Corps Redistribution Center. More and more I wanted to get back into the Army and do something toward helping win the war.

Hundreds and thousands of Air Corps officers and men who had been returned from combat were being processed at the Redistribution Center in Miami. The finest hotels on Miami Beach had been taken over by the Army to give the returning "heroes" a vacation and a rest. Every form of amusement was available, including swimming on the beaches, sailboating, fishing, tennis; there were dozens of bars and night clubs where liquor flowed freely. Millions of dollars of the soldiers' and the taxpayer's money went down the drain in a misguided effort to make the boys with the rows of ribbons on their chests get used to being back home. For most of the fellows it was more foreign than anything they had experienced overseas. For myself, I was more than a little relieved when, after six weeks of being redistributed, I was assigned back to my old navigation school in Coral Gables, Florida, for a refresher course in navigation.

Back at Coral Gables and the University of Miami I immediately set out to see if I could find my old navigation instructor, Charlie Lunn. I waited for a few moments in his private office until I heard heavy footsteps coming down the hall, and then saw Charlie's big frame in the doorway. His jaw dropped and a blank look came over his face as he stared at me; then he said, "Why, Whit, whatever happened to you?"

"What do you mean, what happened to me?" I asked. Then I realized that he was looking down at the brass bars upon my shoulders. What puzzled him was that I was still a second lieutenant after thirty-three months of commissioned service.

"Why, Boselli, Terzian, Trenkle, Hoffman, and all the rest of them are majors by now," he explained.

Funny, nobody at home had noticed that I was still a second lieutenant, and I myself had not given it a thought up to that time. Charlie was interested in the progress of "his boys" and was truly distressed that a member of the first class of navigators he had trained for the Army had done so poorly. After a brief explanation of the troubles I had had, Charlie's attitude was different. "Well, Whit, the first thing you have got to do is to learn how to navigate again. I will assign an instructor to you, and you can take as much time as you need to get back into the swing of things."

A few days later I found myself a student navigator again, going through the routine we had gone through back in 1940. The school had grown from our small class of fifty cadets to several hundred who were training there. Charlie Lunn had trained more than fifty thousand navigation cadets for the Army and Navy and for the British government. He had made a truly great contribution to the war effort.

While I was poring over my maps a few days later, the door swung open and in walked Ted Boselli, one of my original classmates who had also been in the 19th Bombardment Group in California before the war. At the time we had flown to the Pacific, Ted had been navigating the Averill Harriman expedition to Moscow. After a hilarious greeting we folded up the maps and took off for Miami to celebrate.

In the course of the evening I learned that Boselli

was assigned to President Roosevelt's personal crew and that he was devoting his time to navigating the *Sacred Cow*, the President's private plane, and hauling dignitaries to all parts of the globe.

"We're going to Washington tomorrow to pick up Eleanor and take her on a trip to South America. We'll be coming back here in a couple of days. Why don't you just come along for the ride?"

It seemed like a good idea at the time, but the next day, when I was faced with the problem of getting Charlie Lunn's permission to make the trip, it seemed different.

"Go ahead," Charlie said. "You can learn more navigation riding in an airplane than you can ever learn in a classroom."

The next day we climbed aboard the big plane at Miami International Airport and flew directly to Washington. There I was able to locate the family of Bill Harris, the Marine who had made the swim from Corregidor with me. It turned out that Bill's faith in his father was more than just the feeling every boy has that his father is the greatest man in the world. Back on Corregidor, Bill had told me that his father had flown more hours than any man in the Army, Navy, or Marines, and that some day he would become a general. It had come true, and Bill's father was the top Marine air general in the United States.

General Harris was back in the Pacific, at that time, but I had a long visit with Bill's mother and his charming sister, Nancy. When I gave them a detailed account of what had happened to Bill and me, Mrs. Harris asked, "Why didn't you just beat him over the head and bring him with you?"

They had no later word from Bill than what I was able to give them, but we all had faith that he was somewhere in the Pacific, still alive and still trying to get home.

At National Airport in Washington the next day, we waited while a big black limousine pulled up beside the plane with President Roosevelt, Mrs. Roosevelt, and Anna Boettiger. Mrs. Roosevelt boarded the plane, and we all waved good-by to the President and took off for Miami.

In flight I sat across from Mrs. Roosevelt. We talked at length about her sons, who were also in military service and doing very well. One of her sons, like me, was a navigator, and he rapidly rose to the rank of general. In response to her questions I told her of some of my experiences in the Pacific, but warned her that they were secret and could not be published.

A couple of days later her newspaper column gave the following report:

MY DAY

BY ELEANOR ROOSEVELT

MIAMI, FLA., Monday—Exactly at noon on March 4th, Miss Thompson and I left Washington. It was raining. The President and Anna and one or two others came to see us off. On the way down in the plane, I had a chance to talk with several of my fellow passengers. Among them was a young navigator who had been on a bomber plane in the Philippines. He was missing for two years, and as he told me the story, I kept thinking of what his family must have gone through. How hard it must have been to keep up hope during such a long period of anxiety without a word of any kind.

He described calling up his family when he was back here and free to call them. He told them he would be home the following Monday morning. Then he said, "They met every train between that time and when I arrived." I can understand that. It must have been like having someone come back from the dead. He looked well, and I asked him if going through so many strange experiences did not give him a tremendous amount of self-confidence. I should think that after having lived through so much, nothing would seem beyond one's powers.

Back in Coral Gables I continued my refresher course under the tutelage of Charlie Lunn, working navigational ground missions in the mornings and flying out over the ocean afternoons and evenings in Pan-American flying boats.

The stay in the Coral Gables-Miami area offered all the pleasures God left to man on this earth. Yet I was not satisfied. I felt I must get back into the war and do my part. Two years had passed, and I had not flown a single combat mission. Finally, when my navigation refresher course was finished, orders came through assigning me to a military outfit. They read:

Lieutenant Edgar D. Whitcomb, 0409910, AC (N) . . . is relieved of duty and assignment at this station, is assigned and will proceed immediately on permanent change of station to the 2nd Ferrying Group, New Castle Army Air Base, Wilmington, Delaware . . . Officer has escaped from enemy territory and . . . is not to be returned overseas . . .

What did that mean? I read it over again. "Is not to be returned overseas." That was what the colonel in the Pentagon Building had told me, but it looked different on official orders. My big plans for returning to the Pacific seemed doomed. It was not that I wanted to be a hero, because I had long ago learned that the self-respect a man feels far outweighs the thoughts a million other people may have about him. I had been through that in the months of living in Shanghai, among hundreds of people who whispered rumors that I had jumped ship or been a deserter from the Army. That had been hard to take, but down inside myself I knew the truth and was proud beyond expression.

At New Castle Army Air Base I found myself under the command of Colonel James W. Chapman, Jr. The Colonel's foreign transport mission had established a fine record, flying more than a hundred C-54 transport planes from New Castle Army Air Base across the middle Atlantic Ocean and North Africa to India for a period of eighteen months without losing a plane, passenger, or crew member. He was a fine gentleman and an outstanding officer who had formerly been with the 19th Bombardment Group in California and who had piloted the Harriman expedition to Moscow which Boselli had navigated.

For me it was a ridiculous position, being a navigator and assigned to a foreign tranport operation with the restriction that I could not leave the continental limits of the United States. Being a "desk jockey" and listening to the fliers' tales of their experiences in Africa, the Middle East, and India did not suit my fancy; and it was with some little difficulty and the assistance of Colonel Chapman that I finally obtained a new set of secret orders which read:

Lieutenant Edgar D. Whitcomb, 0409910, AC N . . . you having previously (been) restricted from duty over-seas . . . are hereby authorized to make operational trips to theaters outside the continental United States other than the Asiatic Theater.

Within hours after receiving the orders I was on my way, flying out across Atlantic, and for almost a year I shuttled back and forth between New York, Newfoundland, the Azores, Casablanca, Tripoli, Cairo, Abadan, and finally Paris. Our cargoes on the giant C-54 transports included airplane engines, rockets, wounded soldiers, and U.S.O. troops. After one hectic trip from Casablanca to Newfoundland, the glamorous Marlene Dietrich mistook me for the ship's commander, and on the ground at Newfoundland gave me an affectionate kiss in gratitude for the ride across the Atlantic.

In Casablanca our crew members visited the native markets; in Tripoli we enjoyed the Italian resort hotels with their colorful flower gardens along the Mediterranean; in Cairo we stopped at Shepheard's Hotel and then rode camels out to see the ancient wonders of the Nile, the pyramids and the sphinx; and at Abadan we sat and perspired from midnight until two o'clock in the morning, until our plane was ready to take us back into the sky and away from the terrible heat.

Although our planes flew on into India from Abadan, I was prohibited from making that trip because it was in the Asiatic Theater. Even though I received my promotion to captain, I resented not being able to go back.

Between trips over the Atlantic I completed a course in the Command and General Staff School at Fort Leavenworth, Kansas. It was there I first became aware of the vastness of the American military operation and of the tremendous industrial output of our nation. It was gratifying to realize the great power the United States had built up, and it made me feel good to know that the nation was at last achieving the power it should have possessed at the outbreak of the war.

In our classrooms we had maps of the Philippines and of Formosa, and on paper we carried out five hundred plane raids on the enemy bases on Formosa. As staff officers, we were trained in the coordination between ground, air, and sea forces in a beachhead operation. Upon completion of the course, most of the officers were to be sent to overseas commands for assignment as staff officers in the various headquarters, but that was not for me. I would be returned to New Castle Army Air Base, where I would continue to navigate C-54 transport planes across the Atlantic, for there was no place for an officer who was an ex-prisoner of war. For me the wonderful training at Command and General Staff School was like learning how to fly with the knowledge that I would never be allowed inside an airplane.

At some time near the end of the course I made up my mind that I was going back to the Pacific if it were within my power to do so. In desperation I wrote to my old friend Carl Mydans, who was back with the MacArthur Command again, taking pictures for *Life* magazine.

"When you see the good general, please tell him that you have a friend who has a score to settle out there and that he would appreciate it very much if it could be arranged for him to return to the Pacific," I wrote. The possibility was vague, but it seemed to me that General MacArthur would be the one person who would understand my feelings.

I went back to flying the Atlantic again with Foreign Transport Operations, and subsequently received an appointment to the Air Forces Staff Course, which was a finishing school for Command and General Staff School students from the Air Corps. It was the early part of 1945. The American forces had been on the continent of Europe for more than six months, General MacArthur had been back in the Philippines for more than three months, and the possibility of my getting back to the Philippines before the war ended was fading rapidly. Then came the blow which all but destroyed any chance I might have had to return. While in Washington, D.C., with the Air Forces Staff group, I received a phone call from the base personnel officer at New Castle Army Air Base. It was Lieutenant Mark Porter from Richmond, Indiana, and an old friend.

"Say, Captain, I really got you out of a bad spot," he said triumphantly.

"What's that?"

"A request came through from General George C. Kenney in the Pacific for your transfer to a tactical outfit in the Far East Air Forces, and I told him that you were not available," was the answer.

"My God, man, I've been working to get that assignment for months. You say you told him that I was not available?"

"Sure. I thought I was doing you a favor."

"Well, if there is any way you can get in contact with him again, I would appreciate it if you would tell him that I am available," I requested.

"I will do what I can for you," he promised.

I was both encouraged and discouraged at what had happened. Carl Mydans had contacted General Kenney in the Pacific, and General Kenney had requested my assignment to the Far East Air Forces. If he could do it once, he could do it again.

In April, 1945, I was on my way again flying out across the Atlantic for the thirteenth time and on the way to Paris, but I was not just an ordinary navigator. I was a graduate of the Army Command and General Staff School, where select officers, including West Point graduates, were sent to be "finished." More than that, I was a graduate of the Army Air Forces Staff Course, with the best training the Air Corps had to offer in staff work.

In spite of my bitterness over the situation, I found Paris completely as it was supposed to be, gay and wonderful beyond words. We spent three nights and days in the glamorous city before we realized that the only part of Paris we had seen was the beat which we traveled to get from the Excelsior Hotel to the Lido Club and back. The club had everything that anyone could wish for, so why travel farther, we reasoned. It seemed that at any hour of the night a man could sit and pick out half a dozen women as beautiful as any six Hollywood movie stars you could name. It also seemed, if you were so inclined, that you could take out the most beautiful one of any half dozen you saw for *deux mille francs* (about twenty dollars).

At the historic Notre Dame Cathedral I prayed on Easter Sunday, just as I had once prayed on Easter Sunday at the little church service at Army Hospital Number Two on Bataan, that peace would come soon to the world.

Back in the United States a few days later I was summoned to headquarters on very important business. In the personnel section I was greeted with a smile by Lieutenant Mark Porter. "Is this what you've been looking for?" he asked, handing me a set of orders.

I could not believe my eyes as I read:

Captain Edgar D. Whitcomb, 0409910, AC (N) . . . this base is relieved of duty and assignment thereto, and is assigned to the Far East Air Force, Leyte, Philippine Islands, for recommended duty with the 5th Bomber Command for permanent change of station . . .

The day seemed brighter and I felt stronger as I headed for the barracks to start packing my belongings. I had waited and worked for sixteen months to get those orders, and I was going to be on my way before somebody changed them.

What makes a person want to give up a comparatively secure life and go back to war is a thing that is beyond all reason or explanation. It is not the desire to do something great or to become a hero. One stands a much greater chance of meeting death face to face than of accomplishing a heroic feat. I knew it was not a matter of bravery, because I had been frightened many, many times to the point where I thought I would die from fright. At the time I was trying to get my orders to go back overseas, I knew that Croxton, Hovette, and Pease, who had escaped from Corregidor by submarine to rejoin the 19th

Group, had lost their lives fighting in the South Pacific. I knew that Ed Green, my pilot on the first flight from the States to the Philippines, had returned for a second tour of duty in the Pacific and had been shot down over New Guinea. I also knew that Mike Walsh, my pilot at the time of the outbreak of the war at Clark Field, had returned for a second tour of duty in B-29's and had been shot down on his first raid over Tokyo. And I knew of a large number of others whose luck had run out on their second tour of duty. The finest fellows I had ever known in my life had died or been taken prisoner at the hands of the enemy. It was my duty to carry on the fight as best I could.

It was in the early part of May, 1945, that I again took off from Hamilton Field, winged out over San Francisco Bay and the Golden Gate Bridge, and once again headed across the wide Pacific. The trip was different in every way from the first flight we had made. In October, 1941, we had made the first mass flight across the Pacific. In May, 1945, hundreds of planes were flying the Pacific every day. Guam, Saipan, and Tinian each had more bombers than the entire Air Corps had at the outbreak of the war. Then, as we approached Leyte, surface vessels, including battleships, carriers, transports, and cruisers, were visible as far as we could see in every direction for more than half an hour of our flight.

The armed might which the United States had amassed to carry the war in the Pacific to a successful conclusion was beyond all comprehension. A fraction of the might we had in 1945 would easily have stemmed the Japanese tide which had swept down over the Pacific Islands in 1941. When we finally landed at Clark Field, it seemed that all my dreams had come true. There were P-51's, P-38's, P-47's, B-17's, and B-24's spread out across the Luzon plains as far as a person could see. That display of air power made our little effort back in December of 1941 seem insignificant. I felt as if I were from another age, for I knew very little about the type of war the Air Corps was fighting. They had fought their way up from the southern islands under the magnificent generalship of MacArthur and Kenney, and the terrible dreadnaught of war was preparing to move northward to Japan.

Like any newcomer from the States, I was given the fast shuffle from headquarters in the Far East Air Forces, to Fifth Air Force Headquarters, to the V Bomber Command Headquarters, to the 345th Bomb Group Headquarters, and finally to the 499th Bombardment Squadron at San Marcelino, about thirty-five miles southeast of Clark Field near Subic Bay. For a navigator, that was comparable to being a private in the rear ranks—about as low in the ladder of command as it was possible to go. But I learned that I was assigned to one of the "fightingest" air outfits in the entire Pacific.

The 345th Bomb Group was known as the "Air Apaches" and its planes, with fierce monsters painted on their noses, had rained death and destruction upon the enemy from Australia to the China coast. It was the Air Apaches who had sunk thousands of tons of shipping in Manila Bay, swept across Clark Field in two waves of thirty planes at treetop level, wingtip to wingtip, destroying hundreds of planes on the ground with the fire from the eight fifty-caliber machine guns on each plane. It was also the Air Apaches who had helped soften up Corregidor for the invasion by the American paratroops. Had I been assigned to the outfit a few weeks earlier, I would have been able to participate in those raids.

The 345th was commanded by twenty-seven-year-old full colonel by the name of Colthorp who had a reputation for flying on only the rough missions. In other words, when word got around that "the old man" was leading a raid, the boys sat up and took notice. It was certain to be a tough one. With that type of commander, it was not surprising to find that the morale of the officers and men was high, and I was constantly amazed at the bravery of the crews. They seemed willing and eager to go on raids even though they were averaging a loss of one to three planes and crews per mission of twenty-five planes.

The living conditions were much improved over ours during the first tour three years before. There were tents and Army cots for everybody, and some of the more enterprising men had electric lights, radios, refrigerators, and air mattresses on their cots. How different was that life from the life we had endured just twenty miles down the coast at Cabcaben Field on Bataan!

I had been with the squadron about two days when I was told to attend my first briefing for a mission. More than three years had passed, yet I was completely new, for I had never flown a mission. At last I was going to get to do the thing I had been trained for—navigate a bombing mission.

The crew members gathered together in the operations tent. The briefing officer pointed to a map and said, "Our target for tomorrow is on Formosa. All squadrons at full strength take off at first light. You will carry a full load of para-frag bombs and form your squadrons in flight. The group will cross the coast of Formosa here (he pointed to the map) at two thousand feet. Turn south here at fifteen hundred feet. That's about five miles north of target. Kagitown is your target. Hit it at minimum altitude, then head back for the coast. Avoid this air field to the south of Kagitown. Juke Box Three will be at 23 degrees, 15 minutes north and 119 degrees and 44 minutes east. Any questions?"

There were no questions, so we were dismissed. Outside the tent, I inquired of one of the other navigators, "I don't want to seem stupid, but would you please tell me what this Juke Box Three affair is?"

"Oh," he laughed, "that is the location of a friendly sub where you can ditch in case you run into trouble."

"That's reassuring. Does it happen often?"

"Oh, sure. They're pulling our men out of the drink all of the time. They also have an air-sea rescue squadron equipped with flying boats which you can contact in case of trouble."

I thanked him for the information and walked back to my tent alone. It was one of those typical Filippino evenings, with a soft breeze blowing in from the sea and faint stars beginning to peek out of the clear sky above. To the east, mysterious Mount Pinatubo was silhouetted against the evening sky, and I knew that there were Japs hiding in the mountains just as we had hidden there before. Just a few miles to the south of our camp was the barrio of Moron, where Bill Harris and I had argued at length with the Filipinos. They had insisted that we should remain with them until the Americans returned to the islands, but we had told them that it was our duty to return to the American Forces. I thought it was ironic that we would have been back in the fight sooner if we had remained there, rather than attempting to go to China or get back to the United States.

That night in my sleep my will to fight forsook me. I was not just frightened; I was scared. During the night I flew the mission to Kagitown ten thousand times. We were shot down, we crashed, we burned, we got lost, and everything under the sun happened to us. Do people ever refuse to fly on these missions? I asked myself. I had never heard of it in the Fighting Air Apaches. The wounded were very rarely brought back; when a plane was hit at minimum altitude, it simply "augered" in. That was the expression they used, or they would simply say, "Smitty hung his jock today." There was little sorrow or mourning about it. It was simply something that happened, and the fellows were used to it. They were less concerned when a plane carried five of their buddies to a flaming death than we had been when one of our classmates washed out of cadet training back in the States. What

276

were they made of? I wondered. I wondered if any of them were thinking the same thing that I was thinking: that tomorrow we would be going on a real bombing mission, and we might not come back. Only a person who had gone through such a thing could understand the feeling.

Came the dawn, I felt as though I had not slept a wink all night, but with the light of a new day I was not scared any longer. Again I was looking forward to the mission to Formosa.

In the gray of dawn on May 11, 1945, we roared down the runway loaded with bombs on our way to Kagitown. We circled around to the right after take-off. Below, I could see Subic Bay, where Harris and I had sneaked our sailboat out past Grande Island one dark and stormy night many, many months before. As we looked down, the bay was choked with American warships of all descriptions. We were on the offensive, and I felt strong and hopeful. When we gained our altitude and turned on course, we could see the sun breaking out over the eastern horizon far across the mountains of Luzon. To the north ahead of us were heavy patches of clouds.

After awhile other B-25's of our squadron came nosing up to join us in a loose formation. The paintings on the sides of the ships were ghastly, and they gave the plane the appearance of a deadly monster or huge fowl with its beak open ready to devour its prey.

We plowed on through several bundles of rain clouds and soon broke out into the clear tropical sky from which we could see Lingayen Gulf, the city of Baguio to the east, the mountains of Luzon, and a number of small islands as we progressed to the north. After a couple of hours we could see the island of Formosa ahead of us. To the right I could make out the port of Takao, where the *Maya Maru* had put into port on our way to Shanghai in 1942. Then, farther north, the pilot turned and pointed down outside his window. I jammed my face against the window, expecting to see enemy fighters coming up after us, but instead I saw a long, sleek gray submarine circling leisurely in the water below us. A quick glance at my map told me that it was Juke Box Three waiting for any of us who might not get through the mission in good condition.

The crew grew more serious a few minutes later as we made a ninety-degree turn to the right and crossed the coastline. We scanned the skies for enemy fighters and watched the ground for landmarks which would point out the place where we should turn onto our target.

It was a tense moment when we made another ninety-degree turn just five miles north of Kagitown, and started downhill so that we would be as low as possible over the target. We barreled in on the town. The air speed indicator climbed from 200 to 210, 220, 230, 240, and then to 250 miles per hour as we flashed over the rooftops of the town. Streets, houses, trees, and people flashed by below us. As the co-pilot hit the machine gun button, our eight fifty-caliber machine guns spurted flame and deadly missiles out in front of the ship. Off to the right our wing man was also spurting out burst after burst of yellow flame. From under his belly, white parachutes darted and exploded in flashes. They were the small fragmentation bombs with parachutes attached to hold them back so they would not explode under the plane. In a few breathless moments we were past the target area and heading back to sea, but each plane hugged the ground all the way to the coast and blasted every building or moving vehicle in its path. A few minutes later we were over the sea and climbing to gain altitude for our flight back home to San Marcelino.

Back on the ground after our seven-hour mission, we learned that all planes had returned safely and only a few had suffered damage from ground fire, and a couple had sighted enemy aircraft.

During the next few days I flew a couple of ground

support missions, one being a night harassing mission over the mountains to the north and east of Manila. On the other mission we bombed and strafed a location near Aparri at the north end of the island. The war was going great, and I was feeling good.

A few days after my first mission I was sitting in front of my tent visiting with some of the fellows from the squadron when a messenger appeared.

"Colonel Colthorp wants to see you at headquarters right away," he announced. I could not imagine what the Colonel would want to see me about, but I hurried to his office immediately.

I saluted and said, "I understand you want to see me, sir."

"Yes, Whitcomb. Sit down," he invited. "I see by your records that you have a good deal of staff training."

"Yes, sir. I studied it, but I never thought I would get a chance to use it outside the United States."

"Well, how would you like to have a job in the Fifth Air Force Operations Section as an assistant operations officer in charge of training and training aids?"

"Nothing would suit me better."

"There is a great deal of work and responsibility to it. You will be in charge of training and training aids in the entire Fifth Air Force," he warned me.

"I would surely like to try it," I told him. I was on the move again, this time back to Clark Field where the Fifth Air Force headquarters was located.

The new job was pleasant and interesting. In the Fifth Air Force headquarters we were able to get a better picture of what was going on in the war. It became obvious to everyone that the power of the enemy was broken and that it would be but a matter of days until he was forced to his knees. Our planes and the Navy had destroyed the Japanese lines of communications, and the B-29's were pulverizing the industries on the islands of Japan.

In July, 1945, we moved from the Philippines onto the island of Okinawa, where our planes were better able to reach Japan and the coast of China.

Then one morning in early August, 1945, word reached us by radio that a new bomb, more powerful than anything the world had ever known, had completely destroyed the Japanese city of Hiroshima. There was much speculation around camp about the truth of the rumor. Before we had convinced ourselves of the truth, a report came that a second bomb had destroyed Nagasaki. It seemed entirely inconceivable that our nation would resort to a method so completely inhumane. All of the men, women, and children of a city of seventy-eight thousand people had been completely annihilated. Whether it was right or wrong, one thing was certain—the war with Japan would be over in a very short time.

About a week after the news of the atomic bomb, General Smith, commanding general of the Fifth Fighter Command, asked me to navigate him on a trip back to Clark Field in the Philippines. I was glad to make the trip, because Clark Field had come to seem like home base in the Pacific to me.

While the General was in conference at Clark Field, I took a walk over to the hospital area to visit some friends. There, in a little snack bar, while we were discussing the possibilities of the atomic bomb and the end of the war, the radio blasted out the news that set the whole world off on a wild spree of celebration: "Word has just been received that Japan has offered unconditional surrender." There was a long silence in the room. Then someone shouted, and pandemonium broke out. Amid the wild cheering and laughing I walked out of the hospital, alone and deep in thought. It was a clear, bright day, and the sun shone down from high in the heavens as I made my way along the lonely road to a spot three or four blocks away. There I stood and looked at the desolate ruins of an old building. The rocks of the foundation still remained, and a shattered chimney stood as a monument to what had once been there. It had once been the headquarters of the proud little 19th Bombardment Group.

I had been standing there three years and eight months before, on just such a day, when a mighty armada of Japanese bombers came out of the north and rained death and destruction from the skies. A huge cloud of black smoke had risen to blot out the sun, and it seemed to me that the sun had never really shone again since that day. Out to the east Mount Arayat towered majestically above the Luzon plains, looking down on us mortals below, and it seemed that only God and I and the mountain knew what had happened there.

Roy C. Bennett, the Manila newspaperman, Ralph Conrad and Frank Bacon, the miners, all of the other civilians and the Army nurses we left in Santo Tomas Internment Camp were liberated when the American Rangers invaded Manila.

Only a few of the friends we left behind on Bataan and Corregidor ever saw the United States again. Those reported lost in prison camps and on prison ships included Jack Mann, Al Manning, Gunner Farrell, Bromeyer, Charles Miller, "Mo" Daly, John Jones, "Buckshot" Burgess, Graham, Evans, and Jim Dey. W. E. (Ed) Dyess, Colin Kelly, Warner Croxton, Ed Green, Pat McIntyre, Tex Gary, Birrell (Mike) Walsh, Boyd D. (Buzz) Wagner, Harold H. George, "Pinkie" Hovette, and Pease were reported to have been shot or killed in airplane accidents.

Dayton Drachenberg, the photographic officer from Rosenberg, Texas, survived the war because he was too ill to be taken to Japan. The ship on which he would have sailed was sunk by American planes, which sent hundreds of American prisoners of war to the bottom of the sea.

Had I been able to foresee the fate of William Harris, Reid Chamberlain, and T. O. Armstrong, the Marines who sailed away and left me in the Philippines, I might well have rejoiced at being left behind. Several weeks after they left me back in the summer of 1942, they acquired a power-driven boat and tried to sail across the sea to China. They drifted for twenty-nine days in a storm-tossed sea with a dead engine, part of the time without food or water. The treacherous monsoons of the China Sea carried them back to the southern part of the Philippine Islands, where the weary and discouraged travelers parted company to join up with different guerrilla bands.

Private T. O. Armstrong was the one Chamberlain described as a "tall, well-built, blond Norwegian weighing about 180 pounds. He is a wild, cocky chap who thinks there isn't anything in the world he can't lick. However, he's very good natured and loses his temper only when he is called 'Swede.' We always called him 'Army.'"

After separating from the others, Private Armstrong literally disappeared from the face of the earth somewhere in the vast expanse of the South Pacific. Whether he met a terrible death at the hands of the enemy, or was killed by greedy natives for his shoes or gun, or whether his boat was swamped far at sea, will never be known.

Much more is known about the other two, since their careers, although short, were much more colorful. Corporal Reid Carlos Chamberlain, the Californian who looked more like a movie star than a fighting Marine, had the good fortune to be picked up by an American submarine in the southern islands and returned safely to Australia. There General MacArthur pinned a Distinguished Service Cross on his chest and sent him back to the United States. He was mentioned in General Whitney's book, *MacArthur*.

The Marine Corps, eager to reward a fighter who had the guts to escape and return to duty, sent Corporal Chamberlain to Officers Training School at Quantico. The quiet life of the classroom was too monotonous for this young Marine who for the past couple of years had slept with a gun at his side and fired at every uneasy rustling of bushes in the island jungles. After a few weeks at Quantico he requested duty with a combat outfit in the Pacific. The request was granted, and soon he was on his way to the Pacific where, as a sergeant, he took part in the invasion of Iwo Jima. There his luck ran out when he stopped an enemy bullet on the second day of the invasion. So ended the career of another fighting Marine.

As for William Harris, his was another story. He explained his reason for leaving the guerrilla band in the Philippines thus: "We lost our enthusiasm for this outfit because of the way it was run, and also, we had our Marine Corps spirit aroused again by hearing the news of the landing on Guadalcanal. On these accounts, we decided to make another try for Australia." He almost succeeded in reaching Australia by boat, but misfortune overtook him on the island of Morotai where he stopped for provisions. The natives appeared friendly at first, but later turned on Bill and delivered him to the one Jap who was stationed on the island. At a nearby Japanese headquarters it was learned that Bill was the son of Major General Field Harris (then in command of all United States Marine aviation), and he was flown to Yokohama, where he remained a prisoner until the end of the war. The first anyone in the United States heard from him was when "Pappy" Boynton, the famous Marine air ace, was rescued from prison at the end of the war. In his description of the camp, Boynton told how Harris had been knocked down twenty times with a baseball bat for reading a newspaper, taken out of a trash can.

Later, Bill Harris wrote to me while I was in Japan:

Washington, D.C.
September 16, 1945

Dear Ed,

You can't imagine how I was surprised when I found out how well known you have become to my family. Honestly, the trouble which you took to find my folks to tell them what you knew about me was one of the nicest things that anyone has ever done for me, and I can't begin to tell you how much I appreciate it.

The story which my mother told me about your return was also a big surprise to me. I had always figured that you would get back one way or another, but I never could have dreamed of the way which you actually used. My opinion is that your case was the prize put over on the Japanese.

After I left you, too much happened to me for me to try to tell you more than a bare outline. [When I was recaptured] I was kept in solitary confinement in a cell in Ambon for two months; and then on August 1, 1943, I was flown to Yokohama. I spent all my time until last January after that in a navy questioning camp at Ofuna, Japan. The Japs never sent names back from this place, and that's why my folks were never notified about me. In January I moved to Tokyo and stayed there until August 30, when I got moved out. There in Tokyo I fortunately got a fine grandstand seat for the bombing which never received a direct hit but got a lot of near misses.

After I got freed, I received two big breaks. One was that I got the chance to be present at the ceremonies on the *Missouri* [Japanese surrender]. The other was that I got to fly back across the ocean (from Guam on with my father, as a matter of fact). This last was a break to me both as an experience and as quick transportation.

I have about run down now, and so I guess I'll close. Drop me a line when you can.

Yours,
Bill

This was not the end of Bill's military service, for he was a professional soldier from a military family.

He remained in the Marine Corps and advanced to the rank of Lieutenant Colonel. Then, in the middle of the first winter of the Korean War, a letter came from Bill's mother:

Washington, D.C.
January 22, 1951

Dear Ed:

Thought you would like to know about Bill. He is missing in action in Korea. Seems impossible the same thing could happen twice in a lifetime, but it has happened. He went out to Korea in September, was in command of the Third Battalion, Seventh Regiment [Marines]. His outfit was way up north of the reservoirs and fought their way out. He got back to Hagaru safely. His dad flew up and saw him there, but coming down the mountain from there to Koto his outfit was doing rear guard duty. Firing started in one company. He went back to investigate, and no one ever saw him again. It was five o'clock in the morning and dark. His dad doesn't think there is much chance of his being alive, but of course no one knows. They had such heavy fighting on the reservoirs. He started out with a thousand men and only had 250 when they got back to Hagaru.

Have thought and wondered much about you. It has been so long since I've heard anything about you. Remember me to your mother, and love to you.

Katie Harris

It had been a long, rough road for the tall Kentuckian from the day he left the United States Naval Academy and the Marine Corps School. He had spent the major portion of his adult life in the Pacific, where he fought the Japs on Bataan and Corregidor before he was captured. In his stubborn effort to get back into the fight, he swam eight and one-half hours at night to get away from the prison camp; in his desperate quest for food he killed an old horse, ate green bananas and ants; and, still determined to rejoin his outfit, he drifted for twenty-nine days in the monsoons of the China Sea. He was robbed of his chance to fight back by being captured when on the verge of a successful escape.

In his second tour as a prisoner in World War II, Bill spent two months in solitary confinement and was knocked down twenty times with a baseball bat.

Bill's chance to fight back finally came during the ill-fated Korean War, when he led a battalion of tough Marines into the mountains north of the Thirty-eighth Parallel. There, on a cold, dark December morning in 1950, his long road came to an end.